THE WOODROW WILSONS

THE MACMILLAN COMPANY
NEW YORK · BOSTON · CHICAGO · DALLAS
ATLANTA · SAN FRANCISCO

MACMILLAN & CO., LIMITED
LONDON · BOMBAY · CALCUTTA
MELBOURNE

**THE MACMILLAN COMPANY
OF CANADA, LIMITED**
TORONTO

WOODROW WILSON
In his first year as President of Princeton

The
Woodrow Wilsons

By

Eleanor Wilson McAdoo

In collaboration with

Margaret Y. Gaffey

✳

New York

THE MACMILLAN COMPANY

1937

: Printed in the United States of America :

To

My Father and Mother

CONTENTS

The Hunt House

vii

CONTENTS

Cleveland Lane

Bermuda and Cleveland Lane

The White House

ILLUSTRATIONS

ix

ILLUSTRATIONS

THE WOODROW WILSONS

CHAPTER ONE

The Hunt House

In THE MISTY TANGLE *of impressions and
memories of my earliest childhood, one picture stands
crystal-clear. I am playing with my sisters in a square old-
fashioned room before a bright coal fire. We move to a
window and stand peering out. The panes are frosty and
blurred, and Margaret and Jessie blow and then rub with
their fingers. Using all my strength I can just reach to look
through the spot Jessie has cleared and she puts one arm
about me to steady me. Margaret is energetically rubbing
one place after another and looking through each in turn.
Outside, perched in a row on their fence, are our playmates
and neighbors—the five little Purveses—closely wrapped,
motionless little figures, heads lifted to a leaden sky, mouths
wide open, swallowing snow.*

*A door opens and mother comes into the room, eyes
shining, cheeks pink with excitement. Something tremendous has happened. She is telling us. Her voice is a soft
slow drawl, but the words run together; each sentence
seems one long incomprehensible sound; then "we won,
we won" becomes distinct to me and I repeat it over and
over. Margaret and Jessie are shouting it.*

We are back at the window, mother lifts me in her arms

and throws up the sash. My sisters lean out and shout, "We won, we won". As if by one movement, five heads are lowered, five mouths close, five pairs of eyes widen. The littlest Purves tumbles backwards and remains a small dark spot in the snow. The others pay not the slightest attention to it but continue to stare at us. We stick out our tongues. Mother closes the window, but she is laughing as we turn back to the bright warmth of the fire—and the picture fades.

Years later I learned that we had celebrated Mr. Cleveland's second election to the Presidency. My sisters, older than I, were already staunch little Democrats and our neighbors were Republicans—"enemies".

We waited twenty years to celebrate another Democratic victory when father was elected in 1912.

We had moved to Princeton from Middletown, Connecticut, where I was born, and were living in a white frame house owned by Professor Hunt.

A passion for horses was one of my earliest emotions, and here a shiny Christmas tricycle became a beautiful white charger with colorful trappings and a flowing mane and tail. On his back I went, up the center hall, through the sitting room on the right to the dining room beyond, past the warm tempting fragrance of the kitchen, and up the other side of the house to the nursery. If I crashed into things it was my charger shying at a jump or some unexpected object in his path. I spoke to him, quieted him and we were off again in dizzy circles. Father may have been in his study as I passed but I don't remember; I didn't see

"THE HUNT HOUSE", PRINCETON, NEW JERSEY

Margaret and Jessie
about two and three years old

Eleanor Randolph Wilson ("Nellie")
about two years old

him. Everyone and everything—walls, partitions, windows —faded away, leaving the whole wide world for me to investigate.

Mother seemed to be always there. She must have had her errands and social life outside of the house but I remember always being able to find her when I needed her. That was often, as I was a terrible cry-baby, dissolving into tears at the slightest excuse and running to her to be comforted. To me she was the most beautiful and gentle person in the world; her eyes always seemed to shine with tenderness and laughter, and there was no limit to her understanding.

As I search for my earliest impressions of father, I realize that I was conscious of him first as a voice; the limpid clearness of that voice laughing, singing, explaining things, stirred a sense of beauty in me and gave me a vague but warm feeling of protection and security.

I see him clearly for the first time as I struggled with a pair of white kid gloves. Mother tried to show me how to put them on, and father, who was watching, called me over and took me on his knee. With infinite patience he put one finger after another into the stiff little gloves and carefully eased each one down in turn, repeating, "Keep your thumb out, Nellie," until at last all my fingers were in place, my thumb inserted, and the gloves tightly buttoned. No doubt we walked the mile to church that Sunday morning as usual; I remember only the great discomfort of the gloves and my enormous pride in them.

He played fascinating games with us in those early days. Suddenly and magically he would blow out his cheeks until his face became a great round balloon which I was permitted to pat gently back into shape. He could do the most amazing things with his face. He could gather one cheek in his fingers and pull it out and out like stretched rubber until we screamed in nervous delight. He could drop his chin lower and lower and incredibly lower until we covered our eyes in terror—certain that at last it would touch the floor.

Slapping his hands on his knees, he did the galloping horse. Nearer and nearer, louder and louder, faster and faster came the sound of the hoof beats until the horse was upon us—then it whirled suddenly, turned and galloped away—the sound gradually fading in the distance.

Margaret and Jessie were named after our two grandmothers. When I came along, the third girl, I was a great disappointment. Grandfather Wilson, thoroughly disgusted when he was congratulated on his new grandchild, said, "Oh, it's just another of Woodrow's little annuals". I was named after mother, but as she disliked her name, I was given another version of it and called Eleanor instead of Ellen. Father always called her Nell, so I became little Nell and later Nellie.

They had lots of trouble at the start with Nellie. At night we knelt for prayers and then mother tucked us into our cribs in a row in the nursery. I learned, "Now I lay me down to sleep" with the others and for some time said, "fysha die", quite cheerfully. Then one night Margaret said, "If I should die", more distinctly than usual and I was terror-stricken. I didn't tell anyone, but listened nightly with a sinking heart for the dreadful words which I never again said myself.

After prayers, lights went out. Margaret and Jessie had

learned, after one brief struggle, that they must go quietly to sleep in the dark. Father and mother bore my heart-broken sobbing for some time and then acknowledged themselves defeated. I was sung to and cuddled, and the others benefited by my wickedness, for it gave us the most enchanting memory of our childhood—father, sitting by the nursery fire singing "Sweet and Low", "Watchman, Tell Us of the Night", and a lullaby I have never heard since:

I had four brothers over the sea,
　　Peri, Meri Dictum, Domini.
They each sent a present unto me
　　Partum, Quartum, Peri, Meri, Centum
Peri, Meri Dictum, Domini.

The first brought cherries without any stones,
　　Chorus.
The second brought a chicken without any bones,
　　Chorus.
The third brought a blanket without any thread,
　　Chorus.
The fourth brought a book that couldn't be read.
　　Chorus.

When a cherry's in blossom it hasn't any stone,
　　Chorus.
When a chicken's in the egg, it hasn't any bones,
　　Chorus.
When a blanket's in the loom, it hasn't any thread,
　　Chorus.

5

When a book's in the press, it cannot be read.
   Chorus.
Partum, Quartum, Peri, Meri, Centum,
   Peri, Meri Dictum, Domini.

His voice grew softer and softer—farther and farther away—and we slept.

Mother was very proud of the two little blue-eyed blondes, in the "Kate Greenaway" dresses she had made herself, and the fat dark-haired baby. While we were still too young to go to church, she had for a time no one with whom to leave us, and she used to dress us in our best, put me in the baby carriage and stroll down the street at the exact moment the service was out. Friends stopped to comment and admire and she took us home in triumph. Father teased her about it but she didn't give it up. Those identical dresses were a source of woe to me later, as they were handed down and, until I grew taller than either of my sisters, I never had a new dress. Mother could always manage to make one good dress out of two worn ones.

Father and mother worked with great secrecy at Christmas. We never saw any trace of the tree or of any packages until they appeared in dazzling splendor on Christmas morning. Once I opened my eyes to see them arranging three dolls in three little chairs before the fire. It didn't disturb my belief in Santa Claus in the least; they were simply arranging what Santa had dropped too hurriedly.

I believed in Santa Claus implicitly until I was nine, when Margaret and Jessie broke the news to me "gently". They began by telling me that Santa Claus had spanked me. They insisted that they had seen him spank me. They were so persistent and mysterious that I was finally frightened. Why should Santa Claus spank me? What good was a spanking when I was asleep? At last they told me, "Father and mother are Santa Claus, silly, and mother has spanked you, hasn't she?" Though I rebelled hotly, I felt that they were telling me the truth, and for a long time any mention of Christmas or Santa Claus brought a hot wave of resentment against my sisters.

It was in the Hunt house nursery that I had the Awful Encounter with the Bat. I had seen bats on summer evenings and they had seemed the personification of everything evil and sinister, so when one flew in through the nursery window, I crouched against the wall and screamed in a wild abandon of terror. Suddenly, cast at a strange angle by a small lamp in the hall, father's enormous shadow loomed on the wall. He carried a broom, but I thought it was a sword and I was no longer afraid. Father was protecting me. Father was a giant waging a battle in my defence.

It was in this room also that I managed to push the sharp point of a pencil into my forehead. Maggie Foley, our nurse, drew it out and tried to comfort me by assuring me that I would sprout a pencil tree from the small black spot I still have in my forehead. Possible disfigurement was of much more concern to me than the prospect of providing father with an endless supply of pencils. For a long time I watched nervously for any sign of the first sprout.

Maggie was small, white-haired, with dark blue eyes—rather a "witchy" person and really quite severe. She adored mother and loved me best because I was the baby, and later when she became cook she was beautifully partial. It was always "Nellie" and "the other children". Because I was born in Connecticut, Margaret and Jessie called me a "Yankee". I couldn't have understood what they meant, but the intention at least was unmistakable; and I cried so often and so bitterly that Maggie complained to mother and the teasing stopped. Maggie gave me cakes and cookies, always warning me not to tell the "other children". I was torn between the desire to divide with them and the fear that she would stop giving me things if I did, so I usually ended by taking a good bite, stuffing what was left into the front of my dress and dividing in secret.

I spent hours in the kitchen with Maggie. She sang a song I loved, "Marguerite, my star of hope, Marguerite, don't break my heart". Because I liked it so much, she changed "Marguerite" to "Nellierite"—I thought it was my real name. I, in turn, read to her. "Uncle Remus" was the favorite and as the dialect made it almost impossible for me to read, or for her to understand, there were no tiresome interruptions for comment or discussion. It was altogether a most satisfactory arrangement.

We loved Maggie and always obeyed her; only once do I remember that we openly rebelled. We were on the New Jersey coast for a few weeks one summer, and she kept us away from father and mother as much as she could. This was a new and terrible experience for us. We were particularly humiliated at having to sit with her at the children's table, behind a screen in the dining room at the hotel. We could see father and mother, and the fact that they seemed perfectly contented to be away from us added to our misery. One day when we were on the beach, with Maggie in close attendance, we saw father and mother walking on the shore. I think it was then that I realized for the first time how pretty mother was. She was holding father's arm and carrying a parasol. We escaped and flung ourselves upon them, but when they asked us what had happened it did not occur to us to complain. We were sent right back to Maggie.

Though Margaret, Jessie and I discussed things pretty thoroughly when we were alone, we never complained and usually obeyed instantly. We obeyed Maggie because we were a little afraid of her and liked to keep her in a good humor. With father and mother it was quite different. We knew what they expected of us and we wanted to please them and, above all, not to fall short of what we thought they required of us.

Mother spanked us in the good old-fashioned way, whenever she felt that we deserved it. Her face always got quite pink and she invariably cried, but she never told father. I remember my last spanking. Margaret and I were getting crackers in the pantry; Margaret pushed me and I slapped her face, and then we both howled. Mother came and our guilt was discovered and admitted. I used heart-broken sobs again and the chastisement was brief. Margaret used to say, "How can you be such a baby?" and I answered, "You're silly to be so brave—they forgive you quicker if you cry", but she never would.

Margaret and Jessie never lied. Jessie told the truth by instinct. Margaret was defiantly truthful, but I failed occasionally because of my dread of hurting anyone and because I so terribly wanted to please and to be loved. Once

9

when I cut myself with a sharp penknife and couldn't think of a good lie to explain the terrifying flow of blood, wailing that I couldn't remember how it happened, mother's expression of sorrow gave me my first flash of understanding that a lie could hurt more cruelly than even the bitterest truth.

Margaret was the leader in everything. I looked up to her with awe and admiration; she was so fearless, so energetic, so independent. She mothered me quite fiercely and, though I sometimes rebelled, I secretly loved it. Jessie was beautiful, calm and serene. She had long honey-colored hair and we loved to sneak up behind her, take a handful of it and pull. She had such extraordinary powers of concentration that, if she was reading, she simply didn't know we were there. She made a vague little gesture as though she were brushing away a fly—that was all. She and Margaret were so much alike that when I was very small, I was confused as to which was which and called them both "Margadessie".

Mother and father never complimented us on our appearance. I had long thick hair but was not especially conscious of it until I overheard someone say, "What wonderful hair the child has!" After that it became a source of interest and pride. On tiptoe before my mirror, I tried arranging it in various ways—pulled straight back from my forehead, piled high like mother's, fluffed out over my ears. I was heart-broken when mother said that I was so pale and growing so fast, that she had decided to have it cut; and when the village barber came both mother and I cried as the long strands fell limply to the floor.

Margaret had worn her hair very short for some time.

10

She had fought most of the boys, singly and in groups, until they stopped teasing her about it. When I emerged with a "Dutch bob" and a sinking heart, I hid behind her, waiting for the jeers and knowing that my fiery sister would fight my battles, too. Nothing happened at all and it was a blow to find that I was too insignificant even for insults.

Because Margaret was such a responsible little soul and the quiet village was quite safe for children, we were allowed to run about alone. One day, while we were still some distance from home, a group of rowdy boys shouted, threw stones and followed us. We clung together and ran as fast as we could. When we arrived at the house father, hearing the noise, came out cane in hand. The boys flew at the sight of him and I was filled with pride; he seemed such a majestic avenging figure. He was often stern, but never angry with any of us in his entire life. This was the first time that I had seen him angry at all and realized that his eyes, so warm and blue to us, could be cold and grey like flashing steel.

Rain or shine, Margaret, Jessie and I walked to church with father and mother every Sunday morning. There were two Presbyterian churches—the big one called "The First Church", and the smaller one, "The Second Church", which we attended.

The long hymns and sermons, of which I understood very little, confused and exhausted me. The church was plain and uninteresting, the wooden seats cold and hard, and I spent the time in a sort of hopeless stupor until my great friend, Elizabeth Duffield, whom we called "Duffy", told me what she did to keep awake. Over the pulpit was a long quotation from the Bible, and above this there were stars. The secret was to count the letters, *a*'s and *b*'s and so on down the alphabet—and then to count the stars. I soon found the letters boring and confined myself to the stars— much easier to manage and more attractive. My distaste for mathematics probably dates from this time, although I have always liked to believe that it is a direct inheritance from father who frowned at the prospect of adding even a short column of figures, and sometimes called to us from the next room, "Children, what is seven times eight?" My treble, answering, "Fifty-six", came a full moment after my sisters' confident shouts. He disliked everything relating to personal finances and mother attended to all household money matters.

When an effort was made to merge the two churches we joined the First Church and I was much happier. The interior was all snowy white—there were bright red carpets, and I found the congregation much more interesting. It was here that I later came to watch for the arrival of the lovely Mrs. Cleveland, usually a little late and always exquisitely dressed.

After the service, discreet little groups gathered to chat and then we walked home. Sunday was rather a terrible day. We were permitted no games at all—no charades or songs. We read only religious books that mother had carefully chosen to improve our minds and characters. Until our public life began, no servants were required to work in the house; in fact, no unnecessary work of any sort was done on the Sabbath.

Father and mother loved poetry and took turns reading aloud. Father had a certain spontaneous gaiety, a delicious sense of fun and mischief, and though mother was quiet and took no active part in this, insisting that she was not "gamesome", she was the perfect audience for him.

A distinct rhythm, a deep happy peace permeated the household, that household that attracted an unending stream of relatives and friends, aunts and uncles and cousins of varying ages and degrees of attractiveness, but all joyously welcomed. So much laughter and teasing and warm friendliness, and mother the center of it all—her soft Southern voice with its slow drawl, brown eyes so full of changing lights, a perfect complexion, great masses of copper hair, and bangs to hide what she considered too high a forehead. She was small, eager, intensely alive.

I have never understood how she crowded so many and varied activities into one day. She was a skillful gardener, planning every inch of the garden and watching its progress with untiring interest. She was an excellent cook, teaching Maggie all her secrets so that our meals, though always simple, were delicious. In those early days she made all of our clothes as well as her own—she did exquisite embroidery, made with swift snips of the scissors the most enchanting paper dolls for us, and then advised and guided us in coloring them. She even occasionally stole away to her room to spend a few hours at her painting. I remember "sitting" for her once, hours on end, perched on an improvised dais, very straight and stiff and miserable, longing to get my hands on the bright daubs of color on her palette.

She was father's faithful proof-reader. Sometimes after spending a morning going carefully over his work, they would carry on a conversation at lunch, in proof-reading style.

"The soup comma my dear comma is delicious semi-colon Maggie is an excellent cook period No wonder exclamation You taught her period", he would say and she would answer, "Thank you comma Woodrow period".

Perhaps the most vivid memory is a little figure ensconced in a big chair by the fire in the evening, a huge basket of mending on the table beside her, her soft gaze lifted to us in turn as we plied her with questions about our lessons, her face changing and glowing when father spoke to her.

Most incomprehensible of all was the impression she gave of never being hurried, of always having time to listen and advise. She took perfect care of us, watching our manners, morals and health with unceasing vigilance. Other children were allowed to sit on the grass, but we had small straw mats and were forbidden to sit down without them. Once we disobeyed and then, conscience-stricken, confessed. She marched us promptly upstairs, and rubbed us vigorously with alcohol, paying particular attention to the places where the circulation was most likely to have been impaired by the grass-sitting.

She had a way of putting her hands over her face when she was frightened that disturbed me terribly. Once when we were standing on the upper porch watching an approaching storm, she covered her face in this way and I realized that she was afraid of the lightning. From that time I was terrified of it myself.

We hated to see her leave the house for any reason and I always watched eagerly at a window when I knew it was time for her to be coming home. I ran out once to meet her only to find that it was someone else. Father saw me when I came back, dejected, and asked what had happened. I said, "Oh, I thought it was mother coming and it was only a lady". He waited with me to tell her what he considered a delicious joke on her and it became one of the family favorites.

Every Sunday afternoon we went to her room for our Bible lesson. She taught us the Shorter Catechism, and when we were able to say it all by heart without one slip she gravely presented each of us with a fat Bible, name inscribed on the flyleaf, telling us to regard it as our most priceless possession.

I have never known a woman with more versatile literary taste or one who was better read than she. Poetry and philosophy, history and religion, all the great novels and every book on art she could get her hands on. I remember looking over her shoulder, realizing with self-pity that she, at the moment, was unconscious of my existence, and wondering how she could be so interested in a great heavy volume with no pictures in it.

It was from mother that Jessie had inherited her gift of concentration. We loved to stand around while mother was reading and watch father trying to attract her attention; it became a sort of game. First he would make signs, then clear his throat, then speak to her softly and then louder and louder. We were usually in fits of laughter by the time she looked up and said sweetly, "Were you speaking to me?" and father answered, "We thought we were".

As there was seldom money then for trips to the seashore we spent most of our summers, as well as our winters, at home. After the college closed a drowsy peace descended on the village. In the evenings the grown-ups gathered on the porches, chatting with neighbors, slapping mosquitoes, waiting for the night air to cool the hot bedrooms. The children dashed about playing tag and "Hide 'n' seek", screaming with laughter—calling to one another in the dusk. I was afraid of the dark and often ran back to cling to mother for a moment, until the taunts of my playmates aroused my courage. Father's voice, quiet but distinct, always reassured me.

I was too young then to be interested in their conversation, but one night I heard them talking about a New House and I ran and sat breathlessly on the lowest step, listening with all my ears.

CHAPTER TWO

Library Place

Ever since their marriage, father and mother had dreamed of building their own home. Mother had economized fiercely and father had done an enormous amount of extra literary work and lectured outside of Princeton, to make that dream a reality. So at last they had managed to buy the property next to the Hunt house. It was one of our favorite haunts and we were thrilled to learn that it was ours now and that we could watch our own house being built there.

They had chosen it because it was bordered by meadows against a background of distant hills and included a grove of beautiful trees—pines and oaks in front, a huge sycamore on one side and in the rear a glorious copper beech.

Father, who had always been keenly interested in the study of architecture and had a flair for architectural design, drew the plans. They were so nearly perfect that only a contractor was needed for the final detailed drawings. After a long discussion about the line of the roof, mother made a small clay model of the house. It stood on a table and every morning we ran to look at it again, keeping our hands behind our backs to help overcome the temptation to touch it.

For a whole year we were all absorbed in the planning and building of the new house. From the moment the first piece of sod was turned we three spent every free moment watching its progress inch by inch.

Margaret, who was a fearless climber and explorer, waited impatiently for the framework to be up so she could dash from beam to beam, in constant and glorious danger of breaking her neck. Jessie and I ran about underneath imploring her to come down. I have spent countless hours of my life—under buildings, at the edge of the sea, in the mountains—following Margie, wringing my hands and begging her to "come down" or "come back" or "get off".

As soon as it was possible, mother had a lawn put in and we were given a nickel for every basket of weeds we pulled out of it. She deliberated for some time over the hedge. Preferring box, she eventually chose privet for its quick growth.

When the house was ready, Margaret, Jessie and I carried over our most precious possessions which included the canary, and Puffins, a great fat white cat.

Overnight we found everything in place—furniture, carpets, curtains, even pictures; but mother had such a way of making things run smoothly and keeping us comfortable that it did not seem extraordinary to us. I have many times since profited by the secret of that move. She had thought it "simpler to engage ten movers for one day than one mover for ten days".*

All the principal rooms of the first floor opened into a big room, really a hall, with a large square table in the cen-

* Mrs. Bliss Perry.

18

LIBRARY PLACE HOUSE, PRINCETON

Ellen Axson Wilson
with Margaret as a baby

Ellen Axson Wilson as a young girl
(The "basque" picture)

ter, where we gathered to read and sew. This room became the center of all activity. A head of Hermes stood on the mantel over a large fireplace and on either side were photographs of Jessie, Margaret and me. Professor Harper, one of father's friends, called us "the mantel ornaments", which seemed silly to me, particularly as he repeated it so often and chuckled at his wit.

There were other statues on pedestals in the room, among them the Apollo Belvedere and the Winged Victory. When one of the Victory's wings broke, a man who came to mend it said to mother, "Give me the head, ma'am; I can put that back on too, so you wouldn't hardly notice it". I was impressed with the gentle way mother thanked him and said, quite seriously, "I'm sorry but I haven't the head. I wish I had."

To the left of the big room was a smaller one with satin-covered furniture, which we children found most uncomfortable, but quite grand. We called it the "drawing room", liking the important sound of the word. One of the most irresistible things in this room was a large velvet-covered family album, with many pictures of us as babies that mother had tinted with water-color. We were not allowed to touch it; in fact, we were warned not to touch anything in the room.

There were volumes of poetry scattered about on small tables and here I had my first encounter with modern verse. I found "The Hound of Heaven", a small book exquisitely bound. The title haunted me. What was the Hound of Heaven? Was there a Hound in Heaven, and why? At last, overcome by curiosity, I scrubbed my hands, marched in defiantly, my heart pounding with excitement,

19

picked up the book and found that I couldn't understand a word of it.

Also on the left just behind the drawing room was father's study. It was essentially the room of a scholar and always in perfect order, never a book or paper out of place. A picture of grandfather hung over the mantel and there were crayon enlargements which mother had made, of pictures of the great men whom father most admired— George Washington, Webster, Gladstone, Bagehot, Edmund Burke. There were no other ornaments in the room and no unnecessary furniture. A wide window seat faced the garden; a high, leaded window topped a bookcase on one wall; the other walls were lined to the ceiling with books. The typewriter, on a small table, was always carefully covered when not in use.

The most important thing in the room was the large roll-top desk that father always closed and locked when he stopped working. The sound of that desk closing made us listen sharply, for if it was followed by a soft whistle and the jingle of keys in a sort of jolly accompaniment, it meant that he had finished and would soon come out and play with us. It was the important moment of our day.

In this room father wrote his "History of the American People", and paused many times, threatening to devote himself to writing children's stories, insisting that he was not qualified to do anything more serious.

He was enormously popular with the students; they came in droves to discuss their problems with him, bravely enduring the scrutiny of the assembled family in the main room. We enjoyed watching the awkward, blushing boys slide on the hardwood floors or, better still, on the small rugs that slipped under their feet. I remember one particularly embarrassed youth who slid rug and all across the entire room to the study where father, waiting at the door, held out his arms to catch him.

Father had beautiful hands. Whether opening an egg with precision, unhurriedly slitting an envelope, illustrating a point with a gesture, or patiently untying twenty knots in a string, they moved with deliberate, easy grace. They seemed almost to have a life of their own that was yet a part of the harmony of his character.

All his life he carried a large horse-chestnut in his pocket, his "good-luck piece". Polishing it was a ceremony; the routine never varied and my eyes never missed a detail of it. He took it out slowly, held it off, examined it with care, blew on it, turned it over and over, polishing and repolishing, and then at length, satisfied with its glossy patina, put it slowly back into his pocket.

Opening out from the main room was the dining room, with long glass doors into the garden. Here we had breakfast and lunch with father and mother; supper was in the nursery except on special occasions.

Breakfast was at eight sharp and father was usually the first one down. He ate very little and liked only the simplest food. Before meals he said grace in slow reverent tones: "Bless, O Lord, this food for our use and us to Thy service, for Jesus' sake. Amen."

There was no grace after meals. Instead, father rattled off a ridiculous little jingle in a quick singsong way, "Now chickens, run upstairs wash your face and hands brush your teeth and put your bibs away before I count three— or I'll tickle, pinch and spankdoodle you." We jumped at the first word and were scrambling up the stairs before he finished.

Lunch was at one, and father came home from the college, traveling back and forth on a bicycle, as did nearly everybody in Princeton except mother, who could never be induced to try one.

We were prompt for meals; punctuality was a household tenet, strictly enforced. Father would not accept excuses, warning us again and again that we should allow more than enough time to get ready for a meal or a lesson.

One of his favorite stories was about the Irishman who missed a train. His friend said, "Ah, Pat, you didn't run fast enough", and Pat answered, "Sure, I ran fast enough, but I didn't start soon enough!"

We seldom talked at meals, but listened intently. Father had a delightful way of making an engrossing story from the smallest incident that caught his fancy. He and mother talked before us with the greatest freedom and very early we learned that what they told us or said before us was sacred—never to be repeated elsewhere. Thanks to Margaret's constant warning, "Remember, they can talk before us because they trust us", we were strictly faithful to that trust. No one brought troubles or problems of any sort to be discussed at meals.

Sometimes when father made a rash statement, mother would protest, "Oh, Woodrow, you know you don't mean that." Then father always said with the utmost gravity, "Madam, I was venturing to think that I meant that until I was corrected". The moment mother said, "Oh, Woodrow", we looked expectantly at father, and he seldom disappointed us.

After our supper in the nursery, we loved to go down and sit quietly in the main room, listening to the conversation in the dining room. We had, however, a private code—if we heard our own names mentioned, we fled; to stay there would be eavesdropping. Often we found the appearance of a guest more diverting than his conversation. Having been told that Lowes Dickinson was a most distinguished figure in the literary world, I peeked at him with proper respect and found, to my delight, that he had one hand pushed well down into his shoe. By means of elaborate pantomime, I interested Margaret and Jessie and they came over to the door and peeked with me. He kept his hand in his shoe throughout most of the meal.

The Sidney Webbs were guests that looked promising and exceeded my hopes. After dinner, mother suggested to Mrs. Webb that they leave the men to smoke. Only quick action on Margaret's part prevented me from shrieking when she answered, "But I smoke, myself," and drew out a cigarette. Mother looked stunned; I am certain that she had never before seen a woman smoke. After serious and lengthy consultation, we three decided that here was certainly "the wickedest woman in the whole world."

Though there were cigars in the study for his friends and he had no prejudice against it, father didn't smoke. His mother had cleverly protected him from acquiring the habit. When he was very young, she gave him a large black cigar, asking him to puff it and blow the smoke on her rosebushes to kill the bugs. The bugs survived, but the boy collapsed and never tried to smoke again.

Upstairs in one corner, with windows to the garden, was mother's and father's bedroom. It was a spacious room,

23

simply furnished with plain maple furniture, a tan carpet, creamy curtains, and two large chairs, covered in brown and yellow flowered chintz. There were bookcases here, too, and often glass bowls filled with flowers from the garden—roses or mother's favorites, lilies of the valley.

There were photographs of famous paintings on the walls, among them a Leonardo da Vinci Madonna that father had chosen because he thought it looked like mother. Later they bought fine paintings, gradually acquiring an interesting collection of modern American art, but in those early days they had only carefully chosen and beautifully framed photographs.

Both father's chiffonier and mother's bureau were miracles of neatness. Mother's clothes were kept in a small dressing room at one side and I never saw even so much as a stocking lying about in the room. I remember her shocked expression when Maggie reported that one of the few rich women of the town always dropped her clothes on the floor for her maid to pick up and put away. Mother said, "How disgusting!" and then quickly warned Maggie not to talk about it.

A small hall led into the nursery, and here were cupboards—the medicine closet. Rows and rows of bottles of every size and shape, bandages, liniments and cough syrups—a small drug store. Mother was never without the right medicine at the right time and we never traveled without what we called the "medicine bag", a perfectly equipped first-aid kit, which father always packed with meticulous care.

He took the greatest interest in mother's clothes and often made her walk about in a new dress, telling her what he liked about it and what he thought would improve it. He didn't seem to take much interest in his own clothes, usually wearing grey with a plain blue tie, but his dress clothes were always perfect and I thought him very handsome and distinguished when he went out in the evening. He was particular about his shoes, and polished them himself with great care. One night an English guest, not realizing the simplicity of the household, put his shoes outside his door when he retired for the night, and father shined them beautifully, and quietly put them back.

Mother never used a trace of powder, but once when I opened one of her incredibly neat drawers, I found a rabbit's foot that was unquestionably red at the tip. I put it back, feeling very guilty, and scrutinized her carefully for any evidence that she had used it. Years later she told me that sometimes, when she was going out in the evening, she crushed red rose leaves and rubbed them on her cheeks with the rabbit's foot, keeping it, of course, a dark secret from us.

There were fireplaces in all the rooms downstairs and in every room on the second floor, with the exception of the day nursery. There was also a furnace, but because of the constant need for economy, it was kept burning very low and we were always half-frozen in the early morning and when we went to bed at night. Father stoked the furnace himself and we went along to help. Like a golfer arranging his stance, he took his position; one quick glance and he had his aim, then with a wide easy swing, the coal was tossed straight through the furnace door. Then our work began; scurrying about, we gathered up the few stray pieces of coal that managed to slip from the shovel,

25

threw them into the furnace and, when father had closed the door, made a quick scramble for the dark stairs.

At first we three slept in the night nursery. Jessie was always as neat as a pin; I was fairly neat, but Margaret was terribly untidy. Mother finally promised that she could have a small room on the third floor, all to herself, if she kept it in perfect order. Her passion for being alone was such that she made the room a model of tidiness, to which we were admitted only on special occasions.

Our evenings together in the new house were very happy ones. When we had finished our lessons, we came down for a visit with father and mother; above everything else in the world we loved being with them, hearing them read or listening to their conversation. Time after time, when our playmates called us to join in their games, we huddled together and pretended not to hear.

Mother did most of the reading aloud. Her favorites were Wordsworth, Shakespeare and Browning, and at night she read us to sleep with Chapman's Homer. Long before I was old enough to understand the meaning of the words, I was familiar with the sound of many poems I later came to know and love.

We became rabid romanticists. Making costumes out of everything we could find, we acted our own versions of Shakespeare's plays, the Trojan Wars and the stories of the Knights and Ladies of King Arthur's Court. We inflicted charades upon a patient and sympathetic, if not wildly enthusiastic, audience, of which father was a faithful member.

His performances were solo and spontaneous and he did impersonations. I think the "drunken man" was the gen-

eral favorite. We made him do it over and over, and the whole household responded with shouts of glee. With a slight halt in his walk, an utterly vacuous expression on his face, he mumbled with just the right degree of incoherence. The "heavy Englishman" was the second best. For this he had an incredibly affected accent and an air of insufferable superiority as he stalked about, deftly managing an imaginary monocle. He had any number of dialect stories; a Scotch burr and an Irish brogue were in his repertoire, and he told negro tales to perfection. But best of all were his songs.

His voice, a clear tenor of great sweetness, had another quality that eludes description—a suggestion of undertone that gave it a haunting beauty. He sang so easily, so gaily whenever the mood seized him, walking about or more often sitting in a chair, head thrown back—always without accompaniment. When he was young, he had wanted to study singing, but some doctor persuaded him that if he intended to be a public speaker, it was inadvisable to subject a rather delicate throat to any unnecessary strain and he gave up the idea.

He was the only person in the world who has ever thought that I could sing; and sing I did, in the "part" songs. Margaret, who had a lovely voice from early childhood, was alto, father was tenor, I was soprano, and we imagined the bass. Mother and Jessie were never able to carry a tune; they were the audience from whom we demanded a great deal.

We sang "Sweet and Low", "The Kerry Dance", hymns and many other old favorites. There was a stubborn difference of opinion about the pronunciation of Maxwelton, in the first line of "Annie Laurie". Father insisted that it was Maxelton; so we sang away, Eltons and Weltons trying to shout one another down.

The most interesting thing we attempted was an arrangement of Poe's "Raven", based on a sombre, recurring note. Mother, with the ever-present basket of mending, always sat listening and encouraging us. Only once do I remember that she protested. We had repeated, "Quoth the Raven, 'Nevermo-o-ore' ", at least a hundred times, when she interrupted, with unfamiliar firmness in her voice, "If you sing that once more, I think I'll lose my mind". Father replied, "My dear, the poem has achieved its original purpose, and we'll not sing it again."

We loved the new house; every room was an adventure and a dream realized, but the glory of it all was the garden. Mother was an indefatigable gardener, and there were soon masses of bright flowers, innumerable shrubs and ivy growing on the walls.

Father enjoyed the garden and appreciated mother's skill, but he was hardly an active gardener himself. Once he and I mowed the lawn. He did the work, while I stood inside, leaning through a window encouraging him. With a magnificent dash, he would start across and, whenever I saw that he was slowing up, I called, "Dear father, clever father". Each time he looked up at me, smiled, shook his head and bent down for another attack. At last the lawn was cut, but we were both completely exhausted and, content with the glory of our achievement, never tried it again.

We children spent most of our time in the back garden. Here were sunny spots to play in, cool shade to rest in, trees

28

to climb, deep grass to bury our faces in and watch the small crawling things that only children see. There was a spell over it all, half mystical, half warm, earthy fragrance that has stayed with me through the years.

A large copper beech, spreading its wide arms down close to the ground, made shelter for us; its golden-bronze foliage enclosed a small fairyland. Around the tree's base was a carpet of pine needles that mother had brought from the trees in front, and we gathered more needles and small twigs for walls that provided security and mystery. Through the leaves the sun made dappled patterns on the dark pine floor and here we played and dreamed away the long summer days.

On the other side of the garden was "The Dell"; no doubt it was only a small depression with a few flowering shrubs and mossy slopes, but to us it was an enchanted valley, made thrilling by a Constant Peril. To reach it from our tree house, we had to pass under a mulberry tree, from which fruit fell in great quantities and there, crushed and rotting, attracted buzzing wasps and stinging bees. With pounding hearts, we dashed in wide circles past these Monsters to reach "The Dell".

The garden was full of songbirds; it would have been a paradise for them had it not been for Puffins, the great white cat. With fiendish skill and cruelty, she levied a daily toll. Strewn feathers and wings brought sorrow to us all, until it came to a choice between getting rid of Puffins and losing all the birds. The birds solved the problem while we were still debating it. One morning, hearing a terrific racket in the garden, scoldings, noisy whistling and shrilling, we ran out to find that hundreds of birds had gathered in delegations in separate trees and were flitting back and forth as if in consultation. Puffins was crouched in the center of the lawn, ears back and yellow eyes ablaze. Suddenly, as if by command, the various groups gathered into a flock—a dark, whirling mass—that dived straight at the cowering criminal. A white streak—she dashed for shelter under the steps. There she stayed for two days and, as far as we could see, never killed another bird in the garden.

Puffins was always having litters of kittens and we were shocked when we found that they never grew up, because she invariably killed them before we could take them away from her. She had been such a lively, amusing little ball of fluff when we first got her that we bore with her later, even when she grew into a big fat bad-tempered murderer.

No sisters could have loved one another more than we did, and yet I am sure that no three children ever fought more fiercely. Many of our games were fights. One of the best games was dividing things. Jessie, always first with a new idea, started by saying: "Let's divide. I'll take . . ." (whatever she wanted). Margaret got second choice and I got what was left. We divided the house; Jessie took the lower porch, Margaret the upper, and that left the front steps—no good at all—and the back steps—not much better—for me. Generously they added the kitchen porch, from which Maggie always drove us with a broom. Tears and protests were of no avail. "Maggie will let *you* play there", was the answer.

We divided the universe. Jessie took the sun and sunset; Margaret, the moon and stars; and I was given the sunrise and rainbow. I pointed out the unfairness of it in no

Margaret and Jessie
about four and five

Eleanor Randolph Wilson ("Nellie")
about three years old

Woodrow Wilson
at the time of his marriage

Ellen Axson Wilson
at the time of her marriage

uncertain terms—we never saw the sunrise and seldom a rainbow—but Margaret, who always had the perfect answer, told me that I had been given the most beautiful of all and must be content. We divided the Greek gods and goddesses. Juno and Jupiter were Jessie's; Pallas Athene and Apollo, Margaret's, and Diana and Mercury, mine.

The real fight came when we divided the world. Who should have America? We made so much noise that father heard us, called us into the study and stood us in a row. He listened seriously and patiently, then suggested that we draw straws, and arranged them for us. Jessie got America. Immediately we began an extensive search for maps, each writing her name across her possessions, in large untidy letters. We were not caught until nearly every history and geography in the house was ruined.

One of our great treasures and secrets was "The Thumb Confession Book", a tiny volume full of mysterious questions, such as: "Do you think it is woman's prerogative to pop the question?" We gave this a lot of thought and, still uncertain as to its meaning, wrote "No" and signed our names. The question, "Who, in your opinion, is the world's greatest orator?" was the most important of all, though simple to answer. We wrote "Professor Wilson", and insisted that our friends do the same before we allowed them to see anything else in the book. They were all quite willing, with the exception of the little Purveses, who stubbornly wrote, "Dr. Purves". I used to wonder how other children could be really happy without a father like ours. Even when I was very young, I was conscious of a feeling of satisfaction that I was I, because of him.

One summer we managed to have a glorious vacation in

the Virginia mountains. A little corner of the old South, it was really a farm where we paddled in the brook and ran barefoot over the lovely countryside.

It belonged to Colonel Stribling, a dignified veteran of the Civil War, who had been persuaded to take "paying guests". The huge white house with upper and lower porches, both front and rear, seemed shabby in the daytime, but at night it was aglow with romance—the fragrance of magnolias, the mellow light of oil lamps, young girls in long frilly dresses and flowers in their hair, walking about with their beaux; Negroes singing under the trees and the drawling voices of the grown-ups on the porch, chatting in the dusk.

They called one another "uncle" and "cousin" and "aunt" in that charming Southern way that makes one feel that the South is one happy, congenial family and that to be admitted into that family is the most desirable thing in the world.

It was here that we first met Lucy Marshall Smith and Mary Randolph Smith, of New Orleans. Daughters of a famous Presbyterian minister, they were devoted and inseparable sisters, combining a rare nobility of character with gaiety and wit. A warm bond was established at once between the Wilson family and the Smiths. With great interest, father and mother struggled with them through the maze of family trees until, satisfied that they were related, they became "Cousin Lucy" and "Cousin Mary", "Cousin Ellen" and "Cousin Woodrow". We spent hours with our new cousins, who had an inexhaustible collection of stories and games. It was the beginning of a friendship that was to last all our lives, as from that time on we saw them at least once a year; they came to visit us, no matter where we happened to be.

Cousin Lucy was the "original Wilson man". She predicted that father would one day be President of the United States. I remember the quick flush that came into mother's face, as she watched father shrug his shoulders and dismiss the matter lightly. To me, it seemed quite probable. Of course, he could be President or anything else that he wanted to be.

There were five or six other children at Colonel Stribling's. We found them rather wild and strange. One day we overheard an exasperated parent tell mother that we had such "nice manners" and were "so good". We were puzzled when she answered rather wistfully that at times she feared we were too good.

Father was busy writing in the mornings and we were not allowed to disturb him. Sometimes in the afternoons he walked with us, but more often went off alone on a horse. In the evenings he usually joined in the old-fashioned games, played in the big double parlor.

We sat at one long table in the dining room, Colonel Stribling erect and dignified at the head. And such food! Mountains of chicken, cornbread and beaten biscuits three times a day. A large earthen jar of biscuits was left on the sideboard to comfort hungry children between meals.

Not long after we moved to Library Place, Fräulein Boehm came to be our governess. She was selected by a friend of father's, who was studying at the University of Berlin. Plain and shy, with prominent teeth, she wore her hair in a pompadour with a curled artificial fringe across her forehead, and her hats very high on her head. She had

33

been anxious to leave Germany because she was an old maid and felt in the way, but confessed that when the ship pulled away from the dock, she was heartbroken and wanted to jump overboard. That the Smiths were independent and self-sufficient, though unmarried, was immediately a great comfort to her.

She arrived on a Sunday in summer when we were all out in the garden with the usual Sunday guests. Mother and father did their best to make her feel at home at once; but at luncheon, her first meal in our house, she suddenly looked as though she were going to faint. When mother asked her what was wrong, she only shook her head and looked around the table desperately. We were eating corn on the cob with gusto—butter was dripping from the chins of her new pupils. We giggled. But one gently reproving look from mother suppressed us.

Fräulein's English was excellent. She was to teach us French and German, and it was like mother and father to have feared that she might be offended if she were asked to start with French—so we studied German. She began by making us roll our *r*'s, and, when I found that I could roll mine loudest and longest, I became a nuisance.

She was soon quite happy with us and keenly interested in American family life, often telling us that we should realize and appreciate the American man's consideration for his family, and how different the European attitude was.

We made her talk about Germany as much as we could. One day while I was sitting on her lap, I said, "But you are for America, aren't you, Fräulein? If we had a war with Germany, you would be on our side, wouldn't you?" Instantly she pushed me off and stood up like a little soldier, a strange new expression on her face, as she said, "I would follow my Kaiser." I couldn't understand it at all, but it made me sad; so, as usual, I wept.

We loved Fräulein and soon were absorbed in the study of German. We must have learned quickly for, not long after she came, we were having a particularly noisy fight and father called out, "For heaven's sake, stop quarreling, or if you must quarrel, quarrel in German." Relieved because we knew he couldn't understand and, with hardly a moment's pause, we continued, "Du bist ein Narr; du bist ein Esel." Later he told us that his disapproval was mixed with delight to hear us rattle off German so easily.

There was a queer little organ in the nursery. By a laborious system of pumping, it could be persuaded to emit wheezing sounds. Here Fräulein attempted to introduce us to the subtle enjoyments of music. Margaret took to it at once and sat patiently struggling with scales, very red in the face from pumping. Jessie tried conscientiously, but soon gave up, and I rebelled hotly. I usually wheedled Fräulein into playing to me and singing sentimental little ditties during my lesson hour. I can remember the lump in my throat as we wailed together, "Es war ein armes Veilchen."

We had a day and night nursery in the new house. In the day nursery we had our meals and lessons. The food came up on a "dumb-waiter" and, when Maggie rattled the ropes, we dashed to open the door and see what surprise she had sent. We had oyster stew often and hated it, so we slipped the oysters out of the window when Fräulein wasn't looking. They gathered there in a horrible messy heap. One

35

day we heard mother consulting with the gardener about some strange ugly growth that had appeared in the garden. When we confessed timidly, she only laughed and we had no more oysters in our stews.

From the months of happiness and peace spent in the day nursery, two separate days of horror and one week of perfect bliss stand out vividly.

Margaret took care of the canary; the cage hung near a window. Once, during the summer, when we had several days of unusually warm weather, we had lessons and meals in the garden and didn't use the day nursery at all. About the third day, Margaret remembered the canary. We dashed up the stairs, despair in our hearts; we knew before we opened the door. There on the floor of the cage was a pathetic little heap. Sorrow and remorse overcame us and we could neither sleep nor eat. Margaret was heartbroken. For days she was inconsolable and at night she woke, screaming. Her grief was deep and lasting and, for many years, if she was worried or troubled, she dreamed again of the canary.

The second horror was the fire. We were preparing for supper and I was trying to help Fräulein by removing the dark table cover and replacing it with a tablecloth. I said to Jessie, "Bet I can do it without putting down the lamp." I took the lamp in one hand and the table cover in the other, and dropped the lamp on the floor. Instantly the straw matting was ablaze. I made one desperate attempt to pick up the lamp, burning my hand severely. We all three ran up and down the stairs, screaming, and Fräulein lost her head completely. Mother, as usual, came to the rescue; gathering some rugs left on an upper porch to air, she quietly put out the fire before the alarmed neighbors and the town fire engine arrived.

The room was not badly damaged, but I developed an incurable dread of fire. Through the years I have walked in the night, up to attics, down to basements, listening, sniffing, looking for a fire.

My perfect week was when I had scarlatina and was isolated. At first mother stayed with me, spending every moment in the nursery, with no access to other parts of the house. When she was completely worn out, father relieved her and, for once, I had him all to myself. He sang to me, read to me, played on the floor with me.

We had a number of pieces of tile, left over from some of the new buildings at Princeton, and with these and some blocks, he made castles, colleges and cathedrals—tiny models of his favorite Norman design. He arranged a pulley with a basket, so we could send letters down to Margaret and Jessie, and wrote the letters himself, so that they would be germless. We had our meals together; he fed me, petted me, slept in the bed beside me and my bliss was complete. Then, one day, I was well again and had to share him with the others.

CHAPTER THREE

Library Place

WE WERE ALWAYS tremendously interested in everything relating to father's and mother's lives before we came on the scene. We plied them with questions, particularly about their first meeting. At length father said gravely, "When I decided to get married, I put all the girls in the world in a row and picked out your mother." I believed it implicitly. I could see the endless rows of girls and my little mother, in the tight-fitting basque she wore in our favorite photograph, stepping out of the line when father beckoned.

He had seen her first when he was six years old and she a tiny child of two. Visiting his uncle, James Bones, in Rome, Georgia, the little boy had been fascinated by the bronze-haired baby who lived near by and who had what her "mammy" called "a hole in her cheek"—a deep dimple that came and went according to her mood. He had insisted upon holding her gingerly in his arms for a few moments until his cousin Jessie teased him and called him away to more manly pursuits. But it was not until more than twenty years later that he really met her. He was a struggling young lawyer then who had "hung up his shingle" in Atlanta and had already had his first article,

"Cabinet Government in the United States" published in a magazine. He went again to Rome and was taken by his cousins to the Presbyterian Church to hear mother's father, Edward Axson, preach. Mother came in, dressed in deep mourning, and holding her little brother, Ed, by the hand. Father was enchanted at once but disturbed because he thought that she must be a young widow with a child. He was presented to her after church and saw her again the next evening at the Browers'. After escorting her home, he walked for a long time, his head filled with dreams, and finally found himself standing on a small bridge gazing at the stream below and vowing that some day he would marry "Miss Ellie-Lou". Mother was delighted with him but, true to her strict upbringing, treated him at first with great formality. He told us that her first two notes to him, written in answer to his pressing invitations to walk or drive, began "Mr. Wilson"—they didn't write "dear Mr."—in those days—but the third time she absent-mindedly wrote "Mr. Woodrow" which sent him into ecstasies of hope. Their engagement was a long one. He was making a bare living and mother felt that it was her duty to stay with her father, who developed an incurable melancholia after the death of his wife. Eventually and literally, my grandfather died of a broken heart.

One day mother wrote father, reviewing the hopelessness of the situation and suggesting that the engagement be broken, but he took the first train, ran all the way from the station to her house and, arriving breathless and almost speechless, vowed that he would die if she did not marry him.

Father was born in Staunton, Virginia, on December

28, 1856, and christened Thomas Woodrow. There were two older sisters, Marion and Annie, and a younger brother, Joseph. The family was deeply religious. Grandfather Wilson, a Presbyterian minister, was adored in his parish for his devotion to his work, his kindliness and a certain keen wit. One of the family's favorite stories about him is that one day, after a visit to a parishioner, they walked together to the gate, where grandfather's horse and buggy waited. Patting the horse, the man said, "Your horse looks fine, Dr. Wilson; much better than you do." To which grandfather replied: "Quite so, sir. I take care of my horse, and my parishioners take care of me."

Father loved to hear grandfather read and sat by the hour listening to him. As a result, he did not learn to read easily himself until he was twelve.

At sixteen, he went to Davidson College and dreamed of being an admiral in the navy. From there he went to Princeton and, after graduating, studied law at the University of Virginia. Admitted to the bar, he went to Atlanta with the intention of practicing there, but after a few months, finding "little connection between Law and Justice", he decided to take a postgraduate course at Johns Hopkins. Two years later he joined the faculty of Bryn Mawr as professor of history.

After her father's death, mother went to New York to study painting at the Art Students' League. She had always longed to be an artist, but when father accepted the position at Bryn Mawr, at the magnificent salary of fifteen hundred a year, she came back at once to marry him.

Following a brief honeymoon at Arden in the North Carolina mountains, they went to live in a little house at

Manse in Wilmington, North Carolina, during Grandfather Wilson's occupancy

Front row, left to right: Wilson Howe, George Howe. Second row: Dr. George Howe,
Jessie Howe (Aunt Annie's daughter). Third row: Woodrow Wilson, Aunt Annie (Mrs.
George Howe) and "Little Annie," Grandfather Wilson, Marian Wilson, Joseph Wilson
(W. W.'s brother). Standing: Nannie, Minnie

the edge of a wood at Bryn Mawr. But even in those first years they were not alone; mother's brother, eighteen years younger than she, lived with them. They were both devoted to "little Ed" and told many stories about him.

Once when still quite a small boy, he was sent to market for a basket of eggs. On the way home he was set upon by rough boys. He shouted to them that if they would wait until he had put the eggs in a safe place, he would fight them all—and he did—arriving home badly scratched, his clothes in tatters, but with the eggs intact. The experience was a shock, however, and from it he developed a stammer that he never quite lost.

A cousin of mother's, Mary Hoyt, who was a student at Bryn Mawr, also lived in "the little house in the wood", and Margaret and Jessie were both born during this period. Each time, however, Mother went to stay with her relatives in Gainesville, Georgia, humorously insisting that they "must not be born Yankees".

Throughout their entire lives father and mother remained true to their religious heritage, although mother went through periods of doubt and anxious searching for answers to ultimate questions. She read deeply into Kant and Hegel, and the English and Scotch philosophers, and seemed to arrive at conclusions that satisfied her. Father had a deep and unquestioning faith in God which was based, I think, on an inborn, intuitive sense of His nearness and reality. He never felt the need of proving God's existence. His faith was a dominant, living factor in his life and never failed him to the very end.

He was singularly tolerant, free from any taint of bigotry, and always saw and enjoyed amusing situations,

41

even in matters that concerned his church. When the Presbyterian Synod decided against the doctrine of "infant damnation" and declared the decision retroactive, he laughed and said, "Think of all those dear little babies that have been burning in hell so long; now they will all be released."

Father and mother took an active part in church affairs, but they never sent us to Sunday School. Grandfather Wilson had surprised the good people of his pastorate by arguing that, if they couldn't give their own children religious instruction at home, Sunday School wouldn't help much. Father and his brother and sisters had studied their Bible and their Shorter Catechism, as we did, with their mother.

But in spite of our parents' wise and intelligent instruction, Margaret was secretly haunted for a while by fear of "hell-fire". Terrified by certain Biblical thunderings, she brooded alone over her possible fate. Then a day came when, her face alight with relief, she ran into the nursery where Jessie and I were playing on the floor. "I know something," she cried, "something father and mother don't believe in!"

I gazed up at her enquiringly, but Jessie merely said calmly, "I guess it's only Santa Claus".

Margaret's eyes were shining as she answered, "Oh, no! It isn't Santa Claus—it's something important!" Then suddenly she looked a little frightened and ran away as fast as she had come.

Years afterward I remembered that day and asked her to tell me at last what father and mother didn't believe in. "It was Hell," she said. "I heard them say that it was only a state of mind."

Grandfather Wilson came to live with us after retiring from his pastorate in North Carolina. He used to say, "It's hard for me to become accustomed to being known as Woodrow Wilson's father. I have always been just Joseph Wilson and not somebody's father." But he adored father and was immensely proud of him. Theirs was a rare companionship, founded on deep understanding and mutual respect.

Father's gift of lucid expression in speaking and writing was cultivated to a great extent by grandfather. When father was young, his father constantly interrupted with, "Tommy, what do you mean by that?" And when "Tommy" explained, choosing his words more carefully, he added, "Well, why didn't you say that?" Father tried the system on us with no noticeable results.

Grandfather was a strikingly handsome man, clean-shaven, with a rather Roman nose, heavy eyebrows and a mop of white hair. He and mother were great friends, but we were afraid of him. At the table, he put cake in his water and salt on his strawberries and it drove me frantic. One day I summoned courage to ask him why he did it, but he looked at me sternly and said, "Mind your own business and don't ask silly questions." After that, I tried not to watch when we had strawberries, but it was no use; my eyes were glued to his plate as I sat with set teeth, almost tasting the salt myself. He hated popovers—called them "fake food"—and said he liked to find something inside when he opened a biscuit.

He was much given to puns, his favorite being, "It's a curious thing that a man who cares as much as I do about correct grammar should be forced to make an error every

43

time he says his own name—Joseph R. Wilson—when, as anyone can see, it should be, Joseph Is Wilson."

Father joined—in fact, competed—in the pun-making. Time after time he stood us in a row to ask if we knew "Why Robinson Crusoe?"

One evening grandfather and I were alone in the house. Margaret and Jessie had gone for a walk with father and mother. I answered a tap at the door promptly, thinking they had returned, and a drunken man reeled into the room. I crouched against the wall, too terrified to think what I should do. I must have called out as, presently, grandfather came thundering down the stairs, brandishing a stick and looking like Jehovah himself. I was so overcome by his magnificence that I lost my fear. Striding toward the man, he shouted, "Get out of here, sir." At the word "sir", the drunkard jerked himself together and fled into the night.

It is difficult to remember a time when there were not one or more relatives living with us. Father's sister Annie and her daughter often stayed for months. Annie's husband had died while we were living in the Hunt house. She seemed the perfection of widowhood to me, handsome and dignified, always a little tragic and easily moved to tears. Her weeds fascinated me, and I determined to be a widow when I grew up. The idea appealed to me so much that often, when I was alone, I trailed along with downcast eyes and mournful dignity, drowned in the pleasant despair of the loss of an imaginary husband.

Aunt Annie had a genius for entertaining young people, and we spent hours in her room, while she read to us and invented games. She had two grown sons—Wilson and

44

George—the latter an intimate friend and classmate of Ed Axson's at Princeton.

"Little Annie", two years younger than I, was my play-mate. She was a frail, delicate child with long, golden hair and a clear complexion that we all envied. She wasn't allowed to climb trees or play rough games and, though I was fond of her, I sneaked off occasionally for a few hours' respite from the responsibility of seeing that she didn't fall down, bump her head or skin her knees.

Ed Axson lived at the college, but he also had a small room in the attic at Library Place, where he worked at his "inventions"—mysterious contraptions of wood, wire and bits of cork. Father often went up to the little room to discuss the inventions and watch their progress. We adored Ed and he amused himself by telling us the most fantastic yarns. One was that all girls grow up to be boys and vice versa. I believed it, but was worried at the thought that I might grow a beard. Jessie always laughed and Margaret was doubtful but interested, as she often lamented the fact that she was a girl. Colonel Ed Brown, mother's cousin from Atlanta, with his beautiful wife whom we all adored, stayed for a memorable week. He had a fund of good stories and father was always delighted to see him.

Father's cousins, Helen Bones and Marion Brower, and Mary, Florence, Margaret and Will Hoyt, who were mother's, came frequently for short visits. Father especially enjoyed Helen Bones, a lovely little creature with blue-black hair and great gold-flecked eyes. She took his teasing rapturously and egged him on when he felt foolish, much to everyone's delight.

45

Mother's sister, Margaret Axson, twenty years younger than mother and only four years older than my sister Margaret, lived with us part of the time until she married. We resented her fiercely when we were all children, as she insisted on being called "Aunt Maggie". Margaret Wilson was bitter and persistent in her rebellion, but eventually, to keep peace in the family, we all "Aunt Maggied" her. Later, when we were grown up, we had our revenge, for then she fruitlessly implored us to drop it. Grandmother had died when "Aunt Maggie" was born, so when she was small she believed she was mother's child and, not at all pleased at the prospect of sharing mother, she greeted her first niece by slapping her soundly on her tiny, red face. When she grew up, we admired her tremendously. She was aloof, languid, almost mysterious, wore long ruffled dresses, always had a flower tucked into the heavy knot of hair at the nape of her neck and treated her many beaux with magnificent disdain.

But of all the relatives and friends, Stockton Axson, mother's brother, was father's dearest and closest companion. They had the same sense of fun, the same love of books. "Uncle Stock" was a bachelor and lived in a deliciously untidy apartment. As he was often in poor health, we were constantly taking him soup, jellies, cake and other dainties. Such a fascinating room, littered with books and strewn with cigar ashes! There were nearly always students there and I used to curl up in a corner, listening to the cross-fire of conversation, wretched because I couldn't think suddenly of something brilliant to say, something so astonishing that they would all stop talking and notice me. I vowed to myself that some day I would learn the secret.

Mother was eager for Uncle Stock to marry. She encouraged and advised the many girls who were interested in him, but each time he managed to escape. He had a deep resonant voice and such a jolly chuckle that the house was filled with gaiety and laughter when he came; it is difficult to understand the melancholia from which he suffered so much in later years and which mother alone seemed able to dispel. I realize now what a source of help and strength father and mother were to all these people. Father, much occupied with his own work and duties, seemed always able to make time to talk to them and listen to their troubles. How mother managed to stretch the slender household budget to take care of them all, and how she found room for them, I cannot understand. There was always enough for everyone and everything; and I never heard even a vague hint of money troubles of any sort.

In spite of father's popularity with all ages and types and his rare capacity for companionship, he was a shy person and dreaded meeting strangers. He had any number of excuses—he was "too busy", or "tired" or "indisposed", or just didn't "want to go". Then mother gently explained that there was no escape, that guests were arriving or an engagement had been made. He invariably surrendered and, once the ice was broken, enjoyed himself more than anyone else at the party. It has always amazed me to hear or read that father was "cold" or "grim" or "aloof". Warm, close friendships were a necessity to him, a stimulant that he prized, guarded and requited in full measure.

There was a constant interchange of visits in the widening circle of intimate friends at Princeton. Seldom formal calls, but long chatty visits in the afternoon or early evening, simple dinner parties where conversation was the only form of amusement. There were no movies, no radios, nowhere to go except into the realms of the mind. There is a leisureliness about life in a university town, a gentle rhythm that I have never found anywhere else.

Harry Fine, professor of mathematics, and later dean of his department, lived across the street with his handsome wife and three strenuous children. He was one of father's dearest friends and never wavered in his loyalty and devotion through all the bitter controversies that developed later at the University. He and father often stood for hours before one house or the other, deep in argument or conversation, and so engrossed that they had to be dragged away to dinner like truant boys.

The Hibbens lived on the other side of town. They were good neighbors in the rare sense of the word and invariably the first to appear when anyone was ill or help of any sort was needed. They had one child, Beth, who shocked us all by calling her parents "Jack" and "Jennie".

We all loved Mrs. Ricketts, a widow. Her grown-up daughter, Henrietta, gave charming children's parties and had an inexhaustible supply of interesting stories and games. Mrs. Ricketts was an extraordinary character, an "original" if there ever was one. She was afraid of no one and nothing, except servants; even to talk to one disturbed her terriby. As she had some money that she invested shrewdly, mother accepted her advice about her own modest financial affairs. Mrs. Ricketts had a curious way of walking; quickly, holding her skirt off the ground with both hands and then suddenly dropping it and waving her hands in the air. She could not bear to have her sleeves slip over her wrists and this was her quaint way of keeping them in place. One summer we were all staying at the same hotel in the Adirondacks. Walking up a mountainside one warm afternoon, with father, we saw her ahead, dropping her skirts and waving her hands as usual. Father caught up with her and took her arm. "Can I help you, Mrs. Ricketts?" "Help me? Help me? I don't need any help—I'm only eighty," was her lively answer, and off she dashed so that we had to hurry to keep up with her.

Father and mother, the Hibbens and the Bliss Perrys, who were also intimate friends, used to meet almost every Sunday afternoon for tea at the Rickettses'. Miss Henrietta was a brilliant conversationalist, never hesitating to challenge even the most solemn professorial opinions. I remember seeing the group come out of her gate, their faces alight, and continue a discussion all the way home.

The wedding of Professor Harper and Belle Westcott provided the liveliest excitement of our early childhood. Margaret, Jessie and I, "the mantel ornaments", were their only attendants. But I lost interest in the whole performance when I saw that the bride wore a plain brown dress and, as we followed her up the church aisle to the altar, I tried to slip into the pew where father and mother were sitting. My sisters, each clutching one of my hands, pulled me firmly along.

It would be impossible to enumerate all the friends of those early days. Later, when father became president of the University and the reconstruction struggles began, some of them disagreed with him and dropped away, but the majority kept in touch with him throughout his entire life, notably his friends of the Class of '79. They called themselves "The Witherspoon Gang", having lived in Witherspoon Hall, one of the oldest dormitories at Princeton. They were Robert Bridges, William B. Lee, Edwin Webster, Dr. Hiram Woods, Dr. Charles Mitchell, Judge Robert Henderson, and Charles Talcott. They had frequent reunions and later, when we moved to Prospect, all came together to visit us. I rather dreaded their arrival, as I expected them to be sedate old men, but they were as gay, jolly and friendly as so many young boys.

Father enjoyed the society of women, especially if they were what he called "charming and conversable". He didn't defend himself when we remarked that he seemed to find more beautiful women "conversable" than plain ones. He thought women had "deeper sensibilities", "finer understanding" than most men, and he particularly liked the gaiety, the "lightly turned laughter", so characteristic of Southern women.

He had several deep and lasting friendships with women, writing them long letters and spending hours in their company. These friendships he shared with mother and I never saw her show a trace of jealousy. She knew there was no cause for it. She considered herself a "grave and sober" person and often said, "Since you have married someone who is not gay, I must provide for you friends who are." Mrs. Hibben, the Smiths, Mrs. Reid of Baltimore, Mrs. Toy of Boston, Mrs. Hulbert, all brilliant and charming women, were the ones he liked most.

I remember sitting with him, spellbound, in Mrs. Reid's drawing room, listening to their conversation. He appeared in a new light to me that day. Although I had realized before what an extraordinary person he was, he had been one of us, part of the family, and now he seemed a dazzling stranger. The range and versatility of his mind were revealed in his conversation. Not in the least didactic, never professorial, he spoke with charm and utter candor. He was witty, ridiculous, profound, almost in the same breath. Never a monologuist, he was one of the best listeners I have ever known. Looking at his companion with eager attention, his exceptionally mobile face reflected his own emotions and reactions. I never heard him tell an anecdote that was not apropos. He enjoyed a good story and had a priceless collection stored away in his mind, but he often said, "I have the silliest memory in the world. I never forget a nonsense rhyme, but I don't know one piece of fine poetry by heart."

He had an enchanting manner with small children, treating their remarks with the utmost gravity, then making them scream with laughter at his funny faces.

His mind was so quick that he was impatient of repetition or dullness. I have often heard him say, "I can't understand why people tell me the same thing over and over— I'm really not a fool." Scrupulously considerate of other people's feelings, he was generally able to conceal this impatience from all but those who knew him intimately. But I used to watch when Wilson Howe came to see us. Wilson was handsome, but so slow that father's impatience was betrayed at Wilson's first word.

He used to imitate Margaret Axson's and mother's slow drawl and insisted that mother took longer than anyone else in the world to say things. He was never really impatient with her, except when she kept him waiting. I remember seeing him stand at the foot of the stairs when they were going out, looking very distinguished and a little stern, and I knew he was trying not to call her again. When she came rushing down, pulling on her gloves and explaining breathlessly that she had had to stop to attend to some detail of the household routine, he smiled and it was all over.

He had a hot temper which, however, was so sternly curbed that we never saw him really lose control of it. He never expressed anger about small or personal matters, but only when someone was attacking, unfairly, a cause for which he was fighting. Usually, if he knew that someone was lying, his face would go white and the words would come very quietly and bitingly. Never, even when we were children, did he show irritation, although he sometimes quite sternly expressed his disapproval, and I am certain that he and mother never quarreled in their entire lives. At times they would differ emphatically without reaching an agreement, because they were independent thinkers, but always with good humor and even enjoyment. Mother sometimes grew excited in an argument, because there was a passionate, temperamental element in her nature which she could not always repress, but her excitement never turned into bad temper. Father never found fault with her —what she did was perfection to him. Only one thing she ever did seemed to disturb him vaguely. She had a habit of folding her arms, when she was listening to him, and he often stopped and said, "Don't do that, Nell; it pushes out your upper arm." Mother unfolded her arms quickly, quite likely folding them again in a few moments.

Father had been working so long on his "History of the American People" that we were rather stunned when he came out of the study one day and announced that it was finished. Mother sprang up and kissed him, and we went shouting to Maggie with the great news. Her only thought was for me. "Now Nellie can have her pony!" But I didn't get the pony; we got a new carpet for the hall upstairs, where I had been playing with my wooden horses and carts, making such a racket that it was driving everyone in the house crazy.

The History was immediately popular. It ran through numerous editions and was translated into several foreign languages; but father had no talent for driving a good bargain and there were no large returns.

He had worn himself out with the long task and developed a severe case of writer's cramp, but soon taught himself to write clearly with his left hand. He used an old-fashioned style of shorthand in making notes and rough drafts of his work and this plagued his stenographers, as he persisted in its use all his life. There had been an afternoon when the work had worried him to such an extent that he had behaved like the proverbial absent-minded professor. Going upstairs to dress for dinner, he had undressed completely and climbed into bed. It was not in the least like him and, though mother had laughed and teased him, there was a worried little frown on her brow.

That summer she persuaded him to take a bicycle tour through England and Scotland. They had hoped to go together, but there was only money enough for one and she knew that an ocean voyage would restore his health.

He wrote her long fat letters which she read to us, pausing to skip a page now and then and saying, with a quiet smile, "This part is sacred", but sometimes she would, as if by accident, read us a sentence or two of his love-making.

She couldn't resist letting us a little way into the secret, because she was so proud of being his sweetheart still. She was as cheerful and busy as ever, but everything was dull and changed with father away.

The day he returned, Margaret was exploring a building near by. Jessie and I had been watching her dizzy climb and were transfixed with horror when she suddenly made a wild dash and dropped to the ground, screaming. She had seen father waving his hat out of the window of the town hack as it turned the corner into Library Place.

Our enormous pride in father brought a crisis. Mother came into the nursery one morning looking very serious. "Your father has been told that you are boasting about him. Is it true?" Although I wasn't sure what boasting meant, I promptly denied it. Jessie thought a moment and then said, "I haven't mother", but Margaret burst out with, "Well, mother, I do—I tell them a few things."

Mother sat down, drew us around her and said, "I understand how you feel, but it does embarrass your father, so after this we four will have a beautiful time talking about him as much as we like when we are alone, but not to other people."

Mr. Cleveland came to live in Princeton at the end of his second term in the White House. He lectured at the college and, because he was nervous before what he called an "intellectual audience", often asked father's aid and advice. Sometimes he came to father's study, but more often father went to him. Something in his manner made us timid, and I noticed that even his own children tiptoed when they came into a room where he was and, when we played in the

Cleveland garden, if we found ourselves under his study window, we whispered.

Once, when the whole town was in a furor of excitement over the elections, we summoned courage to ask him for a Parker button. Judge Parker was running for President against Theodore Roosevelt and the Clevelands and we were almost the only Democratic children in a violently Republican neighborhood. Mr. Cleveland pinned on our buttons solemnly and we got away, as quickly as possible, to continue our campaign of shouts and insults with renewed vigor.

Mrs. Cleveland, a great beauty, wore clothes that were a topic of lively discussion among the children, not only because they were smart, but because she had so many. Mother seldom had a new dress; we teased her for years because someone once said, "Mrs. Wilson, every fall you look sweeter in that brown dress." I know that at that time she allowed herself forty dollars a year for her own clothes.

Ruth Cleveland was about my age and we became warm friends. There were two other girls in the family, Esther, a wild-eyed tomboy, and Marion, a frail, dainty child who lisped. Margaret, Jessie and I were playing with them one day when father arrived. He asked about the game and we explained that Esther was Marc Antony, Ruth, Caesar and I, Brutus. Far over on the other side of the room was little Marion. "What are you, Marion?" father asked. "Oh, I'm duth the mob", she lisped.

Once Ruth had a birthday party and, while we were dressing to go, I discovered that I had no present for her. Mother gave me some money and I dashed to the village.

I chose a gaudy little gilt frame and the expression on mother's face when she saw it crushed me. It seemed suddenly the ugliest thing in the world and I was ashamed of my exhibition of bad taste. I went to the party with the hateful object clutched in my hand and gave it to Ruth with all the indifference I could assemble. She looked at it —and said nothing.

At the table my spirits reached a new low at what I considered a serious *faux pas* of Margaret's. She sat at Mrs. Cleveland's right and the salad, elaborately arranged in three half cantaloupes, was passed to her first. She took one of the halves, the child next her hesitated a moment and then did the same, and the third child took all that remained of the salad. After some delay more was produced, a different sort entirely, and placed in the exact center of a large bowl, sans decoration. Then, of course, everyone realized what had happened.

Dr. Wyckoff was a fine example of the now almost obsolete "family physician". He was a gloomy old soul with fierce bristling eyebrows and I shivered every time I saw him. One winter everyone in the house had the grippe. Father, worried because Margaret had a relapse and we seemed doomed to a sort of second round, asked Dr. Wyckoff, "Do you suppose this will go on forever?"

"I see no reason why it should not continue indefinitely, no reason whatever," was his solemn answer.

Father was a staunch champion of the public school. He said that he could tell at once which of his pupils came from public and which from private schools. He believed that the public school developed better habits of study; that it discouraged snobbery and bred confidence in timid pupils.

But the public school at Princeton was in rather a questionable neighborhood and almost inaccessible, so mother and Fräulein taught us until Mrs. Scott opened a small private school. It was three miles away, and until we acquired bicycles, we walked. I hated everything about it except the aviary with its variety of strange bright birds. We were afraid of Mrs. Scott, a tall severe person with a great beak of a nose and a husband who reached to her shoulder, and respectfully called her "Birdie".

The boys at Mrs. Scott's teased Jessie because she was so quiet and gentle. One little brat who sat behind her tied her braids to an ink well and poor Jessie sent the ink flying when she stood up. She didn't fight and cry as Margaret and I did, but once when we were having a lesson in physiology, Mrs. Scott produced a diagram of the human intestines and Jessie fainted neatly at her desk.

Everyone was glad when Miss Fine, a sister of Professor Fine, opened her school. She was a natural teacher and the school was a success from the start.

But my first two years at Miss Fine's were spoiled by a dreadful handicap. My teeth had to be straightened and, in those days, orthodontists had not the skill and delicate contrivances they have today. The wire across my upper teeth protruded at least an eighth of an inch beyond my lips and there were innumerable bits of string attached to it, pulling in every direction. Mother had to retie these strings every night. I felt like a horse with a curb bit. Always shy, I now crept about praying that no one would look at me. Hair in two long tight braids, long black-stockinged legs, a pinafore over my school dress and a mouthful of "hardware", I must have been a startling apparition.

57

Mother liked pinafores, although they were no longer the fashion. That was another cross. There were days when I rebelled and, on my way to school, took off the hated garment, hid it under a hedge and retrieved it on the way home.

We went to a dancing class at the Morgans'. Mr. Morgan was a nephew of J. P. Morgan, and his wife had marvelous clothes and jewels. The magnificent house was set back in a formal park; the imposing entrance and stiff, correct servants awed us and we were never quite comfortable there, in spite of Sara Morgan's fascinating doll house and her lovely parties with Punch and Judy shows and presents for all the guests. We coveted only one thing of all the grandeur that surrounded Sara—a pony cart—in which she seldom asked us to ride unless we begged and begged.

These were happy, carefree days for us. School was out at one and, as we were not required to be home before dark, we ran over the countryside, playing hare and hounds and skating on the brook. For the most part, the residents of the village were professors and their families; later, when Princeton was "discovered", grand country houses were built and the whole atmosphere changed. The streets were full of chugging motors and many of our haunts were desecrated.

We spent six peaceful years at Library Place. But they were vitally important years in the development of father's career. His book, "The State", had come to be used as a text book in many colleges at home and abroad. His lectures at other universities, besides his fine work at Princeton, were building for him a reputation in intellectual circles throughout the country.

In 1896, when Princeton celebrated its Sesquicentennial, father was chosen as principal speaker. When he stood up to make his address, a group of his old classmates rose in a body and cheered, but when he had finished, the whole crowd stood up and shouted. This was, I think, his first ovation. But I was more interested in parades than ovations and, when I saw him marching up Nassau Street, his swinging stride like a happy boy's, I ran along screaming and waving, trying to catch his eye. He was always stirred by a band and loved parades.

Father's appointment to the presidency of Princeton came with thrilling suddenness—at least we three had not heard even a rumor of it. That afternoon I was playing with Sue Fine and Ruth Cleveland. Mrs. Cleveland passed in her carriage; we stopped to watch her go by, as we always did. She called out, "Come here, Nellie," and when I ran over to her she leaned out and said, "Give my love to your father." I thought it queer and naïvely said, "Why?" But she only smiled at me and drove on.

Mother's cheeks were pinker than usual that evening when she told us how it had come about. President Patton had resigned and suggested father as his successor. Without any discussion, and breaking the ancient tradition that the president should be an ordained Presbyterian minister, he had been elected unanimously. Father was calm and said very little, but we knew that he was terribly pleased.

Grandfather, who was ill, sent for us and stood us in a row at the foot of his bed. His deep-set old eyes seemed softer than I had ever seen them as he began, "Never forget what I tell you. Your father is the greatest man I have ever known." Margaret said, "Oh, we know that, grand-

59

father." Frowning at her, he continued, "I've lived a long time, Margaret, and I know what I'm talking about. This is just the beginning of a very great career."

The house was electrified with excitement. Friends crowded in to congratulate father and he assumed a new importance in my eyes. My playmates were curious and envious and I found it difficult to conceal my new sense of pride. Almost at once we began to plan the move to "Prospect," the big stone house in which the presidents of Princeton had always lived.

CHAPTER FOUR

Prospect

With childish thoughtlessness and carried away by the importance of the move, my sisters and I felt no regret at leaving the house we had planned with such eagerness and lived in so happily. But it was a terrible wrench for father and mother. I realize now that this change marked the end of a period of peace and idyllic happiness we were never again to know. This was due, in part, to the fact that we were growing out of our childhood, but the change also brought more work for father, new responsibilities for all of us and, for the first time, the shadow of worry.

Father's love of Princeton was an absorbing factor in his life. He was now to have the opportunity to put into effect many of his plans and dreams. Never prone to dwell in the past, he was confident, full of energy and eager to start.

Mother, proud and happy over his unanimous election, realized that it had opened a way for his brilliant talents, but for her it meant giving up the intimate mode of living she preferred—it meant being forced into the kind of social activity she disliked. Besides she mourned a little over what must necessarily be the end of his career as a "man of letters".

Prospect was on the campus and had no privacy whatever, as the gardens were part of the college grounds. The board of trustees had refused the Pattons enough money for much needed repairs, but they now gave mother a modest sum for that purpose and she did over the entire house with what might easily have been spent on one room. She was absorbed and excited. Homemaking was her forte and this, a glorified form of it, gave her a chance to exercise her amazing efficiency.

At the end of a long day's struggle with plumbers, painters or carpenters, or an exhausting shopping trip, she was never too tired to tell us of the progress she had made or some wonderful bargain she had found. One memorable day, exploring in the dark recesses of the cellar, she unearthed some fine old marble mantels, several carved cornices and two beautiful chandeliers that had been removed from the house and replaced by mid-Victorian monstrosities. When she had given careful instructions as to the cleaning and repairing of these, she disappeared into the cellar in search of more treasure. After that, whenever we went to Prospect and did not find her at once, we knew where she was most likely to be.

Bathrooms were done with tile and glass, and soon the whole place was transformed, radiating the comfort and beauty she had such a genius for creating.

The great main door of Prospect opened into a hall with a very high ceiling, a marble floor and two large marble-top tables. Directly beyond was another hall with a rotunda to the second floor, encircled by an iron balustrade that

"PROSPECT", PRINCETON

ELLEN AXSON WILSON ABOUT 1900

soon became a favorite haunt of ours. From here we could see the guests cross from one room to another and sometimes listen to their conversation as we had done in our own house.

The big drawing room in rose brocade opened into this rotunda hall and had four long French doors leading to a terrace. On the right of this room was a smaller one where mother put the satin-covered furniture from the "drawing room" at Library Place.

Mother and father gave a great deal of thought to the arrangement of the study. It was a room of fine proportions, done in green with bookcases all around the walls, reaching to the ceiling. The long windows framed charming glimpses of the great trees and green lawns of the campus. Here grandfather, Washington, Bagehot and the others looked out of their frames upon new surroundings.

The dining room, spacious and flooded with sunshine, opened into the garden. Mother bought some fine old mahogany pieces for this room and hung a large, very handsome portrait of her grandfather over the mantel. At the top of a long stairway, near the entrance to the dining room, was a huge stained-glass Tiffany window, the gift of two of the trustees. Mother had suggested the design and it seemed the essence of magnificence to me.

Our favorite room was the family sitting room, where there was a big fireplace and all the old familiar tables, chairs, lamps and the shabby antique sofa from the main room of Library Place. They seemed to radiate a friendly warmth, almost a protection against the newness of our surroundings.

There was a tower at one end of the house, with four

rooms one over another. The first was the small drawing room, the second Margaret Axson's bedroom, the third a room father used when he wanted absolute seclusion, and at the top was an empty room opening on the roof. In this "mediaeval tower" we played at Knights and Ladies strutting about in extraordinary costumes.

Mother gave us some of her old things to dress up in, but I always wanted to be a "gentleman and a soldier" and wore an old hat of father's and an improvised sword. Mother made me a dark velvet suit with knee breeches and rhinestone buckles and at Christmas I was given a real sword. I tied it around my waist with a ribbon and wore it constantly, even over my short starched dresses, making a fearful racket as I banged it across the marble floor. Every night before I fell asleep I went over the same story in my mind. I was a soldier, dying on a battlefield and thinking of my beautiful sweetheart, as I murmured, "I die for you".

There were so many bedrooms at Prospect that for once there was sufficient space for all the visiting friends and relatives. But Jessie and I still preferred to room together.

The house had been built in the days when luxurious living was possible and the servants' wing was more than ample—a huge kitchen, pantries, innumerable storerooms. One big room over the kitchen with six windows was at first our play-room, but later it became the billiard room. Father had wanted a billiard table for some time, and mother saved her pennies and surprised him with one. He loved the game, was a skillful player and taught all three of us to play.

We had been terribly excited the day we moved in. The

house was so enormous, the ceilings so high, the cellars so dark and mysterious, that it presented endless possibilities. Then, too, we had found that there were some false windows, probably merely to preserve a certain symmetry on the outside, but we were sure that they were outlets from secret rooms, and we tapped the thick walls hoping to find hidden stairways that led to them.

As it was summer and the college had not opened, the electricity was turned off, and when night came the house lost much of its charm for me. It became unfriendly and gloomy; lamps and candlelight made queer shadows and the strangeness of everything, accentuated in the dim light, filled me with panic. As I sat huddled on the back stairs in tears, a warm whiff from the kitchen attracted me and I went in to see Maggie. She seemed nervous and not at all her usual comforting self; she told me that she thought mother was not happy. On the way to bed, I passed mother's room and heard her crying and father saying, with great tenderness, "I should never have brought you here, darling. We were so happy in our own home."

This was the last straw for me and I crept off to bed more forlorn than ever before in my life. Father's grandeur was swamped in this surge of misery. And where could I hope to find comfort if even mother was crying?

Things were brighter in the morning and our days gradually slipped into some semblance of the happy routine we had always known. Mother began almost at once to do over the garden. A wide driveway swept under the tall elms to the porte-cochère in front, and stone steps in the rear, led down to a big formal "French" garden. Here she let herself go, expending all her energy and imagination. She changed the stiff geometrical design into the typical English garden, the first Princeton had ever seen. A small pool in the center, guarded by four cypresses, was surrounded with a riot of bloom; paths were bordered with masses of multicolor flowers. She believed that a garden should have depth and mystery as well as color, and at the side of the house she planted dogwood, mountain laurel and tall ferns, with little marble benches or a sundial at the end of each vista. She transformed the atmosphere of the whole place completely, without disturbing the dignity of the original plan. One end of the garden was near a dormitory and here mother built a pergola. Before the roses covered it, the students insisted that it was for the "Wilson girls" to do their exercises on; and, if one of us went near it, some youth was sure to pop his head out of a window and ask when we were going to start.

Margaret and Jessie were too dignified now to climb trees. These were left to me and my friends, and we took possession with noisy satisfaction, skinning our knees and tearing our clothes. One tree, called "Cedar of Lebanon", was best of all. I could climb to the very top and it became my sanctuary—I loved the name and made a sort of song of it.

There was an old stable on the grounds, and we climbed a rickety staircase and, crawling through a window at the top, found an apartment which we converted into a club. Here we held important secret meetings, skillfully hidden from the older girls. We fought again the battles of the Yankees and the Rebels and the more recent, less clearly defined skirmishes between Republicans and Democrats. The meetings usually ended abruptly, often with shrieks of

66

"That's a lie". Father heard us once and said, "Don't you know that it is hopeless to argue with anyone about his religious or political convictions?"

The first great excitement after we moved to Prospect was father's inauguration. It was so impressive that I almost forgot that I had a new dress as I stood with my mother and sisters and watched the long academic procession wind across the campus and under the Library Arch to Alexander Hall.

Father looked very impressive in his black gown with velvet bands down the front and on the sleeves, his purple and orange hood, and the "mortar board" with a good tassel. We had watched mother adjust the hood and then, after he had gone in to show grandfather how he looked, he had walked over alone to join the procession.

Against the somber background of black caps and gowns were the blazing colors, indicating different universities and degrees. There were so many celebrities that it was impossible to see them all, but I remember the dark dignity of Booker T. Washington, and J. P. Morgan, whose huge nose filled me with dismay. Grover Cleveland and the Governor of New Jersey led the procession, followed by father and the Chancellor of the State. Father turned and smiled at us as he passed and his eyes seemed bluer than ever.

The deafening and enthusiastic applause that rang through Alexander Hall as he made his address put me into a state of near-collapse. The rest of the day is a blurred memory of crowds—hundreds of people, important ones to be spoken to politely and waited on at the buffet luncheon at Prospect.

Now again, I remembered my new dress as I strutted

about with overwhelming manners. I was disappointed when the guests removed their caps and gowns and became ordinary mortals again. Mother was animated and lovely in a new brown dress—this time with fur—and a sweet little hat with ostrich feathers.

Grandfather had been too ill to attend the ceremonies, but father spent every moment he could spare with him, telling him every detail of his new life and work. Often late at night, when we were in bed, we heard father singing "Crown Him with Many Crowns", "A Mighty Fortress Is our God" and other beautiful old hymns that grandfather loved.

Three months later he died. Father's silent grief was heart-rending, and I was desperate at the realization that, with all my love, I had no way to comfort him. The funeral service was in the study, the coffin resting in a deep recessed window. I was frightened when mother told me to go in, but when I saw the serenity of that beautiful old face, I was comforted. We were glad that he had lived to see the beginning of the realization of his dream for his son.

We still had our long evenings together and Uncle Stock was with us much of the time. He loved to read aloud and did it clearly and with much feeling, but father read so beautifully that I listened to anyone else with tolerance, if not impatience. Those were enchanting hours. Here I was introduced to Keats and Shelley; here for the first time I heard father read his favorite,

Who is the happy Warrior? Who is he
That every man in arms should wish to be?

. . . .

PROSPECT

Whose powers shed round him in the common strife,
Or mild concerns of ordinary life,
A constant influence, a peculiar grace;
But who, if he be called upon to face
Some awful moment to which Heaven has joined
Great issues, good or bad, for human kind,
Is happy as a Lover; and attired
With sudden brightness, like a Man inspired;
And, through the heat of conflict, keeps the law
In calmness made, and sees what he foresaw.

. . . .

Without warning he turned to some such nonsense as
"The Bab Ballads", "The Duke of Plaza-Toro" or Riley's
"Man in the Moon". He read "Mr. Dooley" with his best
brogue, or repeated the latest limerick. He spoke, as he
wrote, in flawless English with no trace of any local accent,
and only one curious idiosyncrasy of speech. He said "he
don't" and "she don't". We teased him about it, but he
scorned explanation or apology and persisted in his use of
this "Southernism".

Nearly every evening, and often at meals, there were
heated arguments or long discussions about the meaning or
derivation of some word or the exact significance of some
phrase and, before these questions were settled to the satisfaction of everyone, there were sometimes eight or nine
books of reference on the floor beside his chair.

A different minister came every Sunday to preach in the
college chapel just outside our gate. He always stayed at
Prospect and usually arrived late Saturday afternoon. After
being shown to his room, he had a chat with father in the

study until dinner was announced. On the way to the dining room came the encounter with the other members of the family, *en masse*. We streamed out of the sitting room, mother, Margaret, Jessie and I, usually Aunt Annie and little Annie and often Margaret Axson or Helen Bones. Father never gave his victim the slightest warning and, if he was young, he was usually overwhelmed with shyness. Father used to say that no man had ever become a great success without having been constantly surrounded by admiring females, and that obviously he had no escape from extraordinary renown by that rule.

As father selected these visiting ministers himself, they were invariably eloquent preachers, but he always managed to suggest tactfully that they should make their sermons as brief as possible. Father's predecessor, Dr. Patton, had once remarked, "No soul was ever saved in Marquand Chapel after twenty minutes"—and it was only on very rare occasions that father himself exceeded the twenty-minute time limit when he made a speech. Mother thought we should be allowed to hear the chapel sermons, but father wanted us to continue to attend the village church, both because he wanted us to keep in touch with church activities and because he felt that the boys in the chapel might prove powerful distractions. It was finally agreed that we should alternate.

One Sunday I had an earache and was pleasantly surprised when mother said I should not go to church. The following Sunday I again had an earache, and again was allowed to stay at home. I tried it once more, but father merely glanced at me and said, "Nellie, get your hat and hurry or you'll be late," plunging me into the depths of humiliation but effecting a speedy and permanent cure.

Mother now began to be busy with lists. She divided the members of the faculty into groups and planned a series of ten dinners. There was much excitement over her new dress. It was green, with white lace at the neck and on the sleeves, and father said it looked like the sea and the foam. She wore this same dress for all ten dinners.

Soon after we moved to Prospect, Aunt Sadie Hoyt came to visit us. She was our only really "fashionable" relative and I had been appalled at the grandeur of her house in Philadelphia when we visited her there. She had all the intricacies of social etiquette at her fingertips and was eager to help and advise mother, who listened with apparent interest to all her suggestions. I noticed that even father was a bit grave and didn't joke with her. We thought her affected and secretly made fun of many of the things she did and said. She talked endlessly about wine and how it should be served. She used a great many French words, pronouncing them in an exaggerated way—"menu" on her lips sounded like "man-who". When father protested mildly to mother over some innovation in the household routine, mother answered him with mock gravity, "Sadie says"—at which father always threw up his hands and laughingly surrendered.

Flat on our tummies, peering down from the rotunda, we watched the first of the ten dinners. The house seemed gay and festive with flowers and lights, but the guests were a great disappointment. They were only the parents of our playmates, all dressed up and being very polite.

71

My fire complex was more active than ever at Prospect. When I was found one night wandering about in the dark basement, mother moved me for a time into a small dressing room that adjoined her room. Father was more than patient with me and explained that there was no danger, as the house was stone, and we had a careful night watchman. But in spite of his repeated assurances, every night before I went to bed, and when no one was watching, I took a good sniff around in the hall.

I was curious about Margaret Axson's system with her beaux. When father was away, she received them in the study and, in a room above, ears glued to the grating of a heating chute, I lay on the floor, hoping to hear the words with which she spurned their proposals and dismissed them.

But my interest in romance received a serious setback one day when a little wizened man and his fat, enormous wife came to call. I sat watching them with suddenly aroused curiosity and, after they had gone, asked, "Why did those two get married, father?" There was a twinkle in his eye but he answered with great gravity, "Never speculate about things like that, Nellie—that way lies madness."

Our first dog was a present from Cousin Wilson Howe's bride, whose name was Virgie. She was very pretty, had golden hair and used "make-up", the first we had seen at close range, and her trousseau, which she good-naturedly displayed to my enraptured eyes, included all the latest styles in ruffles and ribbons and drooping ostrich plumes.

The dog, Sport, was a large greyhound. After Virgie left, mother and father said we must change his name, as they could not bear to hear us say "Sporrrrt" in imitation of our new cousin's gutturals. Mother suggested "Roland", saying, "The names are much the same—here, Spote; here, Roland. They both have the *o* sound."

At first Sport was not allowed to sleep upstairs and was put out in the laundry. One night he appeared at our door and, when we took him back to lock him up, we found the laundry door closed. The mystery was never solved, but after that he was allowed to stay upstairs at night. The students called him "Box on Legs", as he got so fat he could hardly walk. Finally father sent him off to a friend in the country where he could have enough exercise. We missed him terribly, but I think mother was glad to see him go as she was always a little afraid of dogs.

Jessie was determined to be a missionary, when she was old enough. I couldn't bear the idea, so finally promised to give up my plan to be an actress if she would surrender hers; and she agreed, to save me from a fate she considered worse than death. Margaret and I sometimes sampled the wine on the sideboard in the dining room, but Jessie never joined us and, if she caught us, gravely reminded us of the evils of drink.

Jessie's vivid imagination was a constant source of delight. She wrote plays which we and our friends presented before a crowd of admiring parents. She made up some of our games and told me fascinating stories, of her own invention, almost every night before we went to sleep.

The room I shared with her was divided with meticulous precision—all her things on one side and mine on the other. Her small desk was usually locked and once, when I found it open, I could not control my curiosity. In a little drawer I found a neat memorandum of the things to be remembered in her prayers. There was to be much praying for

73

Margaret and me—that we should not quarrel so much and that we should not grow up to be drunkards. Her own trivial delinquencies were listed so quaintly and candidly that I was ashamed and, thrusting the book back, quickly closed the desk.

Weeks before Christmas, Margaret, Jessie and I started working like beavers, making the usual utterly useless and absurd little things. There was a lively spirit of competition and we wanted to prove to mother that the hours she had spent instructing us in sewing, drawing and painting had not been wasted.

We no longer had a tree. As the fireplace could not hold all the stockings, we gathered on the second floor and hung them from the rotunda railing, insisting that the grown-ups hang theirs too, and providing father with a long black one. First we had Christmas carols and then we children brought out our gifts, did all the final marking and tying, and put them in the stockings, adding candies and nuts. Then we were sent off to bed.

Christmas morning we were not allowed to see anything until after breakfast. I have a vivid memory of the agony of sitting through it; the grown-ups eating slowly and taking unnecessary second helpings, quite as though it were an ordinary morning.

Father and mother watched us open our presents before they touched their own. Father gathered his into a neat pile and took them into the study, where he untied and rolled up every bit of string and folded every scrap of paper. This was done partly to tease us and partly because of an inherent distaste for untidiness and confusion.

The midday meal was another protracted affair, and in

the afternoon we went visiting, comparing notes and discussing our presents with our playmates.

In the evening the house was usually full of people and
they all joined in charades. Father dressed himself up in
the most grotesque things imaginable. I remember him in
a hat of mother's, a feather boa and a long velvet curtain
trailing behind him as he walked, one hand held high for
an affected handshake. He was a society woman greeting
"her" friends in a gushing manner and a ridiculous falsetto
voice. He was a very good actor and many times expressed
a humorous wish that he had chosen acting as a career.
Years later, when he was swamped with responsibility and
a little tired or discouraged, he would drop into a chair and
say, "Come along, Nellie, let's run away and go on the
stage. We could do a splendid father-and-daughter act."

We always had a rollicking New Year's Eve. Following
an old Scottish custom, we gathered in the dining room
and, standing on our chairs with one foot on the table,
sang "Auld Lang Syne" at the top of our voices and drank
a toast. Then we dashed to open the front door and let the
Old Year out and the New Year in.

One year a cousin whom we disliked was visiting at
Prospect and we couldn't endure the thought of letting
him witness our precious ceremony, so father hatched a
plot. We were to say good night fairly early and then
sneak back to the dining room before twelve. It worked
perfectly until we began to sing. Then it was impossible
to restrain our spirits and our voices and, of course, our
cousin came down to see what was going on and had to be
let in on the festivities.

The first big social affair of the college year was the

Freshman Reception at Prospect, when all the new boys were introduced to the president and the faculty. The first two or three years I was not allowed to appear. Margaret and Jessie had new dresses and were full of thrilling reports. A sort of forlorn Cinderella, I ate in the kitchen with Maggie, where I found some solace watching the Sophomores trying to steal the ice cream from the back porch, where it was hidden.

When at last I was told I could go to the reception, just a few days off, I was beside myself with excitement. But when Maggie said, "Just think, Nellie, by tomorrow night you'll have a beau", my heart sank. What if not one of the boys asked to call?

Terribly shy, not even the thrill of a new blue dress kept me from being miserable at the party. At last an equally shy and painfully awkward boy managed to stammer out a stilted little speech; he was asking to call. It was all depressingly short of the lively little incident I had pictured, but the party was nearly over, I remembered Maggie and, with more enthusiasm than I felt, urged him to come.

When father was a young professor, he had sometimes coached the football and baseball teams and he never lost his interest in the games. We were all enthusiasts, with the exception of mother, who found the games boring. She made fun of us for taking defeat so much to heart and said of me, "This poor child could never cry more bitterly over life's keenest tragedy than she does over the loss of one game." She watched at the window when it was time for us to be coming home after a football game and could always tell whether we had won or lost, the moment we came in sight, two by two along the road. We made no effort to conceal our emotions—if we won we were gaily triumphant; and, defeated, we lagged along, too dispirited to talk.

Later when Margaret and Jessie went away to college, I missed them so much that father took me more often to the games. It was great fun—"Let's find a band, Nellie", and off we went, swinging along, heads up, and father walking so fast that I had to run to keep up with him. He used to get terribly excited. Holding his cane between his knees, he brought it down with a bang at critical moments, and gave short staccato shouts, making more noise than the noisiest rooter.

I became a hero worshiper and knew all the players by sight and name. Once when we beat Yale, John De Witt was the idol of the campus. We filled our rooms with his pictures and, when Beth Hibben told us one day that he would be at her house for lunch, we hung around outside, green with envy, hoping to catch a glimpse of him. After he left she joined us, but was strangely silent about Johnny. Later we discovered that she was disgusted with him because when he asked her if she were superstitious and she replied eagerly, "Oh, yes," he snapped, "Then you should go down to Stony Brook and spit in the water. I do before every game." We agreed with Beth that this coarseness was not to be tolerated, even in so great a hero. Down came his pictures in our rooms, to be replaced by a set of Fra Angelico angels.

Victories at Princeton were celebrated by torchlight processions. With a band blaring, a swarm of singing students came pouring across the campus to serenade father at Prospect and call him out for a speech. Standing on an upstairs balcony, we watched them come "snake-dancing" through the trees and across the lawn, red torches blazing and wild shouts of triumph breaking through the songs. When father appeared there was a burst of cheering and then sudden silence. It was an impressive tribute to him that, excited as they were, they did not want to miss a word he said; but when the note of boyish triumph came into his voice, they were off again yelling like wild Indians.

I remember the night that I realized for the first time the extraordinary way in which he could affect a crowd, by the mere inflection of that quiet voice. He did not "orate", he hardly made a gesture, and yet he could sway them in whatever direction he desired.

Living right on the campus, with no privacy at all, was a trial, particularly when the crowds came twice a year for the big games, and taking a short cut to the football field, trampled and ruined the garden. So father decided to fence Prospect. That fence was the cause of more bitterness than the most drastic reform he instituted at the college. At Commencement it was torn down by inebriated alumni, who decided that he had no right to put it up. I went out with him in the morning to see the damage and his anger and disgust were something to remember. He didn't speak, but struck at the battered railing with his cane and, when I saw that his eyes were grey and cold, I knew there would be no surrender.

He had the fence rebuilt at once. The next year another attempt was made to tear it down, but he had stationed college proctors to repel the attack. I felt as though we were living in a besieged citadel—but I had faith in the commanding officer.

CHAPTER FIVE

Prospect

W<small>E HAD THREE YEARS</small> at Prospect before
the real fight began. Father's plan for Princeton was very
clear in his mind. For years he had discussed it with his
friends in the faculty and on the board of trustees and
hoped to see it adopted, little thinking that he himself
would have the opportunity to bring it about.

As president, the trustees gave him unprecedented powers and at first he was supported enthusiastically on all
sides. Shortly after his inauguration he made a speech at
the Princeton alumni dinner in New York, clearly out-
lining the plan.

It was, broadly, to make Princeton into a democratic
institution of real learning. It involved a great deal of
money but his audacity was contagious, and he fired
everyone with his enthusiasm.

He reorganized the faculty, reconstructed the curricu-
lum, insisted upon the strict enforcement of rules of
scholarship and inaugurated the preceptorial system. Fifty
young Preceptors, whom he selected, were added to the
faculty to supplement the regular professorial lectures.
Each Preceptor met his students regularly in small groups
to discuss the lectures and the required reading. In this

way all the advantages of a small college were added to those of a big university.

The older girls of the town were keenly interested—fifty young men—prospective beaux!

The students made a song about them:

> *Here's to those Preceptor guys*
> *Fifty stiffs to make us wise.*

As is the custom in most college towns, the girls at Princeton began to go to dances when they were very young. The most formal dances given by the mothers at the Princeton Inn were carefully supervised and chaperoned, but this was not the general custom. We three, however, were always thoroughly chaperoned, even when we went to the small exclusive club dances that we considered the most exciting of all. The big Commencement "Prom" was always preceded by weeks of worry for fear we would not be asked. Here we danced until daylight, then after a dash home to change our clothes, we went canoeing. I invariably fell asleep in the bottom of the canoe, but no power on earth could have prevented me from following the formula to the end.

The telephone was quite an innovation in Princeton and a source of constant worry to us. Father considered it an impertinence for our beaux to telephone and ask if we were at home. He insisted that they should take the trouble to walk over and ask at the door, "like gentlemen". Whenever the telephone rang, there was a scramble to answer it, as we were threatened with a number of unpleasant possibilities.

If, by ill luck, father answered in the study and we heard his brusque "Come and find out", we knew that one of us had lost a beau. If we got to the telephone first and heard father take up the receiver in another room, we whispered cautiously, "Hang up and call back later."

We were never permitted to leave the table to answer a call, but once when a new maid said, "Miss Yessie is wanted in the telephone", even father was so convulsed that Jessie slipped out before he could stop her. Margaret Axson had the perfect system—she answered her calls when and where she chose. At meals, she simply floated out of the room, and if father seemed about to protest she gave him a dazzling smile and a sweetly drawled, "Now, Brother Woodrow".

We did not entertain our beaux in the same room. If two came at once there was an undignified rush for the study, always first choice; the little drawing room was second; and next the big drawing room. If there were more than three beaux, the last one to arrive had to be taken for a stroll in the garden, which had compensations. Though father often liked the young men who called on us, he invariably turned against them if he discovered any sign of sentimental interest on our part. He continued to be polite to them, but always said indignantly to mother, "What on earth does she see in that fool?" And mother would laugh, "Is he a fool because he is interested in your daughter?"

As Theodore Roosevelt was President at the time, the whole place was in a furor when he came to Princeton for one of the big games. Our friends asked us what we were going to say when we were introduced to him, and we gave the matter a lot of thought. I found it particularly perplexing, as I remembered hearing father say to Uncle Stock, when Roosevelt succeeded McKinley, "What will happen to the country—with that mountebank as President?" I wasn't sure just what a mountebank was and the whole thing was rather a problem.

We might have spared ourselves much trouble of mind, for Roosevelt paid no attention to us whatever and had eyes for no one but Margaret Axson, who was very much the belle of the occasion. Altogether we had a disappointing day. Coming home from school, we were stopped at the gate by Secret Service men and had to wait until a servant came from the house to identify us. The house was swarming with noisy strangers, and from upstairs, above all the hubbub, we could hear T. R.'s voice. We decided that he was undignified, much too noisy and not to be compared with father.

After luncheon, the guests went to the game and did not return to Prospect. In talking over the events of the day with father, we found that he was amused and rather disgusted with the precedent that made it customary for the President to go through.a door before a lady. He said it was nonsense. "After all, if a man is a gentleman before he becomes President, he should not cease to be one afterwards."

We had money now for long vacations and, in the summer, father and mother were able to carry out their long-deferred dream of a trip to Europe together. They went in June, after sending us to stay with Aunt Annie in the North Carolina mountains. It was the first time we had been separated from them both and we missed them terribly, in spite of the fun we had on our own vacation. We watched eagerly for their letters, reading them over and over when we were in bed at night. It was the first and only time they ever went together to the Continent.

We spent the summers of 1904 and 1905 at the Muskoka Lakes in Canada. The hotel was a rambling wooden building with wide verandas that provided a magnificent view of the water and surrounding country. We sailed and swam, had picnics in the great forests, and father taught us to paddle a canoe.

One day I wandered off to pick flowers and, coming back, was confronted by a strange sight. On the top of a hill was a row of figures, father, mother, Margaret, Jessie and two friends, all bent double, each solemnly gazing upside down through one curiously crooked arm, at the view. They laughed at my goggle eyes and open mouth, and mother explained that, for some strange reason, colors became more intense and values clearer when seen in that position. So I tried to stand on my own head and fell into a clump of prickly bushes.

The second summer father and mother bought a little island and, almost every day, rowed to it across the lake in a small boat, each pulling a pair of oars. They sat for hours there under the tall pine trees, drinking in the beauty and peace, reading aloud, planning the house they would build.

One afternoon we stood on the hotel porch and watched them coming home in a storm. We did not know until afterwards that they had been in real danger. That night they made a will and explained it to us; the important item in it was that if they should both die, Aunt Annie

83

and Uncle Stock were to be our guardians. The idea of having these two kind and easily managed relatives for guardians presented interesting possibilities, but we were appalled at facing for the first time the horrible idea of losing the two people whom we so adored. For days I followed them around like a puppy, with a vague feeling that they were safe as long as I was with them.

Father's work had increased enormously; besides the ordinary routine of administration, there were lectures to the students which he would not discontinue, new plans for the college, involving among other things a continuous campaign to raise money, and a big correspondence. As the university did not provide a secretary for him, he had to manage with part-time help from students who were working their way through college. Never robust, he began to show the strain. At the end of the second summer in Canada, he was ill and in December went to New York for an operation. Mother went with him and I begged to be allowed to go too, but that, of course, was impossible. We spent the Christmas holidays—three anxious, miserable weeks without them—at Prospect. The operation was followed by an attack of phlebitis and he had a very serious time. When he was able to travel, they went to Florida and I was sent to visit the Hoyts in Baltimore, where I saw "Romeo and Juliet" for the first time and fell madly in love with E. H. Sothern, shocking Cousin Mary profoundly by refusing to go home until I had seen him emerge from the stage door. When father and mother finally came home, she showed the effects of the long siege even more than he; she was very thin and pale.

Father and mother considered a trip abroad an essential

part of our education—to be managed if possible. It was too expensive for us all to go at one time, so we took turns. Margaret and Jessie, who were in the same class, had passed their entrance examinations for the women's college at Baltimore, but Jessie was not strong and the doctor advised keeping her out of school for a year; so father arranged that mother should take her abroad. Cousin Mary Hoyt went with them, and father, Margaret and I went to New York to see them off.

We were in such low spirits after they sailed that he thought a circus might revive us. I was so captivated by the freaks that father had difficulty in persuading me to go in to see the real show. A few days later, Margaret and I broke out with measles. Father used to call Jessie the "germ collector" and we felt a mild sort of triumph that we had, for once, caught something without her help!

Then a cable came, in the code mother and father had improvised, with the news that Jessie had diphtheria. They were in Assisi, far from doctors and nurses, and, for what seemed centuries, cables flew back and forth advising us of her condition and at last came word that she was out of danger. After sending to Rome for a doctor, mother and Cousin Mary had nursed her through the dangerous illness alone.

I do not see how father managed to take care of all the things left on his hands—a household, two sick girls·added to his regular work, and the terrible anxiety about Jessie. We did our best to amuse and distract him, but he was never himself with mother away.

Margaret and I were quite well and able to go to New York with father and greet the returning voyagers at the

85

pier. Jessie was pale and thin, and seemed rather grown up and changed to us. She had brought us innumerable small presents and for weeks kept us entertained with stories of the things she had seen. In the fall she joined Margaret at college and I was left feeling lonely, but rather important, as the only daughter in the house.

Father's plans were progressing smoothly. He had succeeded in tightening up, not only the entrance requirements but discipline and scholarship standards as well, and there were few serious protests. Some of the undergraduates, slow to accept the new idea and unable to get to work, were dropped by the wayside. One indignant alumnus amused us by remarking, "Wilson is spoiling the best country club in America", and the "Princeton Tiger" had a cartoon showing father sitting all alone on the steps of Old Nassau, covered with cobwebs, with the title "Wilson—that's all" (a famous whiskey advertisement of those days).

Every now and then an outraged parent arrived at Prospect to plead for a son's reinstatement. Father said, "Promise me that when you girls grow up you will never be that kind of pestiferous parent—demanding special favor for your child for no reason on earth except that he is your child!"

One day just after the entrance examinations, a man, greatly excited, came to see father, protesting because a certain boy had not been admitted. Father said, "But he didn't pass the examinations." The man was amazed. "He's a wonderful boy and a fine athlete; he would be a credit to Princeton." "But," said father, "I don't think you understand—he did not pass the entrance examinations. If the

Angel Gabriel applied for admission to Princeton and did not pass the entrance examinations, he would not be admitted. He would be wasting his time." The man went away stunned.

But there was a new spirit at Princeton and the majority of the students entered into it enthusiastically. The outside world also was showing interest in this new type of college president. There was much comment and speculation in the newspapers, and he had many requests for speeches from different parts of the country. Father was in good health again and we were enjoying our old tranquillity when, with agonizing suddenness, came a great sorrow.

Mother was in the habit of going to New York or Philadelphia almost every week. On her return father always met her at the train and we gathered round to hear the news of friends she had seen and bargains she had found. One day when I was ill and knew that she had gone, I couldn't understand why she had not said "Goodbye" to me. After several days passed and she didn't come in to see me, I was thoroughly alarmed. Then father told me. Uncle Ed, the brother mother so adored, had been drowned. He had been driving with his young wife and baby, and the horses had bolted, broken through a bridge, and plunged them all into the water.

Mother was utterly crushed. It was weeks and weeks before she attempted to resume her usual tasks. I went driving with her when she was able to be out and, though I tried desperately to interest and distract her, she just nodded at me and looked so heartbroken that I finally gave up my chattering.

In the summer Jessie and I went abroad with the Smiths.

The trip was a disappointment to me, mainly because we had to be so careful about money. Gloomy little *pensions* and simple hotels were just not my idea of the grand tour. The Smiths, determined that we should get the full benefit of travel, trotted us about from one historic spot to another, and at night we tumbled into bed with aching feet, too tired to sleep. In Paris I sometimes succeeded in persuading Jessie to sneak out with me to the nearest *pâtisserie*, where we gorged ourselves and felt very wicked and worldly.

Jessie was never lovelier than at this time; she attracted a lot of attention wherever we went, and in Paris if we stopped to look in a shop window, some dapper Frenchman was sure to stroll back and forth, staring at her. I thought it thrilling and romantic, but it embarrassed Jessie and she always pulled me away quickly.

An invitation to tea with Henry van Dyke's brother Paul was an exciting interlude. He took us to a little place where we had delicious *petits fours*. When we had finished the waitress came to make out the bill and asked how many cakes we had eaten from the huge tray she had left on the table, Jessie said "Five", rather apologetically; Cousin Lucy had eaten two and Cousin Mary, one. I was terribly ashamed but there was no escape for me, and I had to admit that I had eaten—sixteen! Seeing the futility of attempting to apologize for my crime, I resorted to tears. Everyone laughed so good-naturedly that I could not even cry successfully.

Leaving Paris for Germany, we had an early adventure in our compartment on the strange little train. It took some time and all the space on the racks to get our many bags and bundles tucked away. No sooner had we finished than the door opened and a small excited Frenchman put his head in, looked about and then began pulling his bags into the compartment. Without saying a word, he jerked all of our things down on the floor and arranged his neatly where ours had been. Cousin Lucy, who spoke indifferent French, remonstrated with him and he went into a paroxysm of fury. He shook his fists, shouted, pointed at his bags, at ours, at the rack. Cousin Mary took up the argument; her beautiful French, instead of calming him, seemed to make him wilder. We were cringing in our seats, expecting him to strike us when the door opened again and the most incredible apparition appeared. A tall cowboy, booted and spurred and wearing a ten-gallon hat. He was perfectly cool and, leaning against the door, asked in a slow Texas drawl, "What seems to be the trouble here, ladies?" The little man, now silent, looked up at the newcomer. Cousin Mary explained what had happened; then, almost languidly, the cowboy took the Frenchman by the coat collar, deposited him in the corridor and threw his bags after him. Without a word and before we could thank him, he was gone.

Later Jessie and I hunted through the train, but we could find no trace of him and never saw him again. I still cling to the idea that he was an apparition—the perfect answer to the prayers of four American women in distress.

Cousin Lucy knew just two words of German—*wunderschön* and *umsteigen*, which she pronounced *humsteickel*. Every time the train stopped she hopped off and, showing her ticket to the first attendant she found, asked anxiously *"Humsteickel?"* and if the answer was *"Nein"*, she trotted back. *"Wunderschön,"* she pronounced

89

perfectly, but apparently had no idea what it meant. We were being shown through a mediaeval torture chamber, where the guide enjoyed describing the tortures in such vivid detail that Jessie nearly fainted. Cousin Lucy, tears streaming down her cheeks, kept repeating, "*Wunderschön —wunderschön*". At last the guide, furious at his inability to horrify her into silence, shouted, "*Gnädige Frau*, this is a torture chamber; it is not—it was never beautiful".

We were fascinated at the range of Cousin Lucy's imagination. She attached romantic and humorous meanings to the most commonplace occurrences and could make a grand story from the most trivial incident. She had a series of yarns she called, "Bathing through Europe"—various ridiculous adventures she had had while in search of a bath.

We had a happy and hilarious family reunion when we got home and then I was hustled off to school at Raleigh, North Carolina. I didn't want to go to college and father and mother believed that a girl should not be forced to do so. One of mother's dearest friends was married to the head of the school, but the real reason for sending me south was that she did not want me to talk like a "Yankee". I went, determined to acquire an accent like hers, and in a few weeks was more Southern than any Southerner—speaking what father called "educated nigger".

I was late for the fall term and, as I arrived at night, I did not see any of the other pupils until morning. A mosquito bit me while I was asleep, so I appeared at breakfast with a huge swollen nose and utter desperation in my heart. For several weeks I was sure I would die of homesickness and shyness.

Mother came to visit me at Thanksgiving, and while she

sat in my room she could hear the girls talking outside. She was so disappointed at the change since her girlhood that she was tempted to take me away. There was still an accent and a drawl, but the general tone of voice of this new generation was nasal.

One of the teachers, "Miss Katie", a fiery unreconstructed little Rebel, was not at all friendly to me at first. Then a debate was arranged between the two Literary Societies: "*Resolved*, That Robert E. Lee did more for the Confederacy than Jefferson Davis." I was chosen for the affirmative side. She called me and said, "I'm glad that you have been chosen; now you will have a chance to find out something about the South". "But I am a Southerner", I said with feeling. "Father was born in Virginia and mother in Georgia." She melted completely at this and begged me to forgive her for the terrible injustice she had done me, and, from that time on, we were great friends.

I worked very hard for the debate and wrote father for advice. He answered with a long letter full of information, and suggestions. I lost, but was somewhat comforted at being told that my delivery was excellent and that I was obviously the daughter of an orator.

Once a year a vote was taken at the school for the most popular, the most beautiful, and so on. When I was voted the most intelligent, I was secretly pleased though I would have preferred to have been the most beautiful. When father and mother heard of it, they were terribly amused, saying it was a serious reflection on the intelligence of Southern girls in general.

Just before the Christmas holidays, I developed a swelling in my neck. The school doctor thought it was of no importance, but when I got home mother was alarmed and rushed me off to Philadelphia, where it was decided that I must have an operation at once. At first no one was really frightened, as Jessie had had the same operation successfully. But the gland had adhered to the jugular vein and complications developed. I was very ill. Mother went to the hospital and sat for three hours on the floor outside the operating-room door; neither father nor Uncle Stock could persuade her to move until it was all over. I enjoyed the role of convalescent, delighted when I heard anyone say, "We nearly lost Nellie". I cultivated quite a snatched-from-the-grave manner.

I went directly to Prospect from the hospital and father dressed the wound for some time. He did it beautifully. I loved to watch his delicate, supple fingers, and there was something dramatic and fascinating in the fact that one thumb was imperfect; from an old infection, a ridge remained at the tip. In the night, if the wound troubled me, I had only to whisper and father would be there at my door, ready to dress it again.

His hearing was phenomenal. I remember one very cold day in Princeton when he sent me out to look at the thermometer on the terrace. I shut the door carefully to keep out the freezing wind, but while I was gone he said to the family, "It's just eighteen degrees above zero". They thought that he was guessing, but when I came back and announced "Eighteen degrees above zero", they were astonished. He told them that he had heard me whisper to myself as I looked at the thermometer.

The year 1906 brought the first public mention of father as a possible candidate for the Presidency of the United

States. A Southern newspaper referred to him as "the most promising of Southern candidates". A few weeks later, at a dinner given in his honor, at the famous Lotos Club in New York, George Harvey, editor of *Harper's Weekly*, "nominated" him in an apparently serious speech. Mother teased father afterwards for quoting poetry in his speech but he said that he had learned "a great deal more about politics from the poets than from the systematic writers of politics". He laughed at us for taking Harvey's suggestion so seriously and continued unmoved by our excitement, but I gave it a great deal of thought and assigned to myself a pleasant, and not entirely inconspicuous, role in the dazzling future that I pictured.

In the spring of that year, father found one morning that he had lost the sight of one eye, and mother, terribly frightened, went with him at once to Philadelphia to consult a specialist. We were at the door waiting when they returned. Father was calm, even gay, but after one look at mother's face we knew that something dreadful had happened. Not until he had gone upstairs did she tell us that the doctor's verdict was that he must give up all his work, and live a retired life. Worst of all, there was no assurance that he would ever regain his health completely. It is impossible to describe the panic and despair that engulfed us. I crawled into bed to cry through a sleepless night, with Jessie quiet and brave beside me.

We made plans at once to go abroad and spend the summer in the English Lake Country. Father insisted on packing the trunks, as he always had. He sat on a chair, surrounded by our baggage, and we brought him our things and watched him arrange them in his amazingly neat and efficient way. The indispensable medicine bag, of course, received particular attention.

That summer is one of the loveliest memories of my life. We found a little house called "Loughrigg Cottage" in the shadow of Loughrigg Mountain, not more than a short walk from Wordsworth's home at Rydal. Father and mother wandered about in the haunts of their beloved poet and mother painted to her heart's content. My sisters and I climbed the mountains with father, rode on the stage-coaches and had long, unhurried conversations with the people of the countryside, often spending hours on some upland pasture with a shepherd or cowherd.

One day while father was walking alone, a man with a fine rugged face and a mop of tousled gray hair caught up with him, touched his arm and said, "Is this Professor Wilson? My name is Yates. We live near here—we are poor but thank God, not respectable." Father was delighted with him and went to his house, an enchanting cottage he had built with his own hands.

He was a portrait and landscape painter and had a charming wife, a Californian, and one daughter, Mary, who looked like a goddess. She was very tall and wore her hair in two long glistening braids. She knew every secret beauty of the countryside and was anxious to share it with us. She walked with easy wild grace and so swiftly that we had the greatest difficulty in keeping up with her. She never wore a hat and had never had more than two dresses at a time in her life; in the winter she wore a long blue cape made from the wool of one of her pet lambs; she did the shearing and carding herself.

94

PROSPECT

A warm friendship grew up at once between the two families; we spent many of our evenings together, talking, reading aloud or telling stories. We sang all the old songs—English and American—Scotch and Irish; Fred Yates supplied the missing bass, having a great booming voice that nearly drowned us out.

He helped mother with her painting and made pastel portraits of all of us. When he put Margaret and me on one canvas, we decided it was because we were too plain to be interesting. The one he did of mother was remarkable; father had read Browning's "Saul" aloud while she posed, and Yates caught the lovely expression that great poetry always brought to her face. He put a curious little drawing of Saul hanging on his cross in one corner of the canvas.

It rained often but we learned to love it and gathered late in the afternoon, wet and dishevelled, by the huge fire, for high tea with yellow Devonshire cream. Later we played whist with father. Being children of Presbyterian ministers, neither he nor mother had been allowed to touch a card in their youth. He had learned whist at college and taught us the game that summer. It was done with great gravity; we were not allowed to chatter—if anyone spoke unnecessarily, he would say, "The name of this game is 'whist'—it would not have been called that if it were intended to be noisy."

When father had to go to Edinburgh on business and mother told me that I was to go with him, I was at first consumed with pride. Then mother added that I amused him—and that was fatal. At once I was shy and self-conscious and my unceasing efforts to entertain him must have

95

been boring to a degree, although he was gentle and patient, and seemed interested in my reaction to all the new sights.

One Saturday night we walked up High Street and I was scandalized at seeing, for the first time in my life, drunken women as well as men, reeling along. I clung to father's arm until we reached the stone-paved court of Edinburgh Castle, its great bulk towering above us, black against the sunset. He told me all its romantic history as we wandered through the gloomy rooms and peered out the grim high windows. He loved Scotland and said that his Scotch blood was stronger than his Irish. "Whenever the Irish gets too strong in me, the dour Scot sternly reprimands me."

At the end of the summer when it was time for us to return to America, father was in good health again. The doctor's diagnosis proved to be wrong; the restful peace of his beloved Lake Country had restored him completely and, plunging at once into active work, he began his fight to rid Princeton of the evils of the Club system.

CHAPTER SIX

Prospect

THE UPPER CLASS CLUBS took the place of the fraternities and secret societies of other colleges. Prospect Avenue was lined with expensive club-houses and their politics and social activities interfered with and threatened to overshadow the pursuit of learning. New students were forced to "bootlick" to get into a club. Often fathers came, before the elections at the end of the Sophomore year, and attempted to use influence or pressure to have their sons invited to join their own clubs.

The tragedy of the unchosen was repeated every year and many a student's life in college, and even afterward, was injured by what almost amounted to social ostracism. Although many realized that the clubs had become a menace to the main object of a college, no one had attempted to interfere, fearing to lose the contributions of the club alumni.

It was all contrary to father's idea of serious study and true democracy and he determined to change it. His plan was to build a group of quadrangles, each with its own dining-hall, using the old dormitories. Here upper and lower classmen could live together with the younger and unmarried members of the faculty. It was much the same system that had been so successful at Oxford and Cambridge. It was conducive to intelligent conversation and helpful companionship and essentially democratic. Naturally, the first rumor of the plan aroused tremendous excitement and bitter controversy.

Father's devoted friends on the faculty and on the board of trustees were open to new ideas and many of the student clubmen supported him and were ready to accept the plan. But the howl that went up from the alumni reverberated throughout the country and frightened the more conservative of the trustees nearly out of their wits.

I was terribly disturbed about it. I felt that father was right and, when I sat with the family and heard him talk, his enthusiasm completely swayed me. But when I was alone or with my friends, I was filled with misgivings; I so much wanted him to retain his great popularity—and then, too, the club dances were such fun.

I was walking down Prospect Avenue one day with a girl who was visiting from Philadelphia and she asked me to tell her about the clubs. She particularly wanted to know which was "Ivy" and which "Cottage". These were considered the "swankiest". "I don't know one from the other and wouldn't go inside any of them," I said defiantly, but too quickly. The lie worried me as it made me realize how deeply my emotions were involved in the question.

It was a long and bitter fight, involving much for which father was to battle the rest of his life—to preserve intellectual vitality and democracy against the power of money and social privilege. We felt it so keenly that, to a great extent, it changed the tempo of our lives.

In the late afternoons, now, we left our various occupa-

tions and amusements and hurried home to be there before
he arrived. Then we waited; the sound of the heavy front
door opening or closing could be heard in every corner of
the house, and we dashed down the stairs to welcome him
and hear the news.

Mother always listened intently, ready to comfort, reassure or encourage him. He made his reports to her, but he
never forgot that we were there too, letting his glance rest
first on one and then on another of us. His constant aware-
ness of us all was one of his most endearing characteristics.
We were, of course, predisposed to think he was right,
since we loved him, but we had caught from him and
mother the excitement of ideas and we were interested in
his causes for their own sake. He didn't want us, young as
we were, to be blind partisans. He was never too busy to
explain, to help us to understand the idea behind that which
he was trying to do.

I had, however, my moments of seething fury when I
heard that anyone had dared to oppose him. The whole
town was taking sides, even the children. My friends were
divided and we spent much of our time arguing fiercely.

One of the most important undergraduate events in
Princeton was the annual dinner given by the Princetonian,
the college paper. The president was always invited to
speak, but that year all the other speakers were "anti-
Wilson". The dinner was held at the Princeton Inn and I
went with a friend and hid on the wide verandah beside an
open window, where I could see and hear.

They did not attack him directly, but anybody could
see what lay between the lines of the speeches. They were
sneering at his plan to make Princeton a democratic insti-

tution of learning. They were all for keeping Princeton
the charming country club for idle young men it had been
for so many years. I could see father's face, and I was almost frightened. His eyes were steely gray and there was
a curious bulge in his long, fighting lower jaw. When he
began to speak, there was only a little mild applause, but
I forgot that, when I heard his voice, low and clear, saying, "It is my lonely privilege, in gatherings of educated
men, to be the only person who speaks of education." I
had never seen him like this before, never heard just that
quality in his voice, and my heart began to beat fast. He
spoke for only ten minutes; first quiet scorn of the sort of
things that had been said in the preceding speeches, then a
swiftly uttered vision of what Princeton might become if
it would put away childish things and gird itself for a great
battle. When he had finished the undergraduates rose from
their seats—some of them climbed on tables—cheering,
breaking into the famous "locomotive", the Princeton "Sis-
boom-ah", cheering again. But he sat there, grim, unsmil-
ing, perfectly silent. Uncle Stock told us that, walking
home with him afterwards across the campus, he had heard
him muttering, "Damn their eyes—damn their eyes."

Another controversy was developing over the Graduate
College; what sort of Graduate College Princeton should
have and where it should be located. Already there was a
small graduate group with Andrew West as dean. He was
a clever man whose only son, Randolph, gave grand parties
in the big house where they lived. He was considered very
rich and was unpopular with the wives of the professors
for making the wage scale impossibly high—he paid his
cook thirty dollars a month! He had wanted to be president

of Princeton and I believe that jealousy of father was at the bottom of most of the trouble he caused.

Father wanted the Graduate College to be, geographically and in every other sense, the center of the college. He believed, moreover, that it should be controlled by the head of the university, not run separately by the dean and the College Graduate committee. Things seemed to be going his way until William Cooper Procter, the soap man, offered to give $500,000, if an equal amount could be raised in a year and the Graduate College located where Dean West wanted it and run according to his plan. Five hundred thousand dollars was a lot of money and the controversy that had been almost settled was reopened, with Dean West and his supporters in a much stronger position. But father was so firm in his determination to preserve unity in the administration and so reasonable in his arguments that he actually won his point and Procter withdrew his offer. The excitement subsided for a time; our family gatherings were less like councils of war and we were able to resume our old, delightful hours with the poets.

Then one morning I was late for breakfast and as I came down the stairs I heard laughter in the dining room. There was something about it that disturbed me and, when I asked what had happened, they told me that an old man named Wyman had died and left two million dollars to the Graduate College to be administered by Dean West. Father said, "We've beaten the living, but we can't fight the dead—the game is up." But the laughter continued and, although I did not join in it, I recognized for the first time the splendid type of courage that can see humor even in defeat.

Father's courageous stand had won the admiring attention of the whole country and established him as a strong Democrat and a great fighter, a reputation he was never to lose. Rumors that he would enter the political field increased and grew so persistent that we began to realize that they could no longer be entirely ignored. One newspaper said, "It is probable that Wilson's enemies at Princeton will unwittingly kick him upstairs into the White House."

But his heart and mind were still concerned with Princeton. The deepest wound he received in this battle remained with him for life. Jack Hibben, his dear friend and close companion, had failed him, joining the opposition at a crucial moment. For the first time in our lives we had seen him yield at times to sorrow and discouragement and we all believed that an illness which followed, forcing him to go to Bermuda for a long rest, was, to a great extent, due to this break.

Some time later, speaking of some of his opponents on the board of trustees he said, "Professional politicians have little to teach me; they are amateurs compared with some I have dealt with in the Princeton fights." His own honesty and directness made it difficult for him to realize that anyone could be deliberately dishonest or mean, and he told us that he had constantly to remind himself that there were people who could not be trusted. Fortunately, he could "turn off his mind" at will, and had amazing recuperative powers.

It was the custom to walk about in the evenings with our beaux and often we gathered in groups at "Old Nassau" to listen to the "Senior singing". Many of the improvised songs were pertinent or impertinent allusions to mem-

102

STOCKTON AXSON
Mrs. Wilson's brother about 1914

JESSIE WOODROW WILSON

bers of the faculty and changed with the changing senti-
ments of the students. The songs about father were very
complimentary at first, but when he began to tighten up
on the discipline, they were less so. When the public press
referred to him as a possible presidential candidate they
sang:

> *"Here's to Wilson, King divine,*
> *He rules this place along with Fine.*
> *We hear he's soon to leave this town*
> *To try for Teddy Roosevelt's crown."*

But father never lost his hold on the students. Often in
the midst of a bitter fight, they would ask him to come and
talk to them and explain the situation. He appreciated their
confidence; it encouraged and heartened him to realize that
their minds were clear and open to new ideas and that,
though they might disagree with him, there was no bitterness or misunderstanding. They were proud of him, proud
of the way he had turned the eyes of the country to Princeton and of the prominence he had attained as an educator
and administrator.

I was often puzzled by their diffidence when they spoke
to him and one day said to a friend, "What's the matter
with you? When father comes into the room you become
paralyzed and tongue-tied. How can you be afraid of him?
He's the simplest, nicest, most amusing person I know."
The boy said, "I'm not afraid of him, but I love and admire
him so much that I don't want him to know what a fool
I am."

We spent the summers of 1909 and 1910 at Old Lyme, a

sleepy little village near the Connecticut River, which we chose because of its famous artists' colony. The terrible shock of her brother's death and the worry over the difficulties at Princeton had been a severe strain on mother's health and spirits, and she needed, as never before, the relaxation and stimulation that she always found in her painting. She, in turn, wanted to encourage my growing interest in that direction.

We stayed at a lovely old house owned by Miss Florence Griswold, a member of an old New England family and a delightful character. Until we came, her summer boarders were exclusively artists, and they told us later that the news of our impending arrival was not greeted with shouts of joy. They nicknamed us "the row of wooden Wilsons"— were certain that we would be stiff and academic and would ruin the carefree atmosphere of the place. But very soon we were all the best of friends and they particularly enjoyed father and mother. On the porch in the evening after dinner, everyone joined in interesting abstract discussions that rambled off into delightful arguments. As there were many young people in the neighborhood, we went to dances and picnics, paddled about in canoes, sang and flirted on "hayrides", and all the artists wanted to paint Jessie and Margaret Axson.

The most interesting room in this unusual house was the dining room. The walls were paneled from floor to ceiling and most of the panels were painted with pictures done by Miss Griswold's guests. There were many famous signatures in the collection and visitors came often to see them.

I studied with Frank Du Mond and mother, free from all household cares, and knowing that we were all busy and enjoying ourselves, went with an easy mind to spend entire days alone at the work she loved. Father carried her stool and easel and we trooped along to see her safely settled in some lane or meadow. We soaked her with citronella but when we went back for her we invariably found her smudged with paint and bitten by mosquitoes and always astonished that we had come so soon.

When we got back to Miss Florence's the sketch was put up for father to see. He was an intelligent and helpful critic and, though he knew little or nothing of technique, mother relied more on his judgment than on that of any or all of the artists at Old Lyme who sat about arguing for hours upon the comparative merits of different schools of art.

Father played a lot of golf that summer, usually with his friend, Professor Vreeland, whose father-in-law had a private golf course near by.

Our second summer at Lyme was not so perfect. Father had been seriously considering resigning from the presidency of Princeton, but had decided to remain for a time at least. The Graduate College fight was lost but there was still much to be done for the university. The undergraduates had not wavered in their loyalty. At the Commencement exercises in June they had given him such an ovation as had never been heard in dignified Alexander Hall—and on the steps of Old Nassau the seniors sang:

> *"Here's to Wilson, King divine*
> *Who rules this place along with Fine.*
> *We have no fear he'll leave this town*
> *To try for anybody's crown."*

But the pressure from many directions to force him into active politics had reached the boiling point. And now, believing that his fight to free Princeton from the influence of money and privilege was hopelessly lost, he began for the first time to give the matter serious consideration.

Up to this time he had sincerely and vigorously discouraged all political advances. In 1907 he had refused to run for the Senate. In 1908 when a movement was started to nominate him for the vice presidency with Bryan, he left instructions with Uncle Stock, before he sailed for Europe, to refuse to allow them to use his name, adding that he felt "rather like a fool for taking it seriously even for a moment."

But, although he had given himself whole-heartedly to his career as a teacher and college president, he had always believed that the trained university man should be vitally interested in the political affairs of his country and hold himself ready to give advice and help whenever he had an opportunity. On many occasions he had made public speeches full of pungent criticism and counsel.

Colonel Harvey was backing him now with sincerity and renewed enthusiasm. He urged Jim Smith, "Big Boss" of New Jersey, to support father for the governorship and Smith, being a practical politician, after a time agreed. He realized that his own power in the state was weakening and that only a Democratic victory could save him; and he thought that father would be a useful tool. He secretly called him "the Presbyterian priest" and believed that he knew nothing of practical politics.

So there were many family conferences in the big square bedrooms at Miss Florence's and the peaceful days of golf and painting were disturbed by speculation and excitement.

When they finally insisted on knowing what father's attitude would be if the nomination were offered him, he told them frankly that he would accept it only on condition that he be left absolutely free, and with the assurance that Jim Smith would publicly announce that he would not run for the United States Senate. He told us, "I have no wish to be Governor if I am to be tinged with the slightest suspicion of 'boss dictation'".

At the end of June, with the State Democratic Convention only a little over two months ahead and Colonel Harvey begging him to make a decision, he still hesitated. I think that this was the hardest decision of his life; many times in the evening we could hear him in the next room talking with mother for hours at a time. He never made a move of any importance without her approval.

Dinner was served at Miss Florence's on a screened porch overlooking her old-fashioned New England garden, and we always sat a long time afterwards in the candlelight, lost in discussions of art and music. The jolly irresponsible artists knew nothing of the impending crisis in father's affairs. One night while we were still talking, he was called to the telephone and when he returned I heard him say, in a low voice to mother, "It was Colonel Harvey. They have asked me to go to Deal Beach on Sunday for a conference with Watterson and Smith." My heart jumped, because I knew it would mean a final decision.

But he was still reluctant to take the final plunge, reluctant to give up his work at Princeton, and on Saturday, finding that there was no train from Lyme on Sunday, he telegraphed Harvey that he would be unable to attend the conference.

On Sunday morning, just as we were about to start for our usual walk up the tree-shaded street to church, a man dashed up the steps. "Colonel Harvey asked me to drop in and bring you down to Deal Beach for dinner tonight," he said breathlessly. We learned afterwards that he had motored all night to get to Lyme in time.

Father gave up. We helped him pack his bag and I noticed that he seemed more amused than excited or annoyed. It was all tremendously serious and important to me; I wanted him to be governor and was convinced that he had only to say "Yes", to be President of the United States.

The suspense was terrific after he had gone; mother tried to paint, but we were all restless and upset and counted the hours until his return.

Cousin Lucy and Cousin Mary were visiting us and we all gathered in mother's room when he finally arrived. He was as unhurried as usual—throughout his entire life I never saw him excited about his own destiny. He had a calm way of accepting everything, a philosophic sort of fatalism. He came into the room, walked over to the fireplace and sat down on a small steamer trunk. We all spoke at once, "Tell us what happened. What did you decide to do?" "Wait a minute", he said, "I want to show you what I found." And he took a small object from his pocket and put it on the floor in front of him. Mother said, "Please, Woodrow"—but he must first find a golf ball and demonstrate properly the wonders of a new rubber tee. After he had explained it all in detail, he put it back in his pocket and told us what had happened at the meeting.

They had agreed that, if he accepted the nomination, he would be left absolutely free—no pledges of any sort were to be demanded and Smith had further agreed that in no circumstances would he run for the Senate.

Father had told them that he would decide after consulting with his friends on the Princeton board of trustees, but as he knew that they would loyally accept his own judgment, he was committed. He asked us again to tell him frankly what we thought, and listened patiently to what was no more than the enthusiastic prophecies of six adoring women. At length he added with a trace of wistfulness, "Colonel Watterson says it will inevitably lead to the Presidency."

There was not much time now for golf. Nearly every day some one came to talk to father; he wrote innumerable letters to friends explaining the situation and made frequent trips to New York for conferences. We seized every hour we could find to return to the poets, the nonsense rhymes and story-telling, avoiding the subject uppermost in our minds and knowing in our hearts that our peace was gone.

When September came and the Democratic Convention convened in New Jersey, father left us at Old Lyme and went down to Princeton to be near at hand.

It was a stormy session—some of the best men in New Jersey, reformers and liberals, not understanding the situation, still fearing that father might be secretly under the influence of the bosses, opposed him. In the end, after a few hours of intense excitement, he was nominated by a large majority.

His supporters found him on the golf links at Princeton and rushed him to Trenton to make a speech. Standing before the crowd of experienced politicians in his golf clothes and a blue sweater, he spoke clearly and simply and with extraordinary directness. Everyone was cheering wildly as he finished. One old man, who had opposed him bitterly, shouted, "I'm sixty-five years old and still a damn fool."

At Old Lyme we waited impatiently for word from father. His voice was warm and vibrant on the telephone and he seemed gay and cheerful as he gave us the news.

In a few days we were all together again at Prospect, waiting with enthusiasm for the campaign to start.

Having, in our innocence, no idea of the ordeal we were facing, we were due for a shock. A college professor thrust suddenly into active politics made the New Jersey situation more dramatic and interesting than the ordinary gubernatorial campaign.

The old stone house on the quiet campus was besieged by photographers. We were asked to pose, singly and in groups. We shyly but firmly refused all requests for interviews. The telephone rang incessantly and politicians crowded even into the sacred precincts of the study. Jim Smith and Jim Nugent, boss of Newark and called the "Big Fellow", were the first to arrive. Father told us later that they were absurdly quiet when they were first ushered into the peaceful, book-lined room. It was a strange atmosphere for them and he had to make an effort to put these "hard-boiled" men at their ease. "But they treated me like a schoolboy when they got over the professorial atmosphere," he said. He also told us that they seemed astonished at his familiarity with New Jersey affairs and personalities.

We stayed close by most of the day, not daring to leave

the house for fear he might have something new to tell us.

He decided to continue as President of Princeton until he was certain that things were going smoothly and he even gave his lectures on jurisprudence and politics, but near the end of October he sent in his resignation. The trustees accepted it with regret and passed a resolution continuing his salary until the end of the first term, and inviting him to remain at Prospect. He refused to accept the salary but we did remain at Prospect until after his election.

He readjusted the pattern of his days with that extraordinary serenity that always seemed to me little short of miraculous. The secret of it was that he gave himself up completely to the task in hand, dismissed from his mind any worry over the past and, regardless of how important his plans for the future might be, did not permit the details of those plans to intrude themselves into the present.

Mr. Cleveland had been uncomfortable when his audience changed from political to academic, and now father had just the opposite situation to contend with. He began his campaign of speaking with some misgiving. He didn't want us to go to the meetings, particularly mother, whose praise and criticism he valued so highly. When we implored him, he said, "I don't know what sort of politician I'll make. I'm nervous—just plain scared—and if you girls are there, it will be worse."

But we were so anxious to hear him that one night, without letting him know, we went to the Opera House in Trenton and hid behind the curtains in a box. I was in a terrible panic, partly because I knew he was nervous, but mostly for fear he would see us and be disturbed at our being there. I remembered Uncle Stock's behavior when

Margaret Axson and Margaret Wilson had gone, against his urgent request, to hear him lecture in Princeton. He had gazed at them indignantly, then marched down from the platform and told them in a hoarse whisper, "I'll give you each five dollars to get out". I wondered confusedly what bribe father would offer us. But he didn't see us and was amused when we told him about it. From that time on, he didn't mind having the family in the audience.

I have always thought that this campaign was the most stirring that father ever took part in; this may have been partly because it was all so new to us and because his audiences, surprised by this new type of politician, were intensely absorbed and responsive. His speeches, far from being pedantic, as many had expected, were couched in the simplest terms, thoughtful and serious, with an educational purpose, yet lightened by humor and with no trace of the usual political harangue.

We were amused when a New York newspaper criticized his use of English, professing surprise that a school teacher was not always careful about his diction. The next night, without warning to anyone, he began his speech with two or three moments of precise sentences, couched in stilted and exquisitely phrased English. The audience looked dazed and suddenly he laughed, walked to the edge of the platform, and said, "Confidentially, ladies and gentlemen, that's the way the New York —— thinks I should talk to you, but I prefer a more informal way of speaking." A friend of his told me afterwards, "Good heavens, he scared me—I thought he was drunk when he spoke in that strange way!"

One day a friend, coming away from a big meeting in

Newark, heard two rough-looking men talking things over. One said, "That's a smart guy." The other replied, "He's smart as hell. What I don't see is what a fellow as smart as that was doing hanging around a college so long."

Father seemed now to be really enjoying himself, his never-failing humor carrying him over the rough spots. One day he told us that, as he was driving through the streets in a political parade, a small boy had jumped on the running board of the car and demanded, "Which is Wilson?" When father replied meekly, "I am", the boy continued scornfully, "Well, why don't you have a better football team?" Father's amusement at this was tinged with a whimsical feeling of guilt—he still felt responsible for Princeton!

As we had started going to parties when we were fifteen, they had lost some of their glamour by this time and we had all gone seriously to work. Father and mother believed that girls, as well as boys, should learn some vocation; but they did not insist and we were allowed our own preferences in the choice of a career. They gave us advice when we wanted it, financial assistance, and always unflagging interest.

Margaret knew exactly what she wanted—to spend as much time as possible in New York, studying singing and listening to fine music.

I wanted to follow in mother's footsteps and go to the Art Students League; but she thought that the Pennsylvania Academy in Philadelphia was better, and I was very busy, commuting every day from Princeton.

Jessie was talented in many ways; she won the Phi Beta Kappa at college, had a flair for writing and definite talent for drawing, but she still wanted to be a missionary. Mother showed her own fine courage when she consented, without argument, but I know that she was relieved when the Board of Missionaries wouldn't let Jessie go—she was not strong enough, they thought, for such an arduous life. She was terribly disappointed, but Uncle Stock remarked that when we heard the news he had never seen such "unholy glee" in the Wilson family. So Jessie chose settlement work and lived, during the week, at the "Lighthouse" in Philadelphia. But whenever we were at home we congregated in the sitting room to discuss all the latest developments. Mother gave up much of her time to reading newspapers and cutting out all references to father. She sorted these carefully and gave him those she thought he should see.

One afternoon when I was returning on the train, three men got on at a way-station. Two sat behind me and the other settled himself beside me. I pretended to be absorbed in a book but I didn't miss a word. They began abusing father—he was a "dreamer", a "school teacher", he would "ruin the state". Before they left the train, I had a chance to take a good look at the man sitting beside me and recognized Mr. Stokes who had been a Republican Governor of New Jersey.

To amuse the family I made a grand story of the incident, which father thoroughly enjoyed. Mother's amusement was only half-hearted; she could never see much humor in a situation that included criticism of father. A few nights later father spoke in Trenton and there, on the platform with him, sat Stokes, smiling smugly. When we joined father, he introduced him to us and, as I shook hands I said, "I think we shared a seat on the train a few days ago, coming from Philadelphia." He gave me a startled look, turned bright purple and vanished.

On election day father was the only calm person in the house. We stood breathlessly by when he answered the telephone, but he would never give the slightest inkling whether the news was favorable or not, repeating, "Yes, yes," over and over and watching our nervous frenzies with amusement. Even after he hung up, we had to beg for details and, when the news was most encouraging, he invariably warned us not to be too optimistic.

By ten o'clock it was evident that he had been elected— he had swept the state in a tremendous victory. Soon we heard a procession on the campus. A crowd of townspeople joined the students and came swarming over the lawn, shouting and calling for a speech. Friends crowded into the house, but mother in her gentle way got rid of them as soon as possible and sent father to bed. The rest of us sat up for hours, talking it all over. In spite of a happy sense of triumph, we felt an undercurrent of dismay. We would have to leave Prospect! Library Place had been sold and we had no home! Worst of all, our brief taste of publicity had made us afraid that we were not going to like this strange, new political life.

CHAPTER SEVEN

Princeton Inn and Sea Girt

THE MOVE FROM PROSPECT was a difficult ordeal. The attics were full of the inevitable accumulation of more than twenty years at Princeton and everything we owned had to be sorted and packed, or discarded. Mother attacked the job with her usual efficiency and we all worked like beavers. She wouldn't let father do anything, although every day he begged to be allowed to help her. She let him sort his own papers and, the last day, smilingly let him pack the medicine bag, but that was all. Day after day she came down from the attic or up from the cellar, tired and dusty and a little sad, and, shutting herself in her room, bathed, put on a pretty dress and emerged fresh and cheerful, to await his homecoming. She wouldn't allow the dining room or father's study to be touched until the last day. He should have peace and quiet at home as long as she could manage it.

Since there was no governor's "mansion" at Trenton, and to rent a house was beyond our means, we had decided to live at the Princeton Inn, an old-fashioned, rambling place on Nassau Street; so all of our furniture, everything except our most personal possessions, had to be sent to storage. Mother said many times, "I never realized before how dreadful possessions are. I shall never save anything again as long as I live." Finally we were settled in a small sitting room and three bedrooms at the Inn. The first evening we sat and looked at one another in despair. No fireplace, no garden, and meals in a hotel dining room surrounded by other people. How could we bear it? But father would be away all day at Trenton, Jessie spent five days a week at the settlement house, Margaret was practically living in New York to be near her singing teacher, and I was commuting every day to Philadelphia. We pretended that we didn't really need a house.

The problem of meeting new and increasing expenses became serious. Mother kept it from father as much as she could and, as far as I could see, did not allow it to worry her, but for the first time we discussed finances at the family conferences.

As we had only the vaguest idea what the social demands of the new political life would be, we planned to buy dresses only when they were needed for a definite occasion. The first of these, of course, was the inauguration ceremony and the ball afterwards, in January, at Trenton.

I was always keenly interested in clothes, my own and everyone else's. I secretly thought myself an authority on style and was delighted when mother first began to consult me about the family wardrobe. She had excellent taste but no chic and Jessie, who looked perfectly lovely in anything, was absolutely indifferent. She stood patiently for her fittings, book in hand, while mother and I fussed and argued. If we pleaded with her, she would tear herself away from what she was reading, glance in the mirror, smile vaguely and murmur, "Yes, darlings, it's lovely." Only once do I

117

remember that she asserted herself and insisted on spoiling a nice line by having it "built up" at the neck.

Margaret had her own ideas and seldom asked for advice. She bought her dress for the ball in New York, but mother and I spent hours planning what we would wear and how we would make Jessie look even more beautiful than usual.

Princeton people had always a slight contempt for New Jersey's capital city. We thought of Trenton as a drab little town—just a place where undergraduates went to celebrate, untroubled by college proctors, and scarcely bothered to look out of the windows when we passed through on the Philadelphia train. And so I was astonished when I found myself sitting with the family in the huge window of a grand house, looking out on a wide street down which came a brass band with three bass drums, the State Guard in truly magnificent uniforms and father, in a frock coat and tall hat, riding in an open carriage drawn by sleek horses that actually pranced. Crowds lined the streets—enthusiastically cheering and waving flags.

After all, Trenton was a fine city, and this a very grand occasion!

Father's inaugural speech was simple and very much to the point. He had been elected to carry out certain reforms and he intended to waste no time in doing so. Campaign pledges then, as always, were serious matters to him. Even the politicians seemed impressed. We didn't realize that they still complacently believed that he would be unable to carry out his "dreams". They thought him a great orator and a fine "figurehead", but an amateur—the "scholar in politics".

I had my hair done and my first manicure; my ball gown

118

was a dream of blue loveliness, but I was scared stiff that evening as I stood in the receiving line with the family. The world seemed a blaze of light—a terrifying sea of glittering uniforms, in the center of which I was inescapably marooned, wondering what to say and what to do with my hands and my feet.

Then I noticed that the two officers at the door carefully scrutinized everyone passing in and that no one was allowed to carry a muff or even a large handbag. I managed at last to ask someone about it and got the casual answer, "Danger of concealed weapons". My heart pounded. I had not realized that father stood in danger of physical violence.

Then the dancing began and, floating off in the arms of a gorgeous uniform, I forgot everything in playing the interesting role of the governor's youngest daughter.

But through all my pride and satisfaction in father's career, there had been, almost from the beginning, a strong undercurrent of fear. Up to this time it had been fear that his constitution, never robust, would not stand the strain. Now I had a new thought to trouble me.

When a few days after the inauguration a friend said to me, "Everyone knows now that he will be President," I said, "No, I can't bear it—it will kill him," and ran crying from the room. And whenever this prediction was repeated, as it was more and more frequently, I had to struggle against a dreadful apprehension.

Even before the inauguration Jim Smith had repudiated his promise not to run for the Senate and defied father to prevent him. A man, called "Farmer Jim" Martine, had been nominated in the preferential primary and, according to all honest standards, this constituted a "mandate of the

people" which father held sacred. He pointed this out to
Smith in no uncertain terms, but Smith flew into a rage,
called him an "ingrate" and the fight was on.

Father had many conferences with the legislators, talking to them simply and directly, appealing to their sense
of fairness, and when the legislature met Martine was
chosen as Senator from New Jersey. It was highly dramatic—the "amateur" showing his power at the first gun.

Father's friends were jubilant and the Progressives all
over the country tremendously interested. But he himself
was sorry for Jim Smith.

The "Big Boss" had paraded through the streets of Trenton with a brass band and an army of supporters, and the
next day, deserted by all his friends, had left alone for
his home in the country. It was a pathetic picture, but there
was no help for it—he had broken his word and brought
about his own downfall.

That was a busy winter. Father plunged at once into his
plan of reform. There were seven important new laws that
he wanted enacted, called "The Seven Sisters". They com-
prised a new election law, a Corrupt Practices Act, laws
regulating Public Utilities, and an Employers' Liability
Act. New Jersey had long been called the "Mother of
Trusts" and the passing of these laws would effectively re-
move that stigma.

From among the group of reformers father had chosen
Joe Tumulty, a young Irishman, for his private secretary.
Tumulty had bright blue eyes in a round pink face. His
admiration for father was boundless and he and mother
became fast friends. She was his confidante and he discussed everything with her at length. He said often to

father, "I want to talk to Mrs. Wilson—you can't come," and added later, "She's a better politician than you are, Governor."

Mother was, as always, absorbed in every detail of father's plans and, in the winter, since there was no house-keeping and little to do socially, she had more time for herself than she had expected. She spent a good part of it buried in letters and newspapers, and enjoying long chats with father's friends and supporters. The worry and excitement of the campaign slipped from her mind with incredible completeness. When someone mentioned "Viv" Lewis, who had run against father on the Republican ticket and had been the chief topic of conversation and our particular *bête noire* for months, she asked vaguely, "Lewis? Who is Lewis?"

One cartoon pleased her so much that she carried it in her purse for days. It was a parade of Salvation Army lassies—all the "progressive" states singing and beating drums. Bringing up the rear was little New Jersey, running and shouting. The caption was "Little old bad New Jersey—she's joined the Salvation Army".

Every evening when the train from Philadelphia stopped at Trenton, I peered eagerly out the window to see if father would get on. Sometimes he took a later train, but often I would see the little flurry on the platform, the bowing porter, and then father walking down the aisle and looking for me. If he was alone or with some intimate friend, he sat with me, but usually he was surrounded by an importunate group and then he merely said, "Hello", gave me the radiant smile he reserved for his family and sat talking with the men until we got off at the junction. I pretended to read, but really watched him out of the corner of my eye. We always knew when he was tired or annoyed. To other people he seemed as courteous as always and absorbed in what they were saying, but we could recognize the straighter line of his mouth, the slight tenseness which marked his hidden impatience. When I saw that look, only shyness and long training in politeness prevented me from interrupting.

Jim Smith, sulking, would not visit the governor even to argue; but he sent Jim Nugent, and father told us of the interview. Nugent, bitterly opposed to the passage of the election law, accused father of using patronage to put it through. This was too much even for his cool restraint. Very angry, he pointed to the door and said quietly, "Good afternoon, Mr. Nugent". Nugent, in a fury, shouted, "Governor, you're no gentleman". The swift reply, "Mr. Nugent, you're no judge", ended the interview. Nugent tore down the hall on the verge of apoplexy. A few days later one of the evening papers published a cartoon entitled, "Good afternoon, Mr. Nugent", showing the chairman of the Democratic State Committee landing on his face in the street, propelled by a big boot labeled "Wilson".

I think father really enjoyed this first year as Governor. He was putting into effect ideas of government that he had planned, advocated and defended with voice and pen for many years. It amazed me to see that even this radical change into active political life in no way disturbed his patience or his sense of humor. But one day when he had been pestered by a persistent, wild-eyed "progressive", he said, "There should be a sign on the desk of every reformer, 'DON'T BE A DAMNED FOOL'."

The legislators and his new associates were surprised and delighted when he showed sudden flashes of the boyish gaiety we knew so well. At a dinner given by one of the senators, after much good-natured teasing and laughter, he danced a cakewalk, with another senator as a partner.

In March, urged by his friends to make speaking tours outside the state, he went South where he had an enthusiastic reception. But mother, always alert for a chance to advance his interests, heard that Mr. Bryan was coming to Princeton to speak at the Theological Seminary and telegraphed him to get back, if possible, in time to see Bryan.

He returned promptly and "The Great Commoner" came to the simple family dinner mother had tactfully arranged. It proved a happy and important meeting. Avoiding political discussion, the two swapped stories and were both at their very best. An understanding was established between them that evening—something deeper than a political entente. They were both idealists, both relentlessly sincere, and each recognized and respected these traits in the other. Father said later that he had been "completely captivated by the man's personal charm".

Jessie and I were at the dinner but, after acknowledging the introduction, Mr. Bryan ignored us. This made me uncomfortable at first; then I began to study him. I thought his voice one of the most beautiful I had ever heard, but his strange thin-lipped mouth, a long straight line, betrayed his intensity. His absorption in issues and ideals seemed almost fanatical.

Tumulty, terribly excited because things had gone so pleasantly, said to mother, "You have nominated your husband, Mrs. Wilson". Mother smiled—she had done "nothing at all", but we knew that it was one of the many times when her natural sweetness and tact had been of incalculable value to father. She did things so quietly that we seldom saw her hand until later.

There was much discussion now about the advisability of a speaking tour. Mother urged father to go. It proved an interesting trip, signally successful from the start. He had never been west of Denver and was delighted with the country, the desert as well as the vast fertile plains.

His good health and high spirits continued. His friend, Frank Stockbridge, who accompanied him, told us that on a cold morning when the train paused at a small station, he gave a fine exhibition of the Scotch hornpipe, on the platform. Traveling eight thousand miles, he made innumerable speeches. He had little time for letters but he sent us bundles of clippings and kept in close touch with mother by long nightly telegrams.

He had repeatedly said, "I am not thinking of the presidency". This worried mother. She wrote him, "Please, please don't say again that you are not thinking of the presidency. All who know you well know that this is true fundamentally; but superficially, it can't be true and it gives the cynics an opening they seize with glee."

His meaning was perfectly clear to us. All his life there was conflict within him—conflict between two sides of his nature, the thinker and teacher, and the man of action. There had been times when he longed for action and said that he was tired of "merely talking", and other times when he felt that the quiet life of the scholar was an ideal existence. But we knew that he accepted a new responsibility as a duty. He believed that no man had a right to refuse an opportunity to serve the people. This belief was an important part of his life philosophy, but personal ambition was almost non-existent in his nature.

He had a passionate longing to see certain reforms carried out in America, vital and sweeping reforms that he felt were necessary to save the country from disaster. He was too intelligent not to realize his own ability and he knew that he could trust himself—that nothing could deflect him from his purpose. But I think that in his secret heart he would have chosen to be the prophet and counsellor, rather than the executive. He was therefore not "thinking of the presidency"; he was earnestly expounding a great program.

He had, moreover, told us that he dreaded the thought of the White House, realizing that it meant giving up freedom of speech and action and the simple life we all prized so highly. He constantly reminded us of the penalties and heavy responsibilities attached to public life. But he saw mother's point and a little later made a frank announcement that he was definitely a candidate.

He had made it a rule, during his Western trip, not to speak on Sunday, but arriving in Denver on that day, he was met by a large crowd and found the town placarded with the announcement, "Wilson will speak on the Bible". As there was no church large enough to hold the audience, the meeting was held in a huge auditorium. With absolutely no chance to prepare, he made one of the most effective speeches of his whole career. Ray Stannard Baker describes it:

"It was not alone Woodrow Wilson who spoke that night. He had, after all, small need of preparation. It was

125

the Scotch Covenanter deep in the spirit of the man that spoke. It was his father, the Reverend Dr. Joseph Ruggles Wilson, and his grandfather, the Reverend Dr. Thomas Woodrow, it was all the long line of his God-fearing ancestors, who spoke that night. It was what he was—more than statesman, more than educator, more than scholar; it was what he was by heredity, by tradition, by all the religious atmosphere of his early training—that he gave to his vast audience that night. . . .

"For he was talking 'of the Bible as the book of the people, not the book of the minister of the gospel, not the special book of the priest from which to set forth some occult, unknown doctrine withheld from the common understanding of men, but a great book of revelation—the people's book of revelation'." *

The first telephone connection between Denver and New York was made while father was in Denver, and to New York's question, "What's new in Denver?", the reply was "The town's gone wild over Wilson"—a bit of information that even the "New York Times" did not ignore, although it was bitterly opposed to father's candidacy.

He continued on west, talking at many points to enthusiastic audiences. Mother had been afraid that the trip would be a strain for him but it proved a powerful stimulant. On his return he regaled us with tales of his adventures, full of shrewd and amusing comment on politics and politicians. I was surprised and delighted when he said suddenly, "I'm frank to say that I get a wicked pleasure in thinking of the blow my nomination would be to some of

* R. S. Baker, *Woodrow Wilson: Life and Letters*, vol. III, pp. 219-220. Doubleday, Doran & Company.

the gentlemen at Princeton." He sometimes used the word "gentleman" with apparent innocence, but a shade of stress, a subtle emphasis, made it the most cutting and unanswerable insult.

The papers were full of comments on the "conquest of the West" by this "amazing school teacher" but he said, "Crowds and enthusiasm do not mean very much. Mr. Bryan had more of that than anyone else in American politics but he never attained the presidency."

For some time his friends and supporters had clamored for a campaign organization of some sort. He was opposed to the idea; but thousands of letters and requests for copies of his speeches now poured in, and taking care of this huge correspondence became an arduous task. Stockbridge volunteered to do it for a time in his New York office, but soon they were forced to take a room for themselves, with William McCombs as self-appointed manager. Cleveland Dodge gave them a thousand dollars and this was the beginning of the organization that father always, in spite of protests, referred to as his "literary bureau".

We were all dissatisfied and uncomfortable at the Princeton Inn. Hotel life was, for us, simply not living at all and, as I was there more than my sisters, I positively brooded about it. Finally, I decided that something must be done. I knew that we couldn't afford to rent a house, but as the Smiths were planning a long visit to Princeton, I suggested to mother that she write and ask them if they would like to have a house with us, sharing expenses. I found a little place on Cleveland Lane, just behind the Grover Cleveland gardens, with a large studio room that captivated mother at once. There was also a small garden, always so important to her. Father approved of the idea, the Smiths replied immediately that they would be delighted and it was agreed that we should move in the fall.

The State provided the Governor with a summer "mansion" at Sea Girt on the New Jersey coast, and in June we went there in rather a confused state of mind, wondering what was before us and longing for Old Lyme and the jolly artists' colony. The big white house had been New Jersey's contribution to the Chicago World's Fair in 1893, and had later been moved in sections to Sea Girt and put together again. It was attractive mainly because it was flooded with air and sunlight, but it looked rather like a summer boarding house, with its long row of rocking chairs on the wide front porch.

The National Guard Parade Grounds were directly in front, and frequent parades and swarms of casual visitors made it necessary for us to hide in our bedrooms if we wanted any privacy.

I was pleased to find that the center room had a rotunda like the one at Prospect, and again provided a chance to look and listen unseen. Mother brought a truck-load of pictures and rugs, cushions and vases from Princeton. Hermes and the Winged Victory, and the bronze bust of Washington presented to father by his classmates, filled the niches in the wall of the imposing staircase. There was one small statue of Narcissus, *au naturel* in the full sense of the word. It worried Jessie, but we laughed at her until the unmistakably lifted eyebrows of some of the visitors from the country made mother uneasy too, and Narcissus was given a less conspicuous niche upstairs.

128

The small reception room was a monstrosity, with bright gilt chairs and a pinkish-red carpet. Only a conflagration could have improved it, so we ran through it with our eyes closed. We usually had our meals on a screened porch at the back of the house. There was a junction a stone's throw away and we were constantly disturbed by the noise of trains thundering by. Father always looked up and waited with a patient smile until the noise subsided, and then resumed the conversation at the point where he had been interrupted. The "state" dining room had an enormous table and clumsy high-backed chairs. Ronald, the tiny English butler, had almost to climb up the back of them to serve. There were so many unexpected guests that housekeeping was both difficult and expensive and, as there was no more money in the family budget than there had been at Prospect, mother had a real problem. She loved to have the house full of people, particularly our friends, and, of course, the relatives were as welcome as they had always been; but once in a while she said, ruefully, "I never know whether there will be five for luncheon, or twenty."

She was not very happy at Sea Girt. Noise and confusion always disturbed her and she had no chance to paint. Occasionally an amusing incident diverted her. One day a small boy came wandering in and she gave him some cake. He reported to his family that he had been to see the Governor and the Governor had given him some cake, but the Governor's husband was not at home.

My sisters and I enjoyed those summers at Sea Girt enormously. Our only problem was to fit a dozen engagements into one short day. Mother, amused at the seriousness with which we took our parties, said, "If you plan your future lives with one half the care you give to your days here, you will all be brilliant successes."

We had our first automobile, provided by the State and driven by an old Irishman who had been coachman for previous governors. He hated the "contraption", was obviously afraid of it and could never be inveigled into anything resembling speeding. In a long tan duster and huge visored cap, he grimly piloted us about, never exceeding thirty miles an hour. I took the earliest opportunity to drive over to Princeton and display our new grandeur to admiring and envious friends.

The Balkan states were waging one of their periodic wars that summer, and father and Jessie often spent hours in the evening, poring over a big map. Father had a historian's interest in such matters, and Jessie shared his passion for maps. Following every move reported in the press, they changed little pins about while father explained the motives and chances of the contenders. I found it terribly boring and when I begged them to stop and talk about something interesting, father looked up with a twinkle in his eye and said, "Nellie wants to talk politics".

We still managed, though more and more infrequently now, to have our evenings together. Gathering in mother's little sitting room upstairs, we read our old favorites and sang our old songs, deliberately shutting out all problems.

Uncle Stock, keenly interested in every phase of father's progress, and full of Princeton news, visited us often. Aunt Annie and little Annie, who had married at eighteen, came also, and of course the Smiths were there. Cousin Lucy was self-appointed guide. She actually enjoyed showing peo-

ple through the house, and was a godsend to mother.
When the wind blew at night, starting all the rocking
chairs on the porch squeaking and groaning, Cousin Lucy
said it was "the ghosts of all the old ladies that had sat in
them, discussing the private lives of past governors".

Mrs. Hulbert, whom father had met in Bermuda, came
also to stay with us. She was a charming woman, with great
intelligence and humor, and particularly fascinating to me.
Watching her daintily puffing at one cigarette after another, I decided that it was a mistake to think it wrong for
women to smoke, since it was so becoming, and neither
father nor mother seemed shocked. We all enjoyed her
immensely, but her constant suggestions about improving
our appearance got on our nerves at last. She insisted that
Jessie would be more attractive with a sleek coiffure and
long dangling earrings, an idea that horrified us all, as Jessie's great distinction was her clear classic beauty.

I found later that mother did not like to see women
smoke. A Mrs. Wilson Woodrow, the divorced wife of a
cousin of father's, was writing short stories at the time and
many people thought mother the author. We found one
story ending with the sentence—"Free—hell, there ain't no
sich word as 'free' for a woman what kin love". We showed
it to mother, but even this did not bring her to the point
of publicly denying that she had written it.

Later in the summer, however, Mrs. Woodrow wrote an
article defending smoking for women, and that was too
much for mother. She gave her first interview: she hadn't
written the story; she was not Mrs. Wilson Woodrow and
she did not approve of women smoking.

The annual governors' convention, held this year at Sea

Girt, meant more parties, dances and banquets. I was dancing one night with the Governor of Florida when he fell,
dragging us both under a table. He was horrified, of course,
and so relieved when I laughed that he insisted on giving
me a pin—a Florida emblem. Margaret and Jessie made a
beautiful story of how I "went under the table with the
Governor of Florida and came out with a jewel".

The governors were impressive and excessively polite to
one another; but Governor Harmon, of Ohio, then one
of the leading candidates for the presidency, was the most
pompous and ceremonious of all and everyone hopped
about to keep him in a good humor. Old Sam, the colored
majordomo, whose job it was to see that guests were met
and taken about properly, prided himself on keeping things
running smoothly. Once while answering the telephone in
a corner of the living room he began sputtering and then,
dropping the receiver, covered his face with his hands and
groaned, "Oh, Gawd, what shall Ah do? It's dat important
Governor, and dey was no one to meet him." Father went
to his rescue and, when he took the receiver, found Joe
Tumulty on the line delighted at the success of one of his
everlasting practical jokes.

On Sunday afternoons, the National Guard had a dress
parade, which father reviewed on horseback. Crowds came
from near-by resorts, swarmed over the grounds and made
a day of it. Father protested with some heat when he was
told that he must wear a frock coat and high silk hat. "I
shall feel a perfect fool. Why can't I wear sensible riding
clothes?" But it was the "custom" and he submitted.

He sat his horse superbly but as he passed us, long coat
tails flying in the breeze and tall hat a bit awry, he would

GOVERNOR WILSON REVIEWING TROOPS

THE "WHITE HOUSE"

The Governor's summer home at Sea Girt

throw us a glance of whimsical dismay. The officers were delighted to have, at last, a Governor who knew how to ride. They insisted that in other years they had lifted Governors onto their steeds and then stayed very near at hand during the parade, to catch them if they fell off. Father disliked having his quiet Sundays turned into days of noisy festivity; it was a travesty of the old Presbyterian idea of the Sabbath.

He managed to play a good deal of golf that summer and often said that he found it the only sure relaxation, "because while you are playing golf you cannot worry . . . each stroke requires your whole attention and seems the most important thing in life." * He was never a first-class golfer, but liked the game and, if he managed to keep in the eighties, was as happy as a child. We failed him as companions here, for we all disliked golf and gave up our time to swimming, riding and tennis.

Years before, Cleveland Dodge had brought him some fine clubs from Scotland. At the customs a suspicious inspector listened dubiously while Mr. Dodge tried to explain what they were. In desperation, he attempted to demonstrate their use, until the man interrupted him with, "I'll just put them down as agricultural implements."

Dudley Malone, young son-in-law of Senator O'Gorman of New York, and an ardent Wilson supporter, was a frequent visitor at Sea Girt. He was a handsome witty Irishman and father loved him. We sat for hours listening to his stories and his keen amusing remarks about affairs of the day.

I met William G. McAdoo for the first time at Sea Girt.

* Letter to Mrs. Edith G. Reid.

133

He had broken his arm and still carried it in a sling, which I thought most becoming to his tall, youthful figure. Tumulty had told us that the "tunnel man" was interested in father's political activities, and it was arranged for him to come down for a conference. We three peered over the rotunda rail when he and father came into the lower hall. We agreed that he was most attractive and Maragaret asked, "Is he married?" I answered with dignity, "He has a wife, and a houseful of children." When we were introduced he bowed and then, a moment later, walked over and shook hands with me. Later I insisted that he had singled me out but my sisters laughed and said, "Not at all—he didn't notice you at first and didn't want you to feel badly about it, that's all."

Father was delighted with him. A few years before they had ridden down to Princeton on the same train, and walking across the campus together, had talked about the Hudson tunnel and Mac's "Public-be-pleased policy".

My sisters and I were sorry to have the summer end. I, for one, was convinced that an utterly frivolous life was infinitely more attractive than the career of the most successful artist.

In November, Nellie Kintner, a schoolmate of mine, invited me to go with her to visit her cousins in Mexico. Mother and father decided to let me go, thinking that it would be an interesting experience, and that it might also instill some independence in me. Except for my years at boarding school, I had never made a long visit away from home. I was excited at the prospect, but while I was packing I stopped occasionally to cry at the thought of leaving the family. Father protested, "But, Nellie, this is supposed to be a pleasure trip. After all, you don't have to go."

It was an interesting trip. We stayed three weeks in Chihuahua with the Lawrences and went to innumerable parties where the young mining engineers, hungry for the sight of an American girl, treated us like princesses. Swaying along, in Mary Lawrence's little *coche*, we investigated all the highways and byways of the strange little city. Then we visited her sister, Amelia, whose husband was manager of a lumber camp in the mountains, at the edge of a huge cattle ranch.

We spent our time riding over the beautiful country; I learned to fish and hunt and flirted shyly with every unattached man. Here I had what I considered my first serious love affair and, when the revolution against Madero broke out, my joy was complete. Could anything be more thrilling than to be in the midst of a revolution and secretly engaged at the same time? When our beaux came to call in the evening, they unbuckled their pistols and left them in the hall, an added thrill to the romantic picture. When the fighting came dangerously near, an electrified fence was put up around the lumber mill, to protect the women and children. My family did not find the situation so romantic. They had no word from me for a week or two and were terribly concerned.

At last one day we were told that a train was leaving in an hour and that it might be our last chance to get away. We packed in frantic haste and climbed into the train, but toward evening we were held up at another lumber camp, and there we stayed for three days. At last a fierce-looking

Mexican general, weighted down with cartridge belts, arrived one night and gave orders for us to proceed. Fifty miles down the line we stopped again—a bridge was out and we spent the night in a boxcar with a terrific wind blowing and very little food. During the night noisy, drunken soldiers from an encampment on the other side of the bridge wandered around our refuge. I was too ignorant of the true state of affairs to be frightened; to me it was thrilling, a glimpse of a Mexican revolution at close range. But the men in our party were very nervous; they hid their pistols, fearing that they might be confiscated, and did not close their eyes until morning.

At dawn we saw an automobile tearing across the plains toward us. It proved to be a carload of reporters looking for me; I had been reported "lost in Mexico". They took the whole party back in the car, but all four tires blew out before we had gone any distance, and there was nothing to do but ride to the border on the rims. The chauffeur was a wild-looking man with two complete sets of solid gold teeth. We asked him how he dared to go into Mexico with so much wealth. Ten years later, still flashing his gold teeth, he arrived in Los Angeles and asked me to pay for the tires we had ruined on that ride as the reporters had refused to do so.

In El Paso we were enchanted to hear that a posse was being formed to go to our rescue. I went home at once and the family were so glad to see me alive that they listened patiently to a detailed account of my adventures. The story grew in length and strength every day. Of course, the most important part was about my beau. Father was grimly silent on the subject, but mother was most sympathetic and interested. She was, however, secretly worried at the idea of my being engaged to someone she did not know. It preyed on her mind so much that she finally persuaded Uncle Stock to make a trip to see him, and was much relieved to receive a good report.

CHAPTER EIGHT

Cleveland Lane and Sea Girt

THE LITTLE HOUSE in Cleveland Lane proved a great success—half-timbered in the English manner, with bay windows and big fireplaces, it reminded us a little of our own beloved Library Place. Though it was furnished, mother added many of our own things—pictures, rugs and curtains—and filled the house with flowers, so we had a home again and were quite happy.

We acquired a negro butler, who astonished us the first evening by appearing at the head of a small flight of stairs that led to the studio room and announcing in stentorian tones, "Dinner is now being served in the dining room". We could hardly smother our laughter, but father insisted that he should not be corrected. He and I used to go swaying in to dinner as though on a rocking train.

Mother began painting at once. Never having had a real studio before, she was enchanted with the fine north light in the big room.

The Smiths—vivacious little Lucy with her fund of delightful stories, Mary with her quiet wit—were her constant companions. They gave her the most tender love and understanding and kept her amused and happy. Day after day they sat in the studio, Lucy busily mending and darn-

138

ing, Mary reading aloud, and mother, her face smudged with paint, intent on her canvas. I think that if she had not had them with her that winter, the strain of the turbulent political storm, gradually but surely increasing around us, might have broken her down.

Father was being literally pushed by his friends into a more active campaign for the presidency. He was working harder than ever before in his life, continuing to force through his program in New Jersey, and yet finding time for many speaking trips and conferences.

His enemies, thoroughly alarmed at his increasing popularity throughout the country, began to fight him viciously. Jim Nugent created a sensation at a public dinner when he proposed a toast: "Gentlemen, I give you the Governor of New Jersey—" Everyone jumped up, glass in hand, and he continued, "—a liar and an ingrate". There was dead silence. "Do I drink alone?" he asked. Glasses and wine were thrown on the floor and he did drink alone. When father told us of the incident later, he seemed amused, but I was in a rage.

The fight grew in bitterness. They began digging into the past, with pathetically scanty results. Sentences from books he had written years before were twisted and misconstrued; a suitcase was stolen from his room in a hotel. Finally, and probably in desperation, they seized upon the fact that, after he had resigned from the presidency of Princeton, he had applied for a Carnegie pension.

The Carnegie Foundation for the Advancement of Teaching gave a retiring allowance after twenty-five years of distinguished service. It was in no sense a pension for the "superannuated", but was created so that university professors could work in other fields, such as research and public service. Father, who had no private income and had saved practically nothing, had made the application as a matter of routine. When it was denied because of a new ruling barring "a man, however distinguished, who retires from educational work to undertake other work on salary", he had made no protest and dismissed it from his mind.

But a member of the Carnegie Foundation board gave a garbled account of the incident to the "New York Sun," which was bitterly opposed to father at the time, and it made the most of it. We were dumfounded at the misrepresentation that followed. Father's only comment was characteristic. "If all they can think of to injure my candidacy is to accuse me of superannuation, they're in a bad way". The attack died of its own violence and absurdity.

Then the talk about George Harvey's support assumed grotesque and amazing proportions. Harvey called himself the "original Wilson man". The editorial page of his weekly had for some time carried the slogan, "Wilson for President". Now, on all sides, came the question, "How can Wilson be supported by Harvey and still be entirely free, when Harvey is controlled by Wall Street interests?"

Father, of course, believed that Harvey was free of Wall Street control. Soon after his return from his Western tour, he had a talk with Harvey and Colonel Watterson of the Louisville "Courier Journal". Watterson, a shrewd political observer, had already said that he thought it might be wise for Harvey to be a little less aggressive in his support.

After the conference, and just as father was about to leave, Colonel Harvey said:

"Governor, I want to ask you a frank question. Is the support of 'Harper's Weekly' embarrassing your campaign?" Father said, "Colonel, I am sorry you asked me that question." "That's all right," Harvey told him. "What's the answer?" "Well, Colonel, I regret to be compelled to tell you that my friends in the West tell me it is." Harvey answered, in the friendliest way, "I thought you might feel that way about it. We shall have to soft-pedal a bit." And they parted, as father supposed, quite amicably.*

Taking Harvey at his word, father wrote him a few days later thanking him for his support and assuring him of his appreciation. Harvey's reply was mildly sarcastic. Then one day "Harper's Weekly" appeared with father's name removed from the editorial page and the surprising statement that it was removed with deep regret and at Wilson's request. We were stunned—it seemed clearly an attempt to put father in an unfavorable light. I think he was angry, but, above all, he was disappointed—keenly disappointed in the man. It was another example of the thing he had spoken of so often to us, "I can't ever seem to remember that there are people who cannot be trusted."

Mother was deeply concerned as to what effect it would have on his career. She was comforted when Walter Hines Page wrote that he thought it would be a good thing, in the long run, as it certainly indicated that father was clear of boss control.

The next and by far the most exciting of all attempts to make trouble was the publication of a personal letter father had written five years previously to Adrian Joline, a

* From Stockton Axson's report of father's account of the incident.

Princeton trustee, in which he had said, "Would we could discover something at once dignified and effective, to knock Mr. Bryan into a cocked hat." Joline, having broken with father, in one of the Princeton fights, now gave this letter to the press. Naturally, we were disturbed, for to lose Bryan's friendship would have been most unfortunate.

Before it was actually sent, a mutual friend warned father of Joline's intention and suggested that he write and ask him not to do it. But father refused, saying that he was not ashamed of anything he had ever written, and that, although he felt differently now that he really knew Bryan, it had been his honest opinion at the time he wrote the letter and he would take the consequences. Bryan, in the South at the time, was expected to return for the Jackson Day dinner, and everyone was speculating as to what would happen. The day before he left for Washington father said, "Don't be nervous about this. It is only small men who allow such things to affect them and Mr. Bryan is not a small man."

Nevertheless, when Dudley Malone called us from Washington that evening we were elated. Margaret answered the telephone and called to mother, "Come and talk to Dudley; he has good news." He had slipped away from the party to tell us that Bryan had paid father a fine tribute; that, far from being a "break", it had become a Democratic "love feast". There were sensational headlines in some of the leading newspapers the next morning saying that Wilson was now the leading Democratic candidate. The missiles of his opponents had proved boomerangs, and his future had never looked brighter. He told us all about it when he came home. Sitting around the fire in the studio, we listened, enthralled. He had a delightful way of emphasizing high lights, and never failed to find humor in situations of this sort. In a sense, he dramatized them— or perhaps we dramatized him.

All the important leaders of the Democratic party were present at the dinner. Bryan came in late, and everyone watched him as he walked first to Champ Clark and then slowly over to father, put his hand on his shoulder and chatted for a few moments.

Father spoke first. Friends of Jim Nugent seated near by attempted to heckle him, but were promptly shouted down. He made no attempt to explain or apologize, but merely discussed the problems of the day, paying Bryan a fine tribute for his "unselfish devotion" to his principles. And at the end, he voiced a simple plea for harmony in the party. "Let us apologize to each other that we ever suspected or antagonized one another." Bryan's eyes never left father's face, and when the applause died down, he rose and made what was afterwards called his speech of abdication. "The time has come," he said, "for new leaders, free from the asperities of the past." He told a friend after the dinner that father's speech was the greatest in American political history. Here was a man who had been three times a candidate for the presidency, who was still the leader of his party, and when everyone thought that he would be resentful and antagonistic, he had stepped aside with a generous and gracious gesture. Father was deeply touched.

He was never very much disturbed by attacks upon him. After having once discussed an unpleasant occurrence, he seldom referred to it again, although we sometimes knew that he had not completely dismissed it from his mind. He

143

had a habit of taking off his glasses and holding them—in fact, balancing them—on his thumb while he rubbed his eyes slowly. I loved to watch him—his eyes seemed larger and more beautiful then than ever and had a fascinating vagueness. There was a little twitch in his left eye—barely noticeable unless he was worried, when it became slightly exaggerated. When we saw it, we knew that he was feeling things more than he wanted us to know. He wrote an intimate friend, "I don't really mind—but the strongest nerves wince under persistent pressure. All these things, in the long run, discredit only those who do them, but for a little while they are very trying." But we never had the slightest concern that he might not know what to do in a crisis or that he would fail in an emergency—our realization of his courage and honesty was to us a shield, a safeguard.

A few days after the Jackson Day dinner, Jack Hibben was elected President of Princeton. I was so engrossed in the various aspects of the political drama that I felt only a passing irritation at the news and was surprised that father seemed hurt. He felt that all his dreams and hopes for the college were now irreparably lost. Hibben had proven himself timid and conservative, and his election seemed a tragedy.

The Governor of the state always takes part in the inauguration ceremonies at Princeton, but father felt it was impossible for him to do so. He said, "I cannot say what I really think without causing a riot, and if I do not speak my mind, I shall be a hypocrite." Fortunately, he had a speaking engagement outside the state, and he went ahead of time, feeling that in this way his nonappearance at Princeton would be less pointed.

Things were no longer going smoothly in New Jersey. After the early momentum of father's progressive program had been somewhat exhausted and the politicians had recovered from the shock of his new direct methods, they began again to work under cover. Resorting to their old tricks, they had managed to regain control of a majority of the legislature. But this was to be expected, and knowing the fluctuation of public opinion, the difficulty of keeping men's minds steadily on progress, he was not dismayed. He had made politics his lifelong study and was able now to take an active part with philosophic understanding and calm. And this was not like the Princeton controversy, where his old friends and his heart were involved.

We were becoming well versed in politics. I loved to exhibit my new-found knowledge to my friends, talking earnestly and at length about political trends and progressive movements. Even in the midst of this busy and critical period, father continued to explain and discuss things in the family circle.

We understood very well the importance of what was happening in the national field. It was no longer the usual simple battle between progressives and conservatives. The country was ripe for reform and the conservatives had very little chance. But there were progressives in each party—Bryan, Champ Clark and father in the Democratic, and Theodore Roosevelt and La Follette in the Republican ranks.

When we heard that La Follette and father were to speak at the same dinner, given in Philadelphia in February by the Periodical Publishers Association of America, we realized that it would be another critical step in the campaign. I was visiting in Philadelphia, and when I saw the papers, the next morning, I was delighted. They had printed most of father's speech and praised it highly, but there was sharp criticism of La Follette. That night when I got home, father was still away, and I rushed up to mother's room to hear more about it. Father had made a wonderful speech, she said; clear, pungent, witty and brief. Then La Follette had spoken for two hours and ten minutes—a diatribe, a bitter denunciation of the "East" and all its works, including his hosts, the newspaper fraternity. At the end of an hour, the crowd, restless and inattentive, began to leave. She and father, sitting there watching the dreadful failure, had been sick with sympathy for the man they had always admired. It finished La Follette as a presidential candidate, and Roosevelt, who had been holding back, saw his chance and announced soon afterward that his "hat was in the ring". This would inevitably mean a split in the Republican party and bring certain victory to the Democrats. From that moment, the Democratic contest for the nomination became bitter in its intensity.

In November, father met Colonel House for the first time. The Colonel was an astute political observer, active and prominent in his own state of Texas, and for some time mutual friends had been trying to bring about a meeting. Father went to see him in New York, and at once they were aware of a quite extraordinary understanding. Father told us that he felt he had "known Colonel House always". He entered into friendships with his whole heart and with an almost childlike faith, which made his suffering, if they failed him, all the more intense.

When Colonel House came to Princeton we were all

captivated. He was a small man with clear, steady eyes—very quiet and calm, his manner in pleasant contrast to the aggressive self-assertion of most of the politicians we had seen. He listened with flattering attention to what we said, but seldom committed himself. He almost annoyed me with his secretiveness, but I felt that when he knew that father told us everything, he would unbend.

McCombs, who was often ill, became erratic and difficult in his role of self-appointed manager, and the Colonel was very helpful in smoothing matters. He had what almost amounted to genius as a mediator. Father went often to confer with him in New York, and McAdoo was often present at these conferences.

Father spoke often of "Mac" with enthusiasm. "He is an attractive and dynamic person and a tremendous help." When I heard that he was coming to Princeton for dinner and to spend the night, I broke an engagement and stayed at home to see him. I was very curious about the "tunnel man", remembering the extra hand-shake at Sea Girt and all I had heard about his adventures under the Hudson River.

But, obviously intensely interested in father and charmed with mother, he paid very little attention to me. At the end of the evening he told mother that he had to leave on an early train in the morning, and begged her not to trouble about seeing him at breakfast. Mother said, "I will let Nellie be your hostess. She is taking an early train, too, and will see that you are taken care of."

Mac, with true Southern courtesy, professed delight at the prospect, but I was very nervous, wondering if I would be able to entertain him properly. The next morning, pouring coffee, I spilled the cream and dropped the sugar tongs, but in a little while he put me at my ease, talking to me as though I were a wise woman of the world.

In the spring, when the delegates to the convention were chosen, father was urged to make even more speaking trips. Mother accompanied him on a tour through her own state of Georgia, and in one small city a triumphal arch had been erected with "Welcome" on one side and "Mizpah" on the other. Two negroes, sitting on a curbstone, were heard discussing it, and one asked, "But what dat word mean M-I-Z-P-A-H?" The other answered, "Why, don' you know? Dat's Miz Wilson's fust name."

The enthusiasm with which father was received encouraged his friends and supporters, but in only a few states were delegates chosen to support him. Disregarding all pleas to play "machine" politics, he refused to deal with the politicians, and made his appeal directly to the people. They seemed to be for him, but when the time came to choose the delegates, the bosses usually had their way. It was heart-breaking, but he took it with his usual calm and cheerful acceptance. The morning after his defeat in Virginia, his birthplace, he was laid up with a cold and I took his breakfast up to his room. Putting the tray down beside him, I was aware of a pair of twinkling eyes regarding my woe-begone countenance. "You don't seem to think very well of your father as a vote-getter, this morning," he said. Then we laughed together, and I went off with a lighter heart.

Mother was beginning to show the effects of the strain. Uncle Stock had had a nervous breakdown and, with her usual unselfishness, she devoted a great deal of her time

18 Dec., 1911

PRINCETON NEW JERSEY

My darling Nell,

There is nothing to tell you, for you know what the others have written. This is only, a dear message, to say how sadly, I miss my precious little Chum, and how empty it makes my heart feel that she is going to be away at Christmas. God bless you, my sweet little Daughter! A merry Christmas and a happy New Year, full of blessings and happy, hours—even for you! Oh, how I hope that blessings may always and everywhere follow you.

Your loving
Father

Facsimile of letter from Woodrow Wilson to Eleanor Randolph Wilson,
December 18, 1911

HOUSE ON CLEVELAND LANE, PRINCETON

to him, trying to interest him in one thing after another to lift the dark depression that submerged him. The confusion in the house was very trying; it was simply overflowing with letters and newspapers, and she was constantly picking them up and arranging them in neat piles, a resigned look on her face.

After a week-end spent at home, Jessie told me that mother was looking very badly and a few days later, going home from the station at Princeton, I saw a little figure walking slowly ahead of me. I was shocked when I realized that it was mother, whose movements had always been so eager and quick. When I talked to the Smiths about it, I found that they, too, were greatly disturbed and we renewed our efforts to make her take things more easily. My sisters and I had a conference. We seriously considered giving up our work and staying at home with her. Perhaps she wanted us, but would not say so. Each one of us, in turn, hinted to her that we would like to be at home for a while, but she wouldn't hear of it. She was intensely interested in our budding careers, following every step of our progress with eager pride. She was glad that I had chosen the vocation she had dreamed of for herself, and Margaret's singing was a source of pure joy to her. Knowing practically nothing about music, she was yet, of all the family, Margaret's most ardent audience. I saw her, many times, sitting listening and smiling happily, with tears on her cheeks. And she was absorbed in Jessie's work, and proud because she had undertaken it, although she often worried about the strain and distress that such work inevitably brought. I am sure that she had no favorite child, but Jessie's beauty and grave self-forgetful dignity were a constant delight to her. When I was younger, I had moments of passionate jealousy watching mother's expression when she looked at my lovely sister. But I was very proud of Jessie, and as I grew older, my love for her was touched with something close to awe. She was reserved, but her mind was strong and profound, and she had depths of feeling that she could not fully express. When she did succeed in expressing her love, we were deeply touched, and her rare moments of anger always surprised us. It was usually on the heights of the soul that she lived, however, and we all recognized this and adored her as one a little apart from the rest of us, not quite of this earth. I have never seen any other human being in whom the balance of physical, mental and soul beauty was so perfect.

Jessie did her best to prevent her many beaux from falling seriously in love with her, but without success. Often, when she had to refuse a proposal of marriage, she wept softly and steadily throughout the ordeal, although crying was not a habit with her.

That winter, she and I were invited to spend a week-end with a charming old lady at her country place in Pennsylvania. Miss Blanche Nevin had a favorite nephew, and, as she confided afterwards to mother, the moment she saw Jessie she decided that here was the perfect wife for her adored Francis.

We arrived in the evening, and at dinner and all the next day I watched a romance blossoming. Unaware of the plot, they were instantly attracted to each other, and for the first time in our lives Jessie seemed to have forgotten my existence.

"Auntie Blanche" wore innumerable necklaces, bracelets and rings, and a silver snake belt that tinkled and clicked as she walked. One could hear her coming a long way off, but she crept about on tiptoe and dragged me off out of the way, a conspiratorial finger on her lips. On the way back to town, I teased Jessie and tried to question her, but she only looked at me with a vague expression and a lovely blush.

I was suddenly indignant. Was Frank Sayre going to take her away from us? The political turmoil had brought sufficient havoc and change into our peaceful lives, but as long as we stuck together, everything would be all right. It was all very well for me to be engaged. I wasn't going to marry for years. I began to talk to her about the beauty of devoting her life to settlement work, but her parting words, as we separated in Philadelphia, were, "Oh, Nell, he has asked if he might call."

I was not happy at the Art School since father had become so prominent. One girl I liked immensely seemed to be deliberately avoiding me, and when I asked her why, she said: "Your father may be president, and I didn't want you to think I was pursuing you." It was my first encounter with this phase of the disadvantage of being in the public eye. Those you dislike pursue you, and those you like are apt to avoid you. We were all called by our last names at the school. I was "Wilson" at first, and then "Governor", and the young artists did not spare me in the caricatures they loved to make and pin on the walls. I appeared many times—a great grinning face—all teeth.

In May, the primaries were held in New Jersey. We were as nervous as witches all day long. If New Jersey's delegation wasn't going to the Democratic Convention pledged to her own Governor, there was not much hope for him. The bosses had been working "tooth and nail" to send an uninstructed delegation. But father won twenty-four out of the twenty-eight delegates, and on the same day Texas gave him all her forty votes. Things were looking brighter.

CHAPTER NINE

Sea Girt

TEN DAYS BEFORE THE CONVENTION, we went back to Sea Girt. I had begged to be allowed to go to Baltimore, but father wouldn't hear of it. He said that it would be undignified, and when I wailed, "But the other candidates' families are going", he looked at me sternly and said: "Does it follow that you should?"

On Sunday we all went to church, but I couldn't listen to the sermon. I sat quietly enough in my appointed place, but my mind was in a whirl. I was thinking, "Next Sunday we'll be here again, and it will be all over. Will it be victory or defeat? Will I be glad or sad?"

The National Guard Encampment had not begun and we had a quiet peaceful day, strangely and unexpectedly like the old Sundays at Library Place. It was raining and we sat around the fire talking about everything except the convention, each of us carefully concealing her nervousness. Suddenly father said, "Two weeks from today we will either have our sweet Sunday calm again, or an all-day reception with an army of reporters camped on the lawn." Thoughtlessly I asked, "Which would you prefer?" As he answered, "Need you ask?" I realized that the question was unanswered in my own mind. I wanted suc-

153

cess for him, with my whole heart, but the old terror tortured me—it might prove too much for him—he and mother might not be able to bear the burden that success would bring.

That week the Republican Convention met in Chicago, and Roosevelt and La Follette—at each other's throats, but with one cause in common, to defeat Taft and the Old Guard—were making the welkin ring. When Taft was nominated and Teddy, roaring with indignation and injured egotism, announced his plan of forming a new party, we were delighted. With the Republicans split, the Democrats were sure to win in November. Father gave us a delicious imitation of Teddy delivering his hysterical slogan—"We stand at Armageddon and battle for the Lord", and added, "Good old Teddy—what a help he is."

Before the Democrats met, Bryan started the fireworks by attempting to prevent the selection of Alton B. Parker as temporary chairman of the convention. The temporary chairman always makes the "keynote speech" and, as Parker was a recognized reactionary, Bryan believed that "it would be suicidal" to have him named, and telegraphed the various candidates, asking them to declare their position in the matter.

McCombs was in a panic. He knew that if father openly opposed Parker, he would not only offend the New York delegation, but alienate others who might eventually support him. He sent a telegram to Sea Girt suggesting an answer to Bryan. "In the interests of harmony", it began, and was weakly evasive from beginning to end.

We gathered in father's room to discuss the situation.

154

He sat on the edge of the bed and said nothing, including each one of us in his glance of rather whimsical interrogation. We thought we knew what he would do, but it was mother who first said firmly, "There must be no hedging." He smiled at her and said, "You are right, of course."

She was very direct and fearless in making suggestions to him, and she could be critical in the best sense of the word, in spite of the fact that she was always ready to admire everything he did. All the faculties of her mind were dedicated to his service, but they were not under his control. Father said once, "Neither the powers above nor below can shake her when a principle is involved", and she answered in her gentle voice, "What's the use of having a principle if you don't stick to it?"

Father, still sitting on the bed, wrote his answer. It began in the words he had used to mother, "You are quite right"—and stated very plainly that the convention must have a progressive chairman, adding that he was certain that his delegates would be of the same opinion.

He was reading it to us when Tumulty knocked on the door. He wanted to suggest an answer to Bryan's telegram and proceeded to advise father to do what he had already done. Father listened to him, saying at intervals, "Yes, yes, I agree with you", and did not tell him that the answer was already written. I saw him do this many times. He never said, "I have already thought of that myself", but listened patiently and courteously, allowing the adviser to go off without any inkling that the advice was unnecessary. There are many who still believe that they, and they alone, were responsible for many of his important decisions.

With the exception of Burke, of North Dakota, who took the same position, all the other candidates either opposed Bryan or avoided making a direct answer.

Father's definite stand brought him to the forefront as a courageous progressive, a real leader, strengthened Bryan's friendship and focussed the attention of the country on the main issue at Baltimore.

On Tuesday, the 25th of June, the Democratic Convention met. The household was tense with excitement. A private wire from the Wilson headquarters in the Emerson Hotel was installed, with one telephone up in father's room and another in a small booth under the main stairway.

The newspaper men, who had pitched tents on the parade ground, dashed in and out all day, ignoring the doorbell, and bringing us the latest news, with all the wild rumors from the front. Tumulty, sitting with his ear glued to the receiver, heard directly from the Wilson men in Baltimore and reported to us. He must have walked miles every day between booth and living room, and he never sat down at all.

A crowd of Princetonians were making a terrific racket at the Emerson, giving the Princeton Tiger yell and parading through the corridors and out on the streets, with an enormous picture of father. The Clark adherents were just as noisy and more numerous, but Tumulty made light of that.

Mr. Bryan plunged immediately into the battle. He made a speech against Parker, ending with histrionic fervor: "You cannot frighten the Democratic Party with your Ryans nor buy it with your Belmonts". It sent the crowd into a frenzy; the galleries were all for Bryan and they cheered him wildly, and shouted insults at the politicians on the floor. But Parker was elected temporary chairman by a small majority. I was astonished when this was described to us. I had paid little attention to political conventions, but had always thought of them as solemn, dignified affairs. Again I longed to be in Baltimore in the midst of it.

The next news we had was that almost the entire gallery had walked out when Parker made his keynote speech. We were told that the delegates were being deluged with telegrams from all over the country, urging them to support Bryan, and finally Ollie James, a pronounced progressive with a stentorian voice, was made permanent chairman.

Tumulty nearly died of joy when they told him that Newton Baker, by the mere mention of ˙father's name while making a speech against the unit rule, had brought on an unexpected demonstration that lasted thirty-three minutes. Tumulty spent those minutes running between telephone and living room, watch in hand, shouting: "It's still going on! It isn't over yet!"

Bryan now made the startling demand that any delegate controlled by Morgan, Ryan or Belmont should withdraw from the convention. Father's eyes sparkled when he heard this, and he laughed aloud. "The old lion is at his best", he said. After a long debate, it was decided that the convention had no right to expel delegates and Bryan had to withdraw his demand.

Midnight of the first session came, but there was no indication of slowing up. When Champ Clark's name was presented, the demonstration lasted for an hour and five minutes.

Tumulty was still wandering about, looking at his watch, but with a look of agony on his face. Mother began to be worried about him and scolded father for teasing him. Father subsided somewhat, but often when Tumulty came into the room, he could not resist humming Champ Clark's campaign song: "I don't care if he *is* a houn', You gotta quit kickin' my dawg aroun'."

When we heard that Genevieve Clark had been carried around the hall wrapped in an American flag, father said, "Now you will understand why I wouldn't allow any of you to go to the convention. How would you like something of that sort to happen to you?"

At two-fifteen in the morning Judge Westcott, of New Jersey, stood up to present father's name. The shouting started at once, and it was difficult for him to make himself heard above the noise. After many unsuccessful attempts, he delivered his eloquent, if somewhat florid, speech ending, "New Jersey appreciates the honor of placing before this convention as a candidate for the presidency, the seer and philosopher of Princeton—the Princeton schoolmaster —Woodrow Wilson".

The demonstration that followed lasted one hour and fifteen minutes. Tumulty nearly went crazy with joy. When an hour passed—he had been terrified that it would not continue as long as the Clark demonstration—he insisted on going upstairs to tell father, and found that he had gone to bed and was sound asleep. We finally crawled into bed too, so exhausted that we couldn't wait any longer for the first ballot.

It was taken at seven o'clock in the morning, after an all-night session and was most discouraging. Clark had 440½ votes and father 324. Harmon came next with 148, then Underwood with 117½, and the rest were divided among "favorite sons". 544 constituted a majority and 724 were necessary for nomination under the two-thirds rule, so things didn't look very rosy.

Father had reminded us from the start that he did not expect to be nominated and that we must not allow ourselves to be too hopeful, and I knew that he meant just what he said; but in my heart I was still convinced that he would not only be nominated, but elected.

He went calmly off that afternoon for a game of golf, and in the evening after dinner, in mother's small sitting room, read aloud from Morley's "Gladstone." I didn't hear a word of it. The shouting and excitement at the convention were echoing in my mind and I was looking at imaginary pictures: the first, a happy one of victory—a sort of family tableau in which we were all glorified—and the other, defeat. This was much less vivid and I pushed it quickly away.

McCombs kept begging father to make terms with Tammany, but he was wasting his breath. Everyone was speculating about Bryan. Whom was he really for? Did he want it himself? As a member of the Nebraska delegation, he was pledged to Clark, but had never personally committed himself. Father never doubted Bryan's honesty and sincerity, but he too wondered. Why didn't he show his hand?

For three days there was very little change in the vote, but in spite of the suspense we were very cheerful. Father said that it reminded him of the story of two men traveling through the country, who stopped to ask how far they were from their destination. They were told "Twenty miles". They went on for some time and asked again. The answer was "Twenty miles". After traveling a long time they stopped to ask again and the answer was still "Twenty miles". At last one of them exclaimed weakly, "Well, thank God, we're holding our own".

Tumulty's cheeks were pinker and his eyes bluer than ever. He was in such a state that he hardly ate or slept, constantly popping in and out of whatever room we were in, giving us the latest news and always managing to make it sensational—either very good or equally bad. Father lamented the fact that he seemed to have lost his sense of humor. Anyone who opposed Wilson was a "damned crook" to Tumulty. He said it so often that it became a household word, and even mother would say, "Well, I suppose that's another of Tumulty's damned crooks". Nothing could have been quainter than the apologetic inflection she gave to that forbidden word.

On Friday Murphy, of Tammany Hall, turned the New York delegation over to Clark, giving him a majority. It was a bad moment when Tumulty, as white as a sheet, rushed in with the news. We all thought it was the end, as for nearly seventy years the candidate receiving a majority had always been nominated—swept along in the rush for the band wagon.

I looked at father and he smiled; there was almost a touch of relief in his manner, as if he had suddenly seen a vision of returning peace. But mother looked tragic and a little dazed.

The Clark people were staging a wild demonstration,

but this time Tumulty did not look at his watch; he just walked aimlessly about, like a lost child. Mother followed him anxiously, begging him not to mind so much, but he just stared at her, not hearing a word she said.

But, to our amazement, there was no stampede. The Wilson men stood as firm as rock, and the convention adjourned for the night. When we went upstairs to bed, my sisters and I couldn't sleep; and when Margaret wandered into the room I shared with Jessie, we sat and talked. Jessie said, "Well, I never could imagine us in the White House, could you?" and I said, "No, I can't, and that's why I'm sure he won't be nominated". The words were hardly out of my mouth before I knew that I didn't really mean what I had said, and Margaret interrupted, "That's not the way to think of it. Can you imagine father failing in anything?" We agreed that we couldn't, and finally slept fitfully.

Coming down to breakfast early the next morning, I heard father talking on the telephone in the little booth. Margaret said, "It's McCombs. Tumulty says he's terribly excited". When father came out he looked grave but perfectly serene. He hesitated a moment; I knew at once that it was bad news and that he hated to upset us.

McCombs had given up; he was convinced that there was no hope, that Clark's nomination was inevitable, and had asked father to send a telegram releasing his delegates and instructing them how to vote. When we realized that father was ready to send the telegram, we were speechless.

We sat down to breakfast with heavy hearts—all except father. I think that, at that moment, I was prouder of him than I had ever been in my life. He was actually gay, like a boy let out of school, and when, on opening the mail, he found a catalogue advertising coffins, he burst into delighted laughter and said, "This company is certainly prompt in its service. They've got their catalogue here by the first mail. Help me to chose an appropriate coffin for a defeated candidate". Our own laughter had a dismal restraint, but it was impossible to remain heavy-hearted in his presence. He said to mother, "Do you realize that now we can see our beloved Rydal again?"

But later in the morning Mac called on the telephone. McCombs had just told him what he had done, and Mac was indignant; they had almost come to blows. Father came back to us, looking a little dazed. Mac had said, "Your nomination is inevitable, Governor—your delegates will stick, if it takes all summer", and had begged him to call McCombs and tell him not to release the Wilson delegates. We were immediately radiant again and Tumulty's face looked like the rising sun.

Father announced that he needed a vacation and went off to play golf, advising us to also take up some healthy pursuits, but nothing could induce us to leave the proximity of the telephone and the excited reporters.

Suddenly they dashed in and told us that they had a flash that Bryan had changed his vote. We waited breathlessly for the telephone to ring. The news was confirmed. The fiery "Commoner" had announced that he could no longer support a man who had received the votes of the Tammany delegation. Bedlam had broken loose again; there had been wild yells and shouts to try to drown him out, but he had calmly gone on to say that he was casting his vote

162

for Governor Wilson. I had heard so much about his power and influence, so much speculation as to his real preference and what he would do next, that I had a moment of wild exultation; but, to my bitter disappointment, on the next ballot, father had only five more votes. Everything seemed to go on as before; the long roll calls, the tedious bickering, the fluctuations from hope to despair. But little by little father's votes increased and Clark's decreased. Bryan had staged his act during the fourteenth ballot and they had reached the twenty-sixth when they adjourned that night. Father stood 407 and Clark 463. Father remarked, "I've been figuring it out. At this rate I'll be nominated in 175 more ballots".

Margaret was running Tumulty a close race as the sleepless wonder of Sea Girt. Two or three times during those hectic days I heard sounds and crept out of bed to peer over the rotunda. There they sat most of the night, lost in discussion, or merely gazing bleakly and silently into space; and usually, sitting in a straight chair at a respectful distance, was black Sam. His heart was in it too—he worshiped father and hung about day and night to hear the latest news.

The next day was Sunday and again I found myself sitting in church with the family. I was in a sort of daze— a stupor of suspense; I saw a long vista of Sundays stretching ahead and the Democratic Convention still going on, with no end in sight. I remembered the messages from the Wilson men: "We'll stick till hell freezes over"—"We'll fight it out if it takes all summer". And I found myself taking it literally. Would we ever have a normal life again?

At midday dinner, father insisted that we should abide

by the old rule—no political problems at meals—and enter-
tained us delightfully. It was a little as if we were nervous
patients and he the doctor with a beautiful bedside manner. Tumulty couldn't stand it; not even father could make
him relax and, although he didn't interrupt, he hung about
in the hall and refused to sit down with us. After lunch he
gave us a new crop of rumors, most of them quite fantastic.
One moment he said, hopefully, "Wait till the country is
heard from—the damned crooks will be flooded with telegrams; they'll have to give in"; and the next moment he
was swamped with terror, believing that this intervening
Sunday would be fatal—it would give the politicians time
to make their nefarious deals.

The most persistent rumor of all was that Bryan had
deliberately caused a deadlock, to bring about his own
nomination.

On Monday as we sat on the porch in the rocking chairs,
we suddenly saw a flock of reporters dash out of their
tents and run madly towards us. They hadn't noticed that
father wasn't there, and were shouting, "You've passed
him, Governor, you've passed him". Tumulty dived out
of the house, his eyes popping, and we jumped up in a
frenzy of excitement and went to look for father.

In his office, the newspaper men surrounded him and
insisted that he should make a statement. He said, "You
might say that Governor Wilson received the news in a
riot of silence".

Again nothing final happened; just a slow creeping up
of father's votes. I couldn't believe it. Would it never end?

On Tuesday Tumulty told us that he had heard that
McCombs had lost his head completely and, marching up

to Roger Sullivan of Illinois, had shouted, "We've got to have Illinois or I'll withdraw". *He* would withdraw! There was murder in Tumulty's eyes. On the forty-third ballot Sullivan delivered Illinois's fifty-eight votes to Wilson and the stampede began. On the forty-sixth ballot, the flash came that father was nominated.

Tumulty rushed out of the house like a lunatic and, standing on the porch, began waving his arms and making weird signals. From behind a clump of trees came a brass band blaring "Hail to the Chief" and "The Conquering Hero Comes". Father asked him if he had instructed them to slink away silently in case of defeat. He was the only calm person there. Someone said, "Governor, you don't seem a bit excited". And he answered gravely, "I can't effervesce in the face of responsibility". He still kept the same detached attitude toward his personal fortunes that he had shown throughout the whole ordeal. It was as if his inner being remained always untouched by what men call success or failure.

It was impossible to describe the relief I felt. We had been under such a long strain that the end came as a sort of pleasant explosion. That night we slept like the dead.

The next morning we took mother's breakfast up to her room and sat with her while she ate it, all very gay and happy. All that day the house was packed with people arriving hourly from Baltimore. Queer, unshaven men, haggard from the sleepless nights and hectic days of the convention. There were men in every room, telling end-less, amusing yarns about the convention. Dudley Malone, an ardent Catholic, had stopped at church every morning on his way to the convention to light candles before the

saints and make a bargain with God. If they would help
Woodrow Wilson, he would never take another drink or
swear another oath. Then, arriving at the scene of battle
with renewed strength, he had muttered extravagant curses
against his adversaries. Father said, "He 'swore a prayer or
two' every morning."

One man told us that he had bought a "houn' dog", planning to take it into the convention and literally "kick it
around" in the presence of the Clark crowd and that Mac
had said seriously that, if he did, he would be lynched, and
"we can't afford to lose a single Wilson man right now".

It was interesting to notice how many of them indicated
by implication, or quite openly, that if it had not been for
their remarkable foresight, cleverness or courage, father
would never have won the victory. I watched father carefully that day. His walk had its usual spring, alive and
elastic. An unending stream of people poured into Sea
Girt, a seething mass of exultant Democrats, wanting to
shake our hands and congratulate us.

We had become accustomed to reporters, but now the
human interest variety descended upon us in full force.
Father had told us to be good sports and try to be as pleasant as possible, but even he sometimes withdrew into silence, after being subjected to hours of silly personal questions. We, who had been taught to be close-mouthed about
our family affairs, found this prying into our lives strange
and annoying. They did not hesitate to question us about
any and every detail of our lives. What were our favorite
colors, occupations, sports? Did we like to dance? Were we
in love or engaged? Did we intend to marry and, if so,
when?

I was sitting with mother when one particularly persistent woman reporter asked why we never wore jewels.
"Have you some sort of moral prejudice against jewelry,
Mrs. Wilson?" Mother smiled and, as I looked at the hard-
faced, sharp-eyed woman, I realized how impossible it
would be for her to understand why mother had no jewelry. Mother, who had sacrificed for us, so that father might
have the books he needed, the vacations; that we might
study art and singing; that there might always be room in
the house for relatives and friends. I thought of her rigid
economy, her perennial brown dress and hat, and I felt a
wave of dislike for the woman who stubbornly repeated,
"But why, Mrs. Wilson?" Mother said, "No, I have no
prejudice against it; we just haven't any". The simplicity
and gentleness of that answer was a great lesson to me, and
brought quick tears to my eyes.

We never gave interviews, but that didn't interfere in
the least with the literary efforts of the ladies and gentlemen of the press. They simply invented them. We were
startled to read in one paper that we were three "high-
brows", with our noses constantly buried in ponderous
volumes, and in another that we were frivolous and gay,
eager to reach the White House and liven up Washington society. Jessie, who abhorred slang and had great natural dignity, was quoted as saying, "Gee, Pop's a practical
man".

The numerous pictures they took of us, singly and in
groups, were revelations of the power of the camera to
misrepresent. Father and Jessie usually looked human at
least, but mother's sweet little face appeared grim and un-
compromising. I looked like a middle-aged mulatto, and

167

Margaret, the smallest one in the family, took on the grotesque proportions of a militant suffragette in the cartoons. We were most of the time in a state between indignation and laughter.

I trembled for fear my secret engagement would be exposed to this pitiless light.

Father was very courteous and patient when he himself was questioned, but he resented almost fiercely the attempts to pry into family affairs and tried to protect us as much as he could. I have always believed that the first rumors of his "aloofness" and "unfriendliness" were the result of his annoyance at this first onslaught upon us. The newspaper people could not understand the sensitive shyness and delicacy which were an essential part of his character.

He disappeared for a few days to work on his notification day speech, managing a cleverly planned escape with mother and Margaret to Cleve Dodge's yacht. No one knew where he was and the rest of us held the fort at home, watching the preparations for the notification day ceremony, and trying to cope with the continuous confusion in the house. A small platform was built on a knoll and long tables arranged for the luncheon guests. There were consultations with caterers and plans to be made to take care of the crowds.

I realized suddenly that I had no new dress to wear for this important day. I begged mother to let me go to Philadelphia to get one. She said I was like "Miss Flora McFlimsy of Madison Square", who had plenty of clothes, but nothing to wear. But I implored so earnestly that she gave me permission to go. I bought a dark blue dress, gathered at the waist, with short sleeves and a small lace collar. Before I got home I knew it was a failure, and I sat up most of the night trying to fix it, pinning it this way and that, putting the collar back to front and around again. Everything I did seemed to make it worse. It ruined the day for me—I wore it, feeling dowdy and uncomfortable, and certain that everyone was looking at me and thinking, "That youngest of the Governor's daughters is a fright".

I was curious about the defeated candidates, some of whom were present. Oscar Underwood, suave and attractive, Governor Harmon, bluff and hearty; and Champ Clark, giving us his limp handshake and prowling around, silent and a little morose. We all liked Thomas Marshall, the vice presidential nominee, a quiet little man with a fund of dry humor.

I was amazed to see a group of Tammany "braves" grouped around the platform, very pleasant and vociferous in their applause when father stood up to speak. For the first time he read from manuscript, and I could see that it irked him to have to do this; at one point he broke off to say, smiling, "I wish I didn't have to read this".

But it was the real "keynote speech" for the Democratic Party, and he looked very grave and a little stern as he finished. There was a new light in the gray eyes that gazed steadily out over the happy crowd beneath him.

CHAPTER TEN

Cleveland Lane

In OCTOBER we were back in Princeton, absorbed in the excitements and alarms of the election campaign. I didn't go back to the Academy, finding it impossible any longer to keep my mind on art.

Father had always disliked the thought of "stumping" —he believed that a few carefully prepared speeches at important centers would be more effective, but his manager and supporters were so strong for a speaking campaign that he was overruled. The other nominees were stumping extensively. Taft did not attack father, but Roosevelt never missed an opportunity to do so. Father avoided personalities, confining himself to issues, and did not at any time attack his opponents, which seemed to baffle Teddy at times, as he needed a fight to be at his best. It reminded us of father's story about two men debating a very serious subject at a public meeting. When one seemed to be getting the best of the argument, an Irish friend in the gallery shouted, "Hit him, Mike, and make it a fight."

Father's speeches were mainly based on his political philosophy, rather than on promises of what he would do, if elected. He said, "How can anyone honestly present a definite plan?" "A sincere man can only explain the political philosophy which he will apply to the problems when they present themselves"—and again, "As a candidate for the Presidency, I do not want to promise heaven unless I can bring it to you. I can only see a little distance down the road."

There was not enough money to provide the secretaries mother and father needed, and mother had not learned to dictate, so we all helped with the enormous correspondence. We sorted mountains of letters, telegrams and messages of all sorts and took turns sitting at the telephone. When father was at home, we continued to protect him from people as much as we could.

Almost every day his supporters wanted him to make a "statement" answering the criticisms of his opponents. These importunities annoyed him considerably. He thought that answering attacks was utterly useless and, therefore, a waste of time. He believed that if people honestly wanted to know about him, they would take the trouble to look up his record and read his speeches, and then form their own judgments; and that answering unfounded and malicious attacks merely emphasized and helped to spread falsehood, without convincing anyone. If people believed these accusations, it was because they wanted to believe them.

I can remember only one instance of his yielding. We were all astonished at the absurdity and inconsistency of the charges. On the one hand he was accused of being secretly "in league" with the Catholic Church and a member of the Knights of Columbus, and on the other, of being a "black Presbyterian" who, hating the Catholics. would do his utmost, as President, to harm them.

One day I asked, "Father, does anyone believe such foolishness?" He shook his head sadly and said, "It seems so—I suppose I shall have to do something about it." A few days later he wrote a letter to Mac, for subsequent publication:—"My attention has been called to the statement that I have become a member of the Knights of Columbus. This is, of course, not true. I have not been asked to join the order either as an active or an honorary member, and am not eligible, because I am not a Catholic. I must warn my friends everywhere that statements of this kind are all campaign inventions devised to serve a special purpose. This particular statement has been circulated in selected quarters to create the impression that I am trying to identify myself with the great Catholic body. It is a very petty and ridiculous business. I am a normal man, following my own natural course of thought, playing no favorites and trying to treat every creed and class with impartiality and respect."

Many times during the campaign I heard anxious friends say to father that "Teddy" was so fiery and picturesque, so skilled in the art of self-dramatization that he was a dangerous rival. Father did not deny Roosevelt's popularity and influence, but he said, "Are people interested in personalities rather than in principles? If that is true they will not vote for me."

He did not realize how much his personal traits contributed to his success, both as an educator and as a statesman. Direct and frank, lucid and balanced, he inspired confidence. His whole manner was in sharp and pleasant contrast with the empty bombast and devious palaver of the familiar type of political candidate. Moreover, his term as

172

WOODROW WILSON ABOUT 1912
With his sister Annie's grandchild, Josephine Cothran

JESSIE WOODROW WILSON, 1914

Governor of New Jersey had clearly proved that his reform measures were not dreams but convictions that he had the strength and perseverance to enforce. He was a new and refreshing personality on the political stage.

When Roosevelt was wounded by a fanatic in Milwaukee, Tumulty was greatly distressed—not from pity, but because he was certain it would make a martyr of him, and, perhaps, elect him. Father sent a telegram, expressing sympathy, and then announced that he would make no speeches as long as Roosevelt was unable to do so. He laughed as he told us of his decision. I couldn't see why it was funny, and when I questioned him, he said, "Teddy will have apoplexy when he hears of this". We were told that it did enrage him, but he made no comment of any sort.

The shooting incident made father's friends nervous, and they begged him to have a bodyguard. He refused, but Colonel House, without consulting him, sent for Bill MacDonald, a famous ex-captain of the Texas Rangers.

In reply to Colonel House's telegram, "Come at once and bring your artillery", Bill stopped long enough to wire back, "I'm a-comin'", and without baggage or impedimenta of any sort, caught the first train. He thought that his old friend was in trouble.

After getting his instructions from Colonel House in New York, he came to Princeton. He had been warned that the Governor would be "mad as hell" but that this must not be allowed to interfere with his vigilance. He was to stay as close to father as his shadow and leave him only when he retired for the night.

Bill carried his "artillery" on either hip. He was a tall,

lean, friendly soul with a droll way of talking, and father was reconciled to his presence almost at once. We were crazy about him—he put new life into the household.

Colonel House had told us some of Bill's adventures and insisted that he had been shot so many times that his body was full of lead and he would certainly sink if he fell into the water. He said that Bill paid no attention to a little thing like a bullet wound and never had a bullet removed.

We tried to make him tell us about these adventures but he lived entirely in the present and was modest and not very chatty. There had been an occasion when several hundred Mexicans had made a raid across the border and Bill and a handful of his Rangers had sent them flying back. We begged him to tell us about the fight but all he would say was, "We-ell, they had mighty bad luck". We heard afterwards that fifty Mexicans had been killed or wounded, while the Rangers were untouched.

Later, after father was elected and Huerta was making trouble in Mexico, Bill drifted into the Treasury Department one day and asked to see Mac. He said, "If the Chief wants this yere feller Hoo-Urta, I'll deliver him—dead or alive".

Mac said, "That's some job, Bill, and it will take a lot of men, won't it?"

"Naw", drawled Bill, "twenty Texas Rangers."

"Why, it's a thousand miles from Laredo to Mexico City", Mac told him. "I don't see how you could get to first base with twenty Texas Rangers. You'd have to have a lot of regulars with you, wouldn't you?"

"Naw", said Bill contemptuously, "I don't want none of

174

them—I don't want nobody with me that has to toot a bugle before they begin to shoot."

Father and he had long discussions about guns. Bill had an intricate explanation of his preference for the strange sawed-off variety he carried. "When I shoots a fella he falls backwards; other people shoots so they falls on their faces", was his triumphant argument. I didn't understand the advantage of Bill's method but father agreed with him warmly.

Once coming home from a campaign trip the car hit a rut in the road and father was thrown against the top and his head painfully cut. Bill was as cool as could be, did just the right thing—brought father home and did not leave until he was certain that the injury was not serious and father safe in bed for the night. We hadn't the slightest suspicion that Bill was hurt until he failed to appear the next day. He had collapsed as soon as he got to his room; the jolt had opened an old wound, and it was several days before he was able to be up and about again. His only comment was, "Well—that's the first time I've ever been hurt by accident, and I don't like it."

Bill took his job with terrific seriousness. Once, a few days after father and he had gone to a football game, they saw a photograph in a small shop window. It had unquestionably been snapped at the game. Bill was so disturbed about it that father said, "What's the matter, Bill—don't you like to have your picture taken?" Poor Bill could hardly find voice to mutter, "I'm no good, Governor, you ought to get rid of me—I didn't see that fella—I'm no good to you at all." He was so unhappy over what he considered a grave lapse of vigilance that it took days of good-natured teasing on our part to make him forget it.

He was with us until after the election and later father made him United States Marshal in Texas. The last we heard of him was that he had married, and that his honeymoon was a novel combination of business and pleasure. Taking a prisoner to the penitentiary, Bill set forth, the criminal manacled to one arm and his bride coyly clinging to the other.

We were like hens with one lone chick those days. We waited up every night, no matter how late father came in, tried to devise tempting things for him to eat, hovered around to wait on him and run errands, and remembered, although it was very difficult, not to discuss politics at meals. Mother reached the end of each day utterly exhausted, but there was a look of calm certainty on her face, a sort of glow, and she never seemed depressed. The "old sweet peace" was gone forever, but she had accepted that and was eager and interested, if a little tense.

Everyone with whom we talked seemed convinced that father would be elected, although Tumulty still had his moments of anguished worry, and father himself kept telling us that we must not be too confident—that he was not at all sure of victory.

Bryan, generous and whole-hearted in his support, was making an extremely effective campaign and, with the exception of McCombs' behavior—still erratic and uncertain —things seemed smooth after the hectic days before the nomination. McCombs was chairman of the Democratic National Committee and was jealous of everyone, particularly of Mac, who was vice chairman. Because of father's unfailing loyalty to his friends—a trait so strong in him that he was sometimes blind to the fact that some were not real friends—he had refused to get rid of McCombs after the convention. He knew that he was weak and undependable, but he did not doubt his honesty and allegiance and felt that in spite of everything, he should not be humiliated by being cast aside when victory was almost in sight.

It was a difficult situation and caused quite maddening troubles and constant irritations. Later McCombs became so ill that Mac had to take complete charge—much to everyone's relief. Mac came down often to Princeton, very tired and harassed, for a conference with father. I remember seeing them standing together, and hearing father say suddenly: "It's hard on you, my dear fellow, but you're handling it all magnificently. I am very grateful." Then he put his hand on Mac's shoulder for a moment—a gesture he used only to express affectionate appreciation. Mac went away looking as though he could handle a dozen McCombses without half trying.

We didn't go with father on his long trips—it was too expensive—but if he spoke in a near-by city, we went to hear him, usually staying with friends for the night. No matter how many times I saw him on the platform, I was always impressed with his grace and ease, and the fact that he never attempted to "orate". His quiet, almost conversational, tone carried distinctly to every corner of the largest auditorium in the country. This was not an accident —he had spent years training for public speaking.

He knew that it was an art, like any other form of self-expression, and, as such, demanded hard work—men were not born speakers. As a young man, he had taken a course in public speaking, which included not only voice placing, but long practice in how to stand, how to move about and how to use his hands and arms. His teacher had insisted that flowing gestures were essential for dignified and effective public appearance.

There was one exercise which he often showed us that fascinated me, since I always loved to watch his hands. Curling his fingers in his palm, he opened them one by one, beginning with the index finger, with a flowing rhythmic motion that was very attractive. But he used few gestures and these were as simple and natural as his manner of thinking and speaking. I never saw him use an awkward gesture.

The climax of the campaign was the meeting in Madison Square Garden five days before election day, and we all four went to New York and stayed with friends in a big house with an organ in it. Someone played it all through dinner and it seemed to afford an outlet for my pent-up emotions.

While we were dressing that evening, mother noticed that Jessie looked pale. "Are you ill, dear?" she asked. Jessie just bowed her head and didn't answer, and mother hurried off to order some medicine. As soon as she left the room Jessie began to laugh hysterically. "Nellie, mother wants me to take medicine—can one take medicine for love?" And then I knew that my fears were justified— Jessie was really in love with Frank Sayre. I threw my arms around her and we laughed and cried together. When mother came back with the medicine we were perfectly incoherent, and Jessie took it without a murmur.

There was such a crowd milling about outside the Gar-

MARGARET WOODROW WILSON, 1914

ELEANOR RANDOLPH WILSON, 1914

den that we could hardly get in, and were very disheveled and nervous when we finally reached our seats on the platform. Margaret and her escort arrived a few minutes later. They had been told that there was no use trying to find seats and in the excitement no one would listen to the explanation that this was Wilson's daughter and that seats were reserved for them on the platform. They had finally to climb in by a fire-escape and find their way to us after a long, hot struggle. The meeting had already begun. Someone was shouting the virtues of the Democratic Party, but no one was listening to him.

There were sixteen thousand people yelling in a mounting volume of sound "We want Wilson, we want Wilson". Then we heard the crowd outside cheering wildly, and suddenly he was standing in front of us, very straight and quiet. The audience seemed to go mad. They were on their feet, roaring and stamping, cheering and waving flags, and for more than an hour they kept it up. He tried to stop them, but it was impossible and all that time he stood there smiling, looking a little stunned, turning every now and then to glance at his family with a strange, almost enquiring expression as if he were saying, "What are we doing here? But it's fun, isn't it?"

When at last they let him speak, I saw that he was deeply touched—his voice was not quite as steady as usual and I had a moment of panic. Then, by an almost imperceptible movement of his chin, a straightening of his shoulders, I knew that he was in control. "Fellow citizens", he began, "no man could fail to be deeply moved by a demonstration such as we have witnessed tonight, and yet I am the more thrilled by it because I realize that it is a

179

demonstration for a cause and not for a man. All over the country, from one ocean to the other, men are becoming more aware that in less than a week the common people of America will come into their own again." When he had finished the wild cheering began again and I thought they would never let him go.

He spent election day very quietly, staying in bed later than usual, and he was in high spirits at breakfast. He said that he had done what he could, that the result was on the knees of the gods, and that he did not wish to have any messages that were not of vital importance.

He spent most of the day walking with Dudley Malone and Captain Bill, visiting all his favorite haunts in Princeton and near by as if in farewell. For that day, I think, he lived in the past again, going over many incidents of his life as a student, as professor, and later, as President of the University. His love for Princeton had never diminished and he knew that he had reached the end of a chapter of his life, giving up forever the peaceful, simple things he loved so much.

After dinner, he read Browning aloud to us. I don't know about the others, but not even his beautiful voice could hold my attention that night. I kept sliding out of the room and tiptoeing back. I was standing near the door, about to slip into my place, when I heard the first muffled tone of the bell of Old Nassau—in another moment it was ringing like a thing possessed, and we all knew what it meant.

Mother ran to the door. I lost sight of father for a moment, but I remembered that when Tumulty called to her from the group of newspaper men on the porch, "He's elected, Mrs. Wilson!" she came back to the steps of the studio and took father's hand. Neither of them said a word.

I was watching his face, and a surprising change came over it—all the gaiety was gone; suddenly he looked serious and grave. People began crowding around him and I was pushed aside. Then we heard the sound of a procession coming. They were singing "Old Nassau" and many were shouting for a speech. Someone dragged a chair out onto the small porch for him to stand on, and I noticed that it was an old broken rocking chair. I wanted to call attention to it, but it was impossible to make myself heard. The house was a seething mass of people. I ran upstairs to hang out one of the front windows.

In all directions, as far as I could see, there were people coming; swarms had already invaded the little garden and were crowding around the porch. Swaying torches made grotesque circles of light and there, sharply silhouetted in the open doorway, a red glare shining full on his face, was father, utterly, utterly unfamiliar.

The crowd, looking up at him, called on him to speak, but he was silent and those few moments, with the restless throng now suddenly still and motionless, are crystallized in time, for me—sharply separated from all that went before and all that followed.

I had a sense of awe, almost of terror—he was no longer the man with whom we had lived in warm sweet intimacy —he was no longer my father. These people, strangers who had chosen him to be their leader, now claimed him. He belonged to them. I had no part in it. I felt deserted and alone.

And then I heard his voice. Tears of relief welled into my eyes. It was the voice that had sung "Peri, Meri, Dictum, Domini," in my childhood.

181

CHAPTER ELEVEN

Bermuda and Cleveland Lane

THAT NIGHT we were all so completely worn out that we went to bed as soon as we could. Fortunately, as the house was small, we did not have the usual flock of relatives and friends staying with us, but it was only with much skillful maneuvering that we managed to get rid of the mob of excited students and townspeople.

All the next day we struggled with an ocean of mail. Tumulty counted fifteen thousand letters and telegrams in the first few days after father's election. Our little house was a terrible mess and mother, for the first and only time in her life, walked through rooms pretending that she didn't see the confusion and disorder. Even the tables and shelves in the studio were piled high and the easel was pushed aside to make room for efficient young women and their typewriters. Most of the messages were congratulations and jubilant paeans of praise from friends and supporters, but there were many hints or frank declarations that some sort of compensation for work in the campaign was now in order. Again I was disappointed to find that many who had been loudest in protestations of disinterestedness were now most insistent in their requests for rewards, either for themselves or for their friends. These same people, if their leader had been defeated, would have taken refuge in quick flight.

There were also the advisers—an army of men reminding father of the magnitude of the task that lay before him. This irritated him considerably. Always eager and grateful for intelligent advice, he found this stupid elaboration of the obvious hard to bear with patience. He came to us once after a conference and said, with a rueful smile, "I wonder why they supported me if they think me so stupid that I have to be told that there are difficulties ahead of me".

Mother and my sisters and I had our share of letters, too. We were astonished and amused by the variety of petitions, the adulation and advice that poured in from every part of the country. Requests for photographs, for autographs, for jobs, proposals of marriage, enclosing pictures of the gentlemen and statements of their worldly possessions. One had a "cow and five acres of blue-grass". Another was "considered the handsomest man in the county".

There were times when we were helpless with laughter, and other times when we felt terribly burdened by this glimpse of all the troubles and longings in the world. A silk manufacturing company wrote to me, enclosing samples of colors and asking me to pick my favorite as they wanted to name it after me. In spite of the family jeers, I complied, but Alice Roosevelt had long ago pre-empted my beloved blue, so I chose a lovely flame-color. The silk company, however, advertised a hideous magenta red as the fashionable new "Nell Rose", and I was annoyed out of all proportion, especially later when tradespeople dragged out bolts of it whenever they saw me coming.

In a few days father told us that he thought a trip to Bermuda would be an excellent tonic for us all, an escape from the confusion and publicity—a real change and rest—and it would give him time to think things out clearly, plan his organization and catch up with his correspondence. We all liked the idea, but Margaret felt that she should not miss the last chance at singing lessons before going to the White House, and accordingly arranged to stay in New York while we were away.

Mother, Jessie and I went shopping! For the first time in our lives we bought what we wanted without having to dwell too carefully on the price. Mrs. Sheridan, a friend of mother's, who had exquisite taste and knew all the best shops in New York, was our guide. I was second in command. One new dress had always been a thrill for me and to choose a complete wardrobe was simply my idea of heaven. In one smart shop an overpoweringly elegant saleswoman looked at us appraisingly and, smiling insipidly, said she understood just what we wanted—"something quite chaste for the young ladies". Nothing could have been more at variance with my personal taste, but I restrained my annoyance and took a mild revenge by shaking my head vaguely at everything she brought out for us.

Mother was embarrassed because she couldn't charge even a bolt of ribbon or a box of handkerchiefs, without bringing a bowing floor-walker and a curious crowd around at the first mention of her name. She went at last to the bank and got enough cash to pay, at least, for the smaller items on our list, and we made better progress; but when we got back to Princeton and recounted our adven-

184

tures to father, she said ruefully, "Oh, Woodrow, we felt like animals in a zoo!"

We were never alone now. Even our close friends, anxious to help and with the best intentions, added to the confusion. Father was in Trenton most of the time, working sometimes far into the night, arranging for things to run smoothly in his absence. We had only occasional glimpses of him.

On his way home one day he met a young man he had never seen before, coming out of the house. He smiled at him politely in passing, and the young man tipped his hat and strode hurriedly away. That evening father asked mother who the nice-looking sandy-haired boy was, and mother was intensely amused. "You'd better stop and make his acquaintance the next time," she said. "That's Frank Sayre, and I think you're going to be his father-in-law." She spent the next hour assuring him that Frank was in every way suited to be Jessie's husband, but for all her eloquence, he met Frank at first with the unnatural stiffness he always displayed toward all who dared to court his daughters. But he couldn't keep it up. Frank was magnetic and unusually intelligent, and father grew very fond of him.

There were crowds at the house when, ten days after the election, we left for Bermuda—crowds at the pier. A secretary, two Secret Service men and a veritable troop of newspaper correspondents went with us and, aboard ship, everyone watched father, followed him, talked to him whenever a chance presented itself. It was impossible for him to have a moment alone, unless he locked himself in his cabin. But

I enjoyed every minute of it. Floating joyously on the stream of excitement, I forgot every fear and worry and reveled in the moment.

If I wore high heels, father and I were the same height; so, when I walked on deck with him, I wore low heels and maneuvered so that the slant of the ship made him appear taller. I had a childish impulse to want him to tower above me—above everything.

Another crowd at the pier when we reached Bermuda, but these were quiet Britons, standing back respectfully, with their hats off, frankly curious, but treating us like royalty. I found myself walking with unnatural dignity, and decided that I preferred our own shouting, friendly democrats at home.

Mrs. Hulbert had lent us Green Cove Cottage, and its restfulness was reassuring. An attractive little white house with heavy green shutters, it had a wide verandah from which Jessie and I could jump straight into the blue waters of the bay. We had our meals on this verandah and found it a useful hiding place, as it could be reached only by going through the house.

We were enthralled by the spell of the place. It was another world—a world moving in a slower tempo—charming, leisurely and permeated with the fragrance of tropical flowers and luxurious vegetation. The little white houses nestling in walled gardens and covered with flaming bougainvillaea, the coral cliffs, the quaint fishing villages by the deep blue water, enchanted us.

Father knew it well and showed us all his favorite views and the hidden beauties he had discovered on his previous visits. They have performed a miracle in Bermuda—no automobiles are allowed there, even to this day—so we drove over the white coral roads in little rubber-tired carriages, or explored the byways on bicycles. Two or three times, father, Jessie and I took sandwiches and stole away for a whole day of bicycle riding—lying, when we were tired, on the beach or in some tropical glade—silently drinking in the heavenly quiet and peace.

The residents of the Island were hospitable, yet most considerate. They knew that father had come seeking seclusion, and they did all they could to help him find it. Jessie and I had the time of our lives. There were innumerable parties. The officers of the Coldstream Guards stationed there were our particular cavaliers, and a week or two after our arrival, they gave a ball for us. Father and mother didn't go. Except for one state dinner and a few small informal ones, they took no part in the social whirl. I was uncomfortable and very shy at first. I found the English custom of speaking to guests at a party, without being introduced, embarrassing, and I couldn't get used to the tea-drinking fetish. Jessie's calm poise remained unshaken.

Mother was very happy in Bermuda and went off alone, for long afternoons to paint, as she had done in Old Lyme. Sometimes I gave up frivolity and went sketching with her, and later at tea we propped our canvases up on chairs for father's frank and thoughtful criticism.

He played golf in his few leisure hours, but every morning he shut himself up in his room, with Charles Swem, his secretary, and worked over his correspondence. He always dictated continuously, without hesitation, and Swem had taken prizes as one of the swiftest stenographers in the country, so they got through a prodigious amount of work. He answered personally all the messages from his friends, carried on a correspondence with some of the finest minds in America, seeking advice and enlightenment on important domestic questions; wrote to Curtis Guild, Ambassador to Russia, to Sun Yat-sen, the Chinese leader, and authorities on European conditions, and sent letters to trusted friends asking for information about the men he had in mind for the Cabinet. Sometimes he read aloud to us the comments on each man in question and then gave us vivid word pictures of his appearance, general characteristics and mannerisms. It was an especial gift of his, to describe people so vividly that they seemed almost to be in the room with us. We were interested in a series of charts he made in his usual methodical way and in his own fine script—a page for each man under consideration: the name at the top of the page; underneath on the right, details of the man's career and his qualifications. In parallel columns on the left were any reasons that might be considered against the appointment.

We were as curious as everyone else about his final selections for the Cabinet, and I said to him, "You've always told us things before—don't you trust us any more?" But he said that he hadn't yet made up his own mind, and was amused by our impatience. I continued to pester him, however, and one evening I said, "Well, I don't really care about any of the others, if you'll just make that nice Mr. McAdoo Secretary of the Treasury." He laughed and said to mother, "Just imagine! Nell wants me to appoint a man to a Cabinet position because he is attractive to the ladies." It became a family joke and father often said,

"What's the matter, Nell? Are you afraid I've appointed someone else to the Treasury?"

But it was quiet thinking and planning that chiefly occupied him in the seclusion of Bermuda, "this calm, clear land" * as he called it, and to re-inform and clarify his own mind he went carefully over the reports of his campaign speeches which were to be published in book form, under the title of "The New Freedom". He had promised certain great reforms, and he took time now to study them again, with great pains and unflagging patience. He was certainly not having a holiday, but for his trained mind, calm uninterrupted thought was never a labor, and just to be away from clamoring crowds was a rest and relaxation.

The reporters were busier than ever, trying to get stories about us. There were rumors of attachments, and even engagements, ridiculous yarns that changed from day to day. I danced one night at the hotel with a Princeton boy, a casual acquaintance who was stopping in Bermuda . . . and the next day American newspapers announced that I was engaged to him. I was embarrassed, but father was incensed. He asked the correspondents to deny the story and they all complied, except one who deliberately sent in another yarn to his paper embellished with the usual nonsense about young love and romance. When father sent for him, he produced a telegram from his office in New York saying, "Send more details about Eleanor Wilson's engagement. Ignore diplomatic denials." Father told him that he might as well take the next ship home as he would never be given another interview.

I was still deeply involved in my Mexican romance and

* Letter to Mrs. Reid.

writing almost daily. Once when several days passed without word from my fiancé, I was certain that some dreadful fate had overtaken him. Father heard me sobbing in the night, and came in to ask what was wrong. He was very sympathetic when the tragedy was explained to him and said that he would send a telegram for me in the morning. I didn't know until weeks later that he said to mother, "If Nell doesn't get her letter, I'm going to throw myself into the sea!"

In spite of all his work and our busy social schedule, we still managed once in a while to have an evening together, reading aloud, talking about the day's adventures, leaning over father's shoulder as he played solitaire.

There was a stock company playing at the small, very primitive theatre in Hamilton, and father and I went two or three times, sitting in the front row, and enjoying every minute of the excruciatingly bad performance.

"I shall never grow up," he told me. "I would rather see poor acting than not go to a play when I have a chance." I felt exactly the same way but mother and Jessie didn't have our powers of endurance. I was secretly glad to have him all to myself.

He had the unusual gift of being able to control his mind and nerves to such an extent that sleep came whenever he willed it. He used to say that he "pulled down the curtains" of his mind. Often between important conferences, he would take a ten or fifteen minute nap that completely refreshed him, and he was able to wake at exactly the time he had set for himself, day or night.

In spite of the long strain of the campaign he was extraordinarily well, but none of us had ever really stopped worrying about his health since the awful time at Princeton when he had been forbidden active work and condemned to a quiet life in the country. Mother never relaxed her solicitous care; she still planned and supervised every meal, stood guard when he was sleeping and protected him whenever she could from people who might harass him. Whenever he was tired, she stood behind his chair and massaged the back of his neck, often calling us in—much to his amusement—to reassure her that no hollows were appearing there. A doctor had told her that as long as the back of the neck remained full and firm, there was no cause for worry.

They knew very well what was ahead—years of the hardest work in the world—the triple role that the American people demand of their President: to govern the country, to lead the party, and at the same time to be accessible to every American citizen who wants to shake his hand. It did not require months in the White House to prove to father that no one man could do all three things at the same time, successfully. And to him it was quite obvious which of the three roles was least important. Sitting after supper in the candlelight, the water softly beating against the rocks below, and blissful quiet all about us, we discussed the future. He must conserve his strength as never before. All unnecessary social life must be curtailed, speaking trips and hours of hand-shaking eliminated. He not only must attend properly to the duties of the office, but must have time to think. I remember his little dry smile when he said, "One is considered queer in America if one requires time for concentrated thought". But he did not hesitate for a moment in deciding that personal popularity was not worth the price of even the smallest neglect of duty and, even before we left Bermuda, accusations of arrogance, aloofness and unfriendliness began to be spread abroad. People never understood the stern conscience that made him forgo social amenities in order to give himself completely to the great task he had undertaken.

We had just a month in Bermuda and we all hated to leave. Jessie and I had had a glorious time, and both father and mother had benefited greatly.

Returning on the boat David Lawrence, a correspondent whom we had known at Princeton, tried to impress me with the fact that father was making a serious mistake in not being nicer to the Press. He was so persistent that he finally worried me until it occurred to me to wonder why he was telling me, and not going directly to father. I suggested sweetly that he should go to "headquarters", knowing that he wouldn't dare, and was terribly pleased with myself for what I considered the rapid strides I was making in diplomatic finesse.

The confusion at the dock in New York was an unpleasant shock. Again from all parts of the country came the office-seekers, and father was harassed almost beyond endurance by what he called "the prophets of woe". His enemies in financial circles were predicting a panic. The New Jersey bosses, anxious for the Lieutenant Governor to take over the State authority, were demanding that he resign the governorship. Father had determined not to do this, as he still had time to force through certain important reform measures. He did not resign until the first of March, just a few days before the inauguration in Washington.

Sometimes in the days that followed I saw a look of unusual grimness, almost anger, in his face. There was that curious bulge in his jaw that I had seen only once before, at the "Princetonian" dinner when he had defied his enemies.

He announced briefly that he was not yet ready to make any decisions about appointments, and told us that he had decided to make some speeches in which he would not "mince words".

We all went to New York to hear him at the Southern Society dinner at the Waldorf. We were not used to grand hotels and, sitting at lunch that day in one of the ornate dining rooms, I was embarrassed by the obsequious waiters and the unconcealed curiosity of the other guests. Mother looked very pretty, in a new dress and hat, her color high and the dimple much in evidence. Suddenly she leaned over and whispered, like a child, "I don't think these people look so stylish, do you? I'm disappointed." But I knew that she was secretly pleased that we did not look "countrified" in contrast.

We sat in a flag-draped box that night, at one end of the banquet hall. I was wearing my first bunch of orchids, a new dress and my best "society" manner, but when father came in and stood up to speak, after the cheering and excitement had died down, I was unhappy because he was so far away that I couldn't see the expression in his eyes.

There was a tenseness in his attitude, a ringing quality in his voice that thrilled me. He spoke of how he "longed to see in America a passion so great for an idea, that men would be ready to lay down their lives for it."

He said: "Prosperity does not exist for a nation unless it

193

be pervasive. Prosperity is not a thing which can be consumed privately, or by a small number of persons, and the amount of wealth in a nation is very much less important than the accessibility of wealth in a nation. The more people you make it accessible to, the more energy you call forth until presently, if you carry the process far enough, you get almost the zest of a creative act . . . God knows that the poor suffer enough in this country already and a man would hesitate to take a single step that would increase the number of the poor or the burdens of the poor, but we must move for the emancipation of the poor, and that emancipation will come from our own emancipation from the errors of our minds, as to what constitutes prosperity."

Toward the end, when he began to speak of the troublemakers, he did not raise his voice; but people seemed suddenly to sit forward in their chairs and there was intense quiet. "Business cannot be disturbed unless the minds of those who conduct it are disturbed. A panic is merely a state of mind, because obviously when a panic occurs there is just as much wealth in the country the day after the panic as the day before. Nothing in material circumstances has changed, but the whole state of mind of the financial community has changed. They dare not part with their money. They call in their loans. They are excited and they do not always know exactly why. That is a natural panic, but you know there are unnatural panics and some panics are said to occur because certain gentlemen want to create the impression that the wrong thing is going to be done—frankly I do not believe that there is a man living at the present moment who dares use that machinery for that purpose. If he does, I promise him, not for myself but for my countrymen, a gibbet as high as Haman."

There was wild applause, but some of his more timid friends were frightened by his vehemence. I was furious when I saw them shaking their heads. To me, he had never seemed so magnificent.

On the 28th of December he and mother went together to Staunton, Virginia, to celebrate the fifty-sixth anniversary of his birth. They enjoyed this trip and mother was delighted when it was arranged for them to spend the night in the room in the old Presbyterian Manse where father was born.

He was received everywhere on the journey with wild enthusiasm—bands, flowers, triumphal arches, cheering crowds; but one afternoon he slipped off to visit an old aunt whom he had not seen since he was a boy. She was very old and deaf, and used a long black ear-trumpet. After a few minutes of rather difficult conversation, she asked kindly, "Well, Tommy, what are you doing now?" Father said modestly, "I've been elected President, Aunt Janie." "What?" "President." "Well, well," said the old lady querulously, "president of what?" Father seized the trumpet desperately and roared into its black depths, "President of the United States", whereupon she smiled skeptically and dismissed him.

Still struggling with the problem of the Cabinet, he talked freely to us about Bryan, when we were alone in the studio room in Princeton. He admired and trusted Bryan, and knew that he must have a place in the administration. Although he felt that in many ways Bryan would not make a suitable Secretary of State, he could not very well offer him anything less. Bryan himself had not even hinted that he wanted or expected anything. Colonel House was advocating him strongly and so, of course, were his thousands of admirers throughout the country. Letters and telegrams came in floods, reminding father that Bryan had borne the "heat and burden" of three campaigns, that he was the "Great Commoner", the "Peerless Leader". Father hesitated for some time; but mother felt that there was no alternative and finally he made up his mind and asked Bryan to come to Trenton to see him. That night he told us about the interview. It has been very satisfactory. Bryan had been amenable to father's every suggestion, was eager to carry out his ideas about foreign relations and had accepted at once. Father said, "His naïveté is really charming—he was as delighted as a child with a new toy".

This was the only purely political appointment to the Cabinet that father made. The others, with one exception, were chosen from the lists he had made in Bermuda, and entirely on the basis of long consideration and careful investigation as to their fitness for the office. The only one chosen more or less at random was Lindley Garrison, Secretary of War. Father had asked Mitchell Palmer, of Pennsylvania, to take the post but Palmer had declined because he was a Quaker; and on Tumulty's recommendation it was offered to Garrison.

The Cabinet appointments were generally well received, but there was an uproar when he announced that Tumulty was to be his private secretary. Tumulty was "young and inexperienced in national politics", said the busybodies, and there were numerous protests because he was a Catholic. When father received a letter asking if he wanted to have "the secrets of the White House relayed to Rome", he tossed it into the waste basket with one terse comment—"Asinine." Mother was eager to have Tumulty appointed. She was, of course, in father's confidence about the Cabinet appointments and so, I believe, was Colonel House, but father told no one else until the day before the inauguration.

The question as to who was to be social secretary had to be solved. Belle Hagner, who was what Washington people called a "cave dweller", meaning a permanent resident of the city, had been Mrs. Theodore Roosevelt's secretary and knew all there was to know about the intricacies of Washington social life. When mother finally decided to ask her to take the job again, I was worried. "She's a close friend of the Roosevelts," I said. "She won't be at all friendly or comfortable with us." But mother laughed at me. "I'm told that she is intelligent and attractive and I'm sure she will soon be our friend too," she said.

But mother was in need of immediate help and asked Helen Bones, our favorite cousin, to come and live with us as private and personal secretary. We all breathed sighs of relief and pleasure when she arrived. She worked like a small steam engine plowing through the stacks of letters, and she still teased and laughed with father, as she had done in the old days at Library Place.

I was not yet satisfied with my wardrobe and dashed off whenever I could, to Philadelphia, to buy another hat or a pair of slippers, staying with my friends, Mrs. Hall and her daughter. One day Ruth and I boarded a street car, and found it so crowded that we had to sit in separate seats. When the man next to her got out, Ruth called to me, "Nell! Here's a seat". Whereupon the woman behind her glared at me and sputtered, "It makes me sick—since the newspapers have been full of the Wilsons, all the girls call themselves 'Nell'." I slumped down beside Ruth and we giggled like children.

One day mother went off to New York by herself on a mysterious errand, and that night gave us each what she called an "inauguration present"—the first jewelry that we had ever had. I was overwhelmed by mine, a bar pin, carved, and set with small diamonds. Jessie and Margaret both received necklaces of seed pearls. When we asked what she had bought for herself, she was astonished. She hadn't thought of that. So the next day father bought her a diamond pendant. It was always called, in the family circle, the "crown jewel".

I invited all my friends to see my "trousseau", a bright blue broadcloth suit, and a hat heavily bedecked with flowers for the inauguration ceremonies; two afternoon dresses, two dinner dresses and, the joy and pride of my heart, a pale blue satin trimmed with pearls for the Inaugural Ball. The day it was delivered, mother told us that father had decided that there would be no Inaugural Ball. He thought it was not in keeping with simple democratic ideals, and in spite of loud outcries and protests from Washington society and tradespeople, he stuck to his decision. I shed some secret tears; I knew he was right, but wished desperately that he wouldn't be so Jeffersonian.

For the first time in his life father had to borrow a considerable sum of money from a bank—five thousand dollars. He hated to do it, but we could not have made the move to Washington without it.

On the third of March, with motor cars standing in line, a crowd around the house and Secret Service men waiting on the door-step, father and mother suddenly rebelled and, leaving us to follow, walked alone to the station where the special train was waiting. On the way, old friends stopped them to say "Good-bye", among them Dr. McKenzie, a Presbyterian minister. Father listened to his congratulations, and then said gravely, "I appreciate your good wishes, but had you not better pray for me?"

He had refused the usual military escort, but was delighted when the Princeton students asked if they might accompany him with their own special band.

It seemed as if everyone in Princeton was there to see us off, and as if at least half were going too. The "special" had nine cars, and was jammed with boys singing "Old Nassau" at the top of their lungs. My friends were terribly excited and pleased, and we all scrambled aboard and explored every corner of the private car at the end.

I had decided to be dignified, but found it too difficult, so I concentrated on merely trying to conceal my pride and self-satisfaction. I believed that Duffy and the others would be disgusted, if they found out how I felt.

We stood on the back platform when the train pulled out and, although father and mother were smiling and waving, I thought they both looked very wistful as the lovely classic towers of Princeton faded in the distance.

CHAPTER TWELVE

The White House

THERE WERE CROWDS all along the line, but the train rushed shrieking through the stations, and all we could see was a blur of faces and waving flags. The big Washington terminal was a sea of people, but the Secret Service men hurried us through to the President's entrance where automobiles were waiting.

I remember one excited woman who kept dodging in and out, trying to get near and shouting, "Which is Margaret? Which is Jessie? Tell me, which is Eleanor?"

There were not many people on the streets. Washingtonians are used to arriving and departing Presidents, and do not let them interfere with their leisurely business, so we were carried swiftly to the Shoreham Hotel.

I had been in Washington only once before, when on our way to Virginia we had made a brief stop to change trains. I was seven at the time, so my impressions were vague, and now I remembered only that I had stood in the middle of a street holding tightly to father's hand and gazing at the Capitol. I was disappointed this time, and astonished to see, in some places, little sordid shacks jammed in between majestic public buildings.

At the hotel our suite was full of flowers, people and

200

noise. Friends, relatives, newspaper correspondents and Secret Service men crowded around us. We tried vainly to compose ourselves in the midst of indescribable babble and confusion.

Helen Bones tried to find a quiet corner to sort and distribute the tickets for the inauguration ceremonies and finally had, in desperation, to sit on the floor of a bathroom with the General in charge of arrangements.

A small cousin who had been brought from Ohio to see us was wandering mournfully about, her face streaked with tears. When she was at last persuaded to tell what was wrong, she wailed, "Oh, they're just ladies; they haven't any crowns or long trains or anything; they're nothing but ladies."

After an hour or two, mother looked so white and helpless and so tiny that I dragged her away to her room and locked the door, leaving Helen on guard outside to prevent anyone from disturbing her by knocking.

After she had had a short rest, I helped her to dress, as she and father were going to tea with the Tafts at the White House. I arranged her hair and adjusted her prettiest hat at just the right angle. She hardly said a word. When I kissed her and told her how perfectly lovely she looked, I saw the color flood into her cheeks and then, suddenly putting both hands over her face, she burst into tears. I was thunderstruck and for a moment couldn't think what I should do. Then I rushed for some spirits of ammonia and made her drink it.

In a very short while she smiled up at me and assured me that she was "all right", that it was just the noise and confusion, that I must not worry and must be sure not to tell anyone. But I was terribly alarmed. There was almost despair in her sudden break, something I had never seen before.

I went with her to find father, after we had repaired the ravages of the tears and carefully readjusted the hat. My concern about her appearance made her laugh, and I was somewhat comforted as I watched them go. But as soon as they were out of sight, I ran back to her room and locked myself in.

The old terror that it would be too much for them came over me with stabbing sharpness. I was afraid that mother was ill, that she would not live, and I went to pieces. Sobbing hysterically, I walked about the room and then, fearing that someone would hear me, crawled under the bed where I lay pounding on the floor with my hands and crying in black despair, "It will kill them—it will kill them both."

When exhaustion forced me to stop, the sound of my voice, strange and heavy, repeating, "It will kill them both", echoed in my ears and added to my terror. At length I was too weary and wretched to make a sound, and just lay there.

Margaret and Jessie were knocking on the door. The sound was faint and far away at first, but continued louder and louder, until at last I realized what it was and answered. As soon as I could, I got out from my strange retreat and opened the door. If they noticed my swollen eyes, they were too kind to comment, and I said nothing at all about my terrifying experience.

It is difficult for me to believe that in less than three hours I was at a party given by Cousin John Wilson where, in

Woodrow Wilson and Mrs. Wilson leaving house on Cleveland Lane, Princeton, to walk to station the day before the Inauguration at Washington

INAUGURATION CEREMONIES, WASHINGTON, 1913

a divine new dress, I learned to do the fox trot and found the world a rosy place, particularly designed so that I might have a good time.

Mother and father came back from the White House. We leaned out of a window and watched father, escorted by a cheering mob of Princeton students, leave for a dinner at the New Willard, where eight hundred Princeton alumni had gathered to give him a last big send-off. Then we tucked mother into bed and questioned her about their visit with the Tafts.

She had very little to say, but she seemed not at all daunted at the prospect of managing so huge an establishment. Mrs. Taft had told her many housekeeping secrets and details of the routine that she thought might be helpful. The Tafts were charming, friendly and very helpful. Mr. Taft had written father before we left Princeton, telling him what the expenses of the White House were likely to be; how it was possible to save money, and how much and in what way he had been able to save.

When mother was at last asleep, we dashed off to the party and danced until two in the morning.

Dressing for the inauguration the next morning was a lengthy and elaborate performance, complicated by the fact that Margaret's costume had arrived unfinished from New York the day before. There was much frenzied sewing and pinning to be done, and my arms ached from doing my hair four times before I was satisfied. Mother still wore brown, Jessie had a green broadcloth, while Margaret and I stuck to the inevitable blue.

Shortly after eleven we left the Shoreham and drove in one of the White House automobiles, complete with liveried chauffeur and footman, to the Capitol. We had to go by side streets to avoid the crowds on Pennsylvania Avenue, waiting for the Presidential parade.

Arriving at the Capitol, we were escorted to seats in the Senate Gallery, to watch the Vice President being sworn into office. Senator Poindexter, of Washington, was making a tiresome speech. I neither heard nor heeded what he was saying, but nervously watched the hands of the Senate clock crawling slowly toward noon—the hour of the inauguration.

Three times, as the minute hand reached a few seconds before twelve, a man walked over and turned it back, while Senator Poindexter droned on. I was aghast. Were they actually turning back the clock when a President was to be inaugurated? Thousands were waiting for the moment of adjournment, and certainly no one was paying the slightest attention to the speech. Someone near me muttered, "He's a Republican—he's doing it on purpose", and no one seemed surprised.

At last he sat down. Mr. Marshall was sworn in; two by two, the incoming and outgoing Senators marched up to the rostrum together, and then the moment came when we were ushered along the corridors to our seats on the portico of the Capitol.

The day was gloomy and overcast. We watched the procession arrive—father and Mr. Taft in an open carriage drawn by four horses—father smiling and Mr. Taft positively beaming. The cheering that greeted them on all sides was as much for Taft as for father. There were shouts of "You're a darn good loser", and he laughed and waved his hand.

Father looked slender and distinguished, but very grave as he moved into his place. He had asked that mother's small Bible be used that day, and as the Chief Justice held it open before him and he lifted it to his lips, a ray of sunlight broke through the clouds and fell directly upon him. I thought, "That means that he will be successful and happy", and I was no longer conscious of my fears.

Just as he was beginning to speak, people eagerly trying to get as close as possible, pushed through the barriers. When the police attempted to force them back, he said, "Let the people come forward", and they crowded close to the platform, smiling gratefully up at him.

His voice rang out over the extraordinarily quiet crowd, but even on that day, he made not the slightest attempt to orate. I could hardly breathe when he finished, "This is not a day of triumph; it is a day of dedication. Here muster, not the forces of party, but the forces of humanity. Men's hearts wait upon us; men's lives hang in the balance; men's hopes call upon us to say what we will do. Who shall live up to the great trust? Who dares fail to try? I summon all honest men, all patriotic, all forward-looking men, to my side. God helping me, I will not fail them, if they will but counsel and sustain me."

But it is mother who stands out in my memory through the solemnity of the scene and the almost terrifying intensity of father's words. Slipping quietly from her place, she moved swiftly over until she stood directly beneath him. There, utterly oblivious of the thousands watching her, she gazed up at him, like a small child, a look of rapture on her face.

The cheering seemed to come in great waves as father

and Mr. Taft drove off, and a little later we found ourselves again in the big car dashing through side streets. Margaret and Jessie sat on either side of mother, each holding
one of her hands, and Helen Bones and I were on the little
seats, looking into her happy, flushed face. I for one, was
rapturous and wondered how I could ever have worried
about anything.

To avoid the crowds we entered the White House
grounds by the South Gate, arriving at an entrance seldom
used, into what is really a sort of basement. The first thing
that met my eyes was an enormous circular seat, covered
with vivid red velvet. We passed through rooms full of
"collections"—china, glass, ancient furniture and portraits.
It looked like a small museum.

A little elevator, lined with mirrors, carried us to the
main floor, and we were ushered into the Red Room where
Mr. Taft received us. He asked, almost at once, if we
would like to see our rooms, and of course we jumped at
the suggestion.

One of the things I had dreaded was the possibility of
stiff, pompous servants such as had made nightmares of my
dancing class days at the Morgans', but the smiling colored
faces that I now saw for the first time relieved these
fears. "Ike" Hoover, a slender dark-haired man with a
thin face, who was the head usher and majordomo, was
beaming with hospitality.

My first impression of the bedrooms was that they were
terrifyingly large. They were all in suites, with bedroom,
dressing room and bath. The room chosen for Jessie and
me had enormous, old-fashioned wardrobes, a marble
mantel and great carved gilt mirrors. I walked through it

SOUTH PORTICO OF WHITE HOUSE, 1913
Woodrow Wilson at head of steps

Mary Randolph Smith, 1912

Lucy Marshall Smith, 1912

to the little dressing room beyond, and flopped down on the small white iron bed. "This is where I live", I announced. The little room had simple curtains with gay flowers, and the carpet was bright blue. I lived there all the time I was at the White House.

Mother's and father's suite was opposite ours, two bedrooms, a dressing room and two baths. Facing south and overlooking the gardens, the Ellipse and the Washington Monument, it was full of light and air, and there were fires burning in the open grates When we ran in to look, mother was standing at the window, but she turned and put her arms around us and said, "Isn't it lovely, children?" Suddenly I thought, "This is our home—not the grand, overpowering place I thought it would be."

After we had primped and powdered we went down for the buffet luncheon, and my panic returned. There were so many people I didn't know. Father greeted us warmly, and I managed to whisper to him for a moment about his speech.

After that I stayed close to mother and hardly spoke, contenting myself with staring at everyone, and trying to identify the persons whom I knew by reputation. Father had not announced his Cabinet appointments until the day before and, except for Mr. Bryan, Mac, Josephus Daniels and Albert Sidney Burleson, I had never seen any of them. I was very curious about them, and, remembering the elaborate charts father had made in Bermuda and his vivid descriptions of the men he was considering, tried to pick them out of the crowd.

Bryan was sitting in a big chair, surrounded by admirers and eating voraciously; Mac was laughing with three pretty women; Daniels, Secretary of the Navy, twinkling and chatty, had his plump wife beaming at his side, and Burleson, the Postmaster General, looking like a priest and with a large black umbrella hanging on his arm, was whispering to Colonel House. I identified Mr. Redfield, Secretary of Commerce, at once by his pink whiskers which he incessantly brushed back from his mouth with a finger and thumb, and James McReynolds, the Attorney General, because he had the old-fashioned bachelor's rather overwhelming manner towards women.

But I had to ask mother to show me Franklin K. Lane, Secretary of the Interior; David Houston, Secretary of Agriculture; Lindley Garrison, Secretary of War, and William Wilson, Secretary of Labor. They were eventually brought up to be introduced, and I formed a swift and haphazard impression of each in turn. I thought Mr. Lane very attractive, in spite of his large white face and bald head. Mr. Houston seemed stiff and dull; Mr. Wilson, very simple and shy, and Mr. Garrison, just a good-looking man who irritated me with his persiflage. But I knew that they must all be wonderful men since father had picked them, and I was sorry that they all couldn't manage to look wonderful.

After a while I made my way through the crowd around father, and found him talking animatedly with Mr. Taft. I heard Taft say, "Mr. President, I hope you'll be happy here." Father repeated, "Happy?" The usual smile left Taft's face as he answered, "Yes, I know. I'm glad to be going—this is the loneliest place in the world." I looked around at the mob of people, all so polite, so deferential. Yes, I knew what he meant, but *we* wouldn't be lonely—we had each other—no one could take that away from us.

After luncheon we went out to the reviewing stand to watch the parade. It was still cloudy and rather dreary, but my spirits rose at the sight of the gay uniforms and the sound of the stirring music. Father looked happy and smiled at me, as if he remembered our old holidays at Princeton and his "Let's find a band, Nellie".

I heard the Chief Aide say, "He's the first President I've known who looks the part." Soon the sun was shining brightly and every band that went by seemed to play a livelier tune. I was sorry when the parade was over.

It was dusk when we went back into the house and, upstairs in the Oval Room, the big family sitting room, tea was waiting for us, also cousins and aunts, uncles and intimate friends. At first I thought the room very grand and uncomfortable. It was done in rose color and the proportions were exquisite, but the furniture was stiffly arranged and it looked as if no one had ever lived there. The Tafts' things had gone, and ours not yet arrived. But in a few days mother had the furniture rearranged, our own pictures hung, the bookcases filled with our favorite books, and our piano near the windows, making it look almost as home-like as any room we had ever lived in.

The tea party was very jolly. There was a big victrola, the first one I had ever got my hands on, and I kept it going all the time while I danced the fox trot with my young cousins. Why someone didn't protest, or attempt to stop us, I can't imagine.

Cousin Florence Hoyt sent us into gales of laughter with the tale of how she had reached the White House. She was a cripple and had arrived at the station while the inauguration was in progress. By some oversight there was no one to meet her, and not a single taxi in sight. Hobbling out onto the street, she tried to hail a passing car, but nobody noticed her except an old Negro ambling by in a "hot-dog" wagon drawn by a little scarecrow horse. He stopped and asked if he could help, and she said, "Yes", would he drive her where she wanted to go? He heaved her, crutches and all, into the back with the "hot dogs", and they rattled off.

As they neared the White House, Cousin Florence called out, "There's where I want to go, uncle." He rolled his eyes at her in a panic, and began to argue with her as if she were a foolish child. One thing he was firm about; he was going to drive in "de back way", but she finally prevailed upon him to go bravely up to the front steps.

Shaking his head from side to side, the whites of his eyes very much in evidence, he yet managed a grand "Whoa" as he pulled up. Two liveried doormen appeared and stood dumb with astonishment, but Cousin Florence waved gaily at them, calling out that she was Mrs. Wilson's cousin from Baltimore, and they lifted her down, brushed her off, gave the old Negro a grand send-off and, with unimpaired dignity, ushered her into the house.

In the midst of the laughter someone ran in to tell us that Aunt Annie had fallen on the stairs, giving her back a bad twist. Father and mother, terribly distressed, went at once to her room, and in a little while Dr. Cary Grayson, a young medical officer in the Navy, arrived.

They had met him the day before at tea with the Tafts when Mr. Taft had said, "Mr. Wilson, here is an excellent fellow that I hope you will get to know. I regret to say that he is a Democrat and a Virginian, but that's a matter that can't be helped."

After he had taken care of Aunt Annie, Dr. Grayson came into the Oval Room and chatted with us: a charming man with a handsome aristocratic face, speaking "educated nigger" in a soft attractive voice, and with a chuckle that sounded like tearing silk. We were all delighted with him. He became the family physician, and later held the official position of Medical Adviser to the White House. He was one of the dearest and most loyal friends that father or any of us ever had.

At dinner that night there were so many relatives and friends that it was served in the big "State" dining room, where the luncheon had been held. Everybody dressed up and we made quite an occasion of it—our first private meal in the White House. There were masses of roses on the big table; great silver candelabra and the soft candlelight shone on the proud, gay faces of all the Wilsons and Woodrows, the Axsons and Hoyts, as they gazed admiringly at their great man, sitting quietly and more than a little tired, at the head of the table.

CHAPTER THIRTEEN

The White House

Iᴛ ᴡᴀs ꜰᴜɴ ᴛᴏ ᴡᴀᴋᴇ ᴜᴘ in the White House, to jump out of bed, bathe in the gorgeous big bathtub, and laugh with Jessie because we didn't even know where the family dining room was. We had a lady's maid for the first time and I was enormously set up about it. She was only a nice Irish girl who had been our waitress at Princeton and had come down to Washington with us, but now she was lady's maid and almost out of her wits with excitement over being in the White House, which made it all the better. She already knew her way around, having made friends with every member of the household staff, and investigated every corner the day before.

She said, "The cook's wonderful, Miss Nell. She didn't look down her nose at me at all. You'd think she'd act grand, now wouldn't you, being the White House cook?" Finally, still chattering like a magpie, she escorted us to breakfast.

Father and mother, Margaret, the visiting relatives, and Fred Yates who was also a house guest, were already there, and mother, smiling and serene, was pouring coffee at the head of the table.

The room adjoined the big dining room, and had been

212

used for years as a family dining room, but it was on the dark north side of the house, full of hideous mahogany furniture, and there were people constantly passing by the windows. So in a few days we abandoned it, and had all our meals at one end of the big dining room which was very beautiful, and had an enchanting view of the lawns and gardens in the back. It was paneled from floor to ceiling in walnut, had a plain moss-green carpet, and green brocade hangings at the windows and doors. Over the fireplace was an oil painting of President Pierce, and on the walls were heads of animals, Theodore Roosevelt's contribution, elk and deer and strange looking creatures I had never seen before. I hated them, but the room was so huge that they were not oppressive. The sun streamed in long golden shafts through the French windows and one window opened on a terrace, over a wing of the house which led to the President's offices.

We used to assemble for meals a few minutes before the hour and wait for father, knowing that, on the dot, he would appear, walking briskly across the terrace, and sit down to talk delightfully about everything but the business of being President.

That first morning there were hundreds of things to talk over, about Inauguration Day. Father, as usual, had noticed innumerable amusing incidents which he made the most of, but at exactly nine o'clock he left for his office. There was to be a Cabinet meeting at ten, and he had two or three appointments before that.

We decided to waste no time before making a tour of our new home and, calling Hoover, asked him to be our guide. How many times we were to "call Hoover" in the days to come! A really unusual man, he had been usher at the White House since the Cleveland administration and chief usher for four years, and was the most quietly efficient person I have ever known. We used to say that if we asked Hoover to get the moon out of the sky, he would have it in five minutes, neatly wrapped, with no fuss at all.

The big glass and wrought-iron main doors led into a square marble-floored entresol. Here there were two marble-topped tables decorated with ferns, and portraits of Taft and Roosevelt hung on the walls. "Teddy" had obviously assumed his famous belligerent pose for the artist; he was frowning across at mild Mr. Taft, as if he would never forgive him for interfering with his Presidential hopes.

A few weeks after our arrival, as we sat at lunch one day, we heard a terrific crash, and father sent the butler to see what it was. He returned and said, solemnly, "Mr. Hoover says, suh, that Mr. Taft fell down and smashed his glass." Father murmured, "I suppose he couldn't stand it any longer."

A long wide corridor, carpeted in red, ran the length of the house, from the dining room at one end to the famous East Room at the other, where the large receptions were held. Between were three reception rooms—the Green Room next to the East Room, then the oval-shaped Blue Room, and the Red Room which adjoined the dining room. All the rooms were connected by four large double doors.

The East Room was exactly my idea of palatial grandeur: a great expanse of shining floor, two marble fireplaces, three enormous crystal chandeliers, a concert grand piano in gold leaf, at one end, and rows and rows of gilt chairs against the walls. I imagined myself whirling around in the arms of handsome young officers, and passed into the Green Room in a blissful dream.

The Green Room was lovely; there was a beautiful flowered carpet and delicate Empire furniture, but the effect was little spoiled by too many large gilt-framed portraits of Presidents.

I thought the Red Room one of the ugliest I had ever seen. Paneled in magenta-red velours, with a hideous rug on the floor, heavy velvet curtains, overstuffed furniture, and lots of gilt everywhere, it was gloomy beyond words. Also there was, over the fireplace, that enormous portrait of George Washington that makes him look as if his false teeth were about to leap out of his mouth, and I didn't feel in the least like laughing at the first President. However, since the Red Room adjoined the dining room, it was used more than any of the others and we had to get used to it; there was nothing one could do about it, except fill it with flowers and keep a bright fire burning.

The famous Blue Room was my favorite. Used chiefly to receive formal calls from Ambassadors and Ministers, it was paneled in soft blue brocade and the long windows, set in a curving bay, looked straight over the big round pool in the gardens to the Washington Monument, towering above the trees of the Ellipse.

Upstairs there was another long corridor but it had no entrance hall to light it, and its gloom was deepened by a dark red carpet, maroon-colored walls and stiff elaborate tables along the walls and up the center. One end was used as a sort of sitting room and office for the social secretary. Here Belle Hagner had her desk and telephone, and here we all congregated in the morning to settle plans for the day and go over our colossal mail.

In a few weeks mother had some of the Princeton furniture brought down, and put lovely, gay-flowered chintz in the big fan-shaped window. Our own rugs lay on the polished floor and they seemed like the faces of old friends looking up at me.

Mother's room was on the south side of this sitting room, Jessie's and mine on the north. Also on the south side of the house were father's room, with the big carved bed in which Lincoln had slept, the Oval Room, the President's study and Margaret's room—blue and bright and so big that her grand piano was almost lost in one corner.

On the north side were the Rose guest room with its dressing room and bath, the great staircase, another guest room and the housekeeper's apartments.

The President's study was, I think, the most attractive room in the house. It was lined with bookcases and had just a touch of shabbiness about its leather-covered furniture. Here the Cabinet meetings were often held and, sitting in the Oval Room next door, we could hear the Cabinet laughing and swapping stories.

I teased them all about it, "I thought that you solemnly settled the affairs of the world at Cabinet meetings", I said, but they insisted that father always opened the proceedings with the latest anecdote, and that they had to spend all their time until the next meeting, hunting up new ones to tell him.

Mother was disappointed when she found that Watts' famous picture, "Love and Life", no longer hung over the mantelpiece. She knew that it had been a gift to America from Watts himself, during the Hayes administration, and she looked for it eagerly. Hoover told her that it had been sent back to the Corcoran Gallery by the Tafts, but that he would have it returned at once. We found out later that "Love and Life" had had many trips back and forth between the White House and the Gallery, according to the notions of the White House occupants. We were told that Mrs. Hayes had been shocked by the two beautiful, naked figures.

Margaret's room and the Rose guest room at the far end of the corridor had been the President's offices in the days before Theodore Roosevelt had persuaded Congress to appropriate money for the two new wings of the White House, which Stanford White so skillfully designed and executed. But it was not until we stood before the fireplace and read the inscription on a small plaque under the mantel in Margaret's room that I realized the great event that had taken place there.

"In this room Abraham Lincoln signed the Emancipation Proclamation of January 1st, 1863, whereby four million slaves were given their freedom and slavery forever prohibited in these United States."

Cold chills ran up and down my back. We laughed when Helen Bones insisted later that the spot was haunted, but none of us ever quite lost the feeling that there was a special sort of light there.

The whole house was a mass of bloom. Every morning the "flower man", with his little rubber-tired wagon, passed quietly from one room to another, watering the ferns and plants and replenishing the vases with fresh cut flowers from the White House greenhouses.

On his heels came another little wagon with wood for the fireplaces. The "wood man" was a genius—his fires were laid with geometric precision and skill; they always burned cheerily and never smoked or sulked.

Congress appropriates a certain sum each year for the maintenance and upkeep of the house, and mother managed in a short while to save enough to redecorate some of the rooms.

The smaller of the two guest rooms was shadowed by the porte-cochère, and was so dark that even in the daytime the lights had to be turned on. This she did in different shades of bright clear yellow, and when she had finished, it looked as though she had actually brought in the sunlight it had never seen.

Her own room she filled with flowered chintz and gay cushions and lamp-shades, until it looked like an indoor garden. Later she had the enormous attics divided into a series of small, quaintly shaped guest rooms, with their windows opening out on the roof, a fascinating place where one could see the whole city and the Virginia hills across the Potomac. One small attic room had a skylight, and this she made into a studio, hoping that the day would come when she would find time to use it.

We insisted upon seeing the kitchen too, and found it an overwhelming place, with a huge shining stove in the center, and pantries, store rooms and laundries opening out in all directions. The cook, who didn't "look down her nose", stood in starched, immaculate white, surrounded by her minions, her radiant smile making me long to stay and visit with her. There were times when I still missed my cheery days with Maggie and the lovely kitchen smells.

I had a vague recollection of another room, the first we had seen on the day we arrived, but I forgot to ask about it, and it was not until we had lived in the White House for months that I wandered one day, accidentally, into the series of "museum rooms" in the basement. This part was open to the public and, except for a billiard room where father sometimes played in the evenings, was not used by the family at all.

Portraits of Presidents' wives were hidden away there. It seemed amusing to me that only Martha Washington, probably one of the most self-effacing, had a place with the men upstairs. I found at last the round red velvet seat, and there I sat for a long time, remembering that first day and thinking with amazement how much I had changed since then.

It seems fortunate that the White House was built when colonial architecture was in vogue. Nothing can spoil the dignity and charm of the general plan. There is light, space and simplicity in the beautifully proportioned rooms, with their unusually high ceilings and lovely doors and windows that defy the various tastes and whimsical ideas of successive occupants.

For the rest of the day we entertained the never-ending stream of relatives and friends who had come to Washington. Grandfather Wilson's family had evidently been very prolific. Father had told us that he had fifty first cousins, but I had never really taken in that appalling fact until now. And now I was sure that he had been very conservative in his count. Here were cousins and aunts and uncles, of whom I had never heard, and some I never saw or heard of again after that day.

One was a little old lady, in black, who said that she was my great-half-aunt Mary, and she wanted to be shown around. I had already made the rounds a dozen times, but she made me do it again. She grew gloomier and gloomier as we marched through room after room, and made no response whatever to my attempts to impress her with the beauty and historical significance of the lovely old house. Finally, in despair, I led her back to the Red Room where, looking very small and shabby under the big chandelier and the heavy gold picture frames, she sat sighing. At last I heard her mutter, "Well, my dear, it's plain but I guess it's elegant."

Mother had divided the relatives into groups and that day we had what we called the "Woodrow Lunch", thirty-one guests, all Woodrows except Fred Yates and the Smiths. In the evening we had the "Wilson Dinner" of twenty-five, and the next day the "Axson-Hoyt Lunch", after which they managed to tear themselves away. Mother implored the Smiths to stay on a little while longer, and we hated to see Fred Yates go but he said, "I must go—my cup is filled to the brim."

In the late afternoon there was a tea party in the Red Room; officials and their families and our own friends. Mother had chosen for these occasions some lovely, if a bit too picturesque, dresses for Jessie and me. They were long, pleated "Fortuny Gowns", and Jessie looked seraphic in hers—all white with a gold belt that matched her shining hair. Mine was a soft blue and I was mildly pleased when

THE WHITE HOUSE

I looked in the mirror upstairs in my room but, as I walked into the Red Room, I suddenly felt awkward and dowdy; I knew we were "artistic" when we should have been "smart". I envied Margaret who dashed in a little late, in a simple blue suit.

But Charlie Rockwell, one of the young White House aides, who was making the introductions, saved the day for me. He told me all the idiotic rumors they had heard about us, and said that he had brushed up on his Ancient History and Greek, as they were certain that we would appear in thick glasses, straight hair and possibly high buttoned boots. I was greatly amused when he said, "Tell me, can you dance?" I said, "Goodness, we were raised in a college town; I'm a very frivolous person," and he was delighted.

Two or three newspaper women had been invited to tea and one of them got me off in a corner and said, with breathless intensity, "If any of you girls are engaged and I don't find out about it, I shall never, never get over it." I smiled at her, rejoicing in our cleverness; no one had even suspected Jessie's and my secret engagements.

The newspaper people could see us only by invitation, so we were free at last from too persistent questioning; but, whenever they could, they watched our every move. Poor Cary Grayson was suspected of being engaged to each one of us in turn and finally to Helen Bones, and the young Army and Navy men couldn't dance with us twice at a party without starting romantic rumors floating all over Washington.

I was excited when I heard that, besides the three big cars, the White House boasted a small electric, and when the guests departed, I implored mother to let me learn to run it. She gave in with some misgivings, and I dashed out to ask Hoover to have it brought around, with a man to teach me. Soon I found myself sailing magnificently around the Monument grounds, my heart pounding with delicious terror. It was one of those high glass boxes, the newest thing at the time, and it couldn't go over twenty miles an hour, but it seemed to me that we were whizzing along at incredible speed. When I got back to the house I couldn't talk about anything else; of all the grandeur of the new life, this seemed the most alluring.

There were three chauffeurs, and when father wasn't in the cars, they dashed grandly through the streets and sped madly along the country roads. But father would never allow them to exceed the speed limit, and when he discovered that we not only permitted it but reveled in it, he made us promise to mend our ways. He sternly disapproved of taking advantage of power and position, to break even the smallest law.

There was always a footman sitting beside the chauffeur, a brisk young colored man whose duty it was to open the doors and help us to descend, as well as to present cards when we paid calls, and run innumerable errands.

Energetic little Margaret could never get used to this. Before he could leap out, she was already on the pavement, and we would bet on which one would win the race to the store entrance. The footman always tried hard to keep his dignity, but it was difficult when, outdistanced, he returned to the car to find the rest of us rocking with laughter. Margaret always said, "Well, I'm not crippled, am I? I can open doors myself—I always have!"

With the exception of the chauffeurs, the cook and the ladies' maids, all the servants were colored. Coates, the head butler, was a very solemn and dignified person who seldom smiled, and the ushers were, without exception, tall and good-looking. The livery, bottle-green with black and white striped vests and gilt buttons, was very effective. Their jobs were life jobs, and they never left unless they were ill or died. They were undisputed leaders of Washington colored society and headed all the colored organizations. Brown, who was six feet four and had the biggest feet I have ever seen in my life, could sometimes be seen marching at the head of a parade, in the most magnificent uniform ever seen, even in this city of uniforms, and with such dignity as no Ambassador could hope to attain. His side partner at the front door, was the Grand High Commander of the "Chandelier Club", named after the East Room chandeliers. Brooks, the President's valet, was very well educated, speaking with hardly a trace of dialect and performing his duties with unending and meticulous attention to every detail.

Father used to say, "I have no choice, not even in the matter of ties. Brooks just puts things out and I get into them without a word." He was scandalized when he saw father's clothes, and respectfully but firmly suggested that others should be ordered as soon as possible. He recommended the tailor, selected the materials, with mother's help, and superintended the fittings until he was finally satisfied with the result, confiding to mother that since the President was "so much the gentleman", he, Brooks, was happy that he now looked more like one. Father was very patient, but enormously bored with all the fittings; he stipulated that if this had to be done, there must be enough clothes to last throughout his term of office.

There was a fine old Negro, named Richard Green, who had been head messenger at the Treasury Department, and valet to the Secretaries of the Treasury, ever since the time of Secretary Sherman. He was a good Christian and a great Bible-reader, constantly quoting passages to illustrate or prove his point. Later when one of the White House doormen died, father asked Mac if he knew of a good man for the place. Mac said, "I know the best Negro in Washington, Richard Green. I hate to give him up, but it would be a fine promotion for him, and I'll send him over." He called Richard into his office and told him that he had good news for him; the President wanted to make him a White House doorman.

Richard's eyes filled with tears and he stood there perfectly speechless. Mac said, "What on earth's the matter, Richard? I'm telling you that you are to be promoted to the finest position you could ever have." But Richard stammered, "Oh, Mr. Sec'eta'y, let me stay here. I'd rather be a do'keeper in de house of de Lord dan dwell in de tents of wickedness." We laughed over this for years. He hadn't meant to cast aspersions at the White House and its occupants; he was only thinking of his beloved Treasury. They found another man for the White House place.

The housekeeper, Mrs. Jaffray, was a thin prim little woman with a waspish waist and beautifully groomed white hair. She was very, very ladylike, and performed her duties quietly and efficiently, but whenever she had an opportunity, she loved to regale us with stories of her past grandeur. "My uncle, the Bishop" was the hero of most of her tales, and one day we asked her of what he had finally died. "Oh, it was very sad," she said, "he had something the matter with his diocese."

But Ike Hoover outdistanced her when it came to malapropisms. He loved to use long words and enchanted us by his misuse of them. After one of the big White House receptions, some of the Senators criticized the order of precedence in which they had been received. Their comments reached the press, and Hoover was indignant. "They shouldn't be allowed to speak such obscenities," he told us.

One day father was signing an important bill, and as he finished and started to wipe the pen with his usual care, Hoover said, "Please, Mr. President, don't do that. We wish to have unmitigated proof that you really used it." On the day that father decided to take him to Europe when he went to the Peace Conference, I met Hoover on the stairs, beaming with joy and pride, and I said to him, "Are you happy, Hoover?" He flung his arms wide and cried, "I am crucified, Miss Eleanor, positively crucified!"

On the other hand he could perform services that seemed to be beyond the power of more highly educated men. There was a time, for example, when father wanted to use a quotation in a speech and had his secretary call up the Congressional Library to get the exact wording. They sent back word after several hours that they couldn't find it, and Hoover said, "May I try, Mr. President?" In fifteen minutes he had it there, all neatly typed and absolutely accurate. His feeling for father and mother was almost touching. He was loyal to the other Presidents he had served, and we never heard a word of criticism of them, or their families, pass his lips, but he loved father with deep devotion.

When father left the White House, a sick man, he begged to be allowed to go too, to serve him in any capacity however lowly, and broke down completely when he had to be left behind.

I think that none of the White House staff ever became quite reconciled to father's insistence throughout his whole term of office, that even the President must never go through a door or enter a car before a lady. I remember the first time when I watched him leave with mother and Mrs. Hall, who had called and was being given a lift back to her apartment. Brown and Mays were at hand, flinging the big doors wide. Hoover, very dignified, was ushering and the footman was standing at attention beside the car door. When father stepped back and let the ladies go ahead of him, the little ceremony seemed to go to pieces. Hoover stopped in his tracks; the doormen gazed at each other in silent consternation, and the footman, confused, shut the door of the still empty car. I laughed to myself, remembering what he had said years ago in Princeton: "If a man is a gentleman before he becomes President he should not cease to be one afterwards."

The Wilson dinner that second evening was very jolly. Father was in a story-telling mood, and he and Cousin John Wilson matched each other with new ones until we were helpless with laughter.

John Wilson was a delightful person. He called himself the head of the Wilson Clan, and insisted that, on that account, father owed him a certain amount of obedience.

He made him wear a hat when he crossed the terrace, administered noxious doses when he had a cold, and ordered him off to bed if he looked tired. He had been a junior at Princeton when father was a freshman, but because of grandfather's long-ago quarrel with his Northern relatives, they did not discover until John graduated that they were first cousins.

I was indignant because some visiting Governor insisted on seeing father after the Wilson dinner; I wanted the gay family party to continue, but my head was whirling with new impressions, and my eyes drooping with exhaustion and, very early, I climbed into my little white bed and was asleep a few seconds after my head touched the pillow.

CHAPTER FOURTEEN

The White House

Belle Hagner sat at her desk under the fan-shaped window, like the Delphic Oracle. She introduced us to the mysteries of Washington etiquette, and solved all the problems of precedence. She was a grand person, stout and jolly, with a deep voice and a laugh that echoed through the halls. We were friends almost at once, and my sisters and I loved to sit around with her, chatting and laughing and interfering with her work.

She had well-defined ideas about how we should conduct ourselves, and did not hesitate to speak her mind. She believed very strongly in the usefulness and necessity of social observances. If we would be very sociable, invite lots of people to the White House, accept as many invitations as possible, we could offset the "highbrow" stigma, and help father carry out his program.

Father and she had many good-natured arguments. Belle believed that people's vanities and social aspirations must be taken seriously into account; that in the unwritten annals of Washington there were many instances of important measures defeated because of a fancied slight from the White House. But father disliked the idea of being pleasant for policy's sake, and she could not shake his preference for candor and simplicity in human relations. He said, "Let the girls accept as many invitations as they like, but from people they really like—not with any mistaken idea that it will help me." I used to watch them with amusement, as they talked. Belle, beneath her frankness, always seemed to be a little in awe of him. She had a way of opening her eyes very wide and gazing at him with a sort of startled wonder —this college professor who knew nothing about the intrigues and heart-burnings of Society. And he sat patiently regarding her with the little twinkle in his eye which he usually reserved for attractive children.

Mother merely smiled and went serenely on, inviting as many people as possible to the house, and treating them all alike, with simple friendliness.

According to a long-established custom, the President and his wife never go to social functions outside the White House, except a series of dinners given each winter by the Cabinet members. Obviously they could not accept every invitation that would be tendered, and if they picked and chose, the heart-burnings that would ensue would probably burn up the city.

Mother carried out the usual program of dinners, receptions and musicals at the White House, gave two or three tea parties a week, and received callers almost every afternoon. Her swift adaptation to the new life was amazing. She had been entertaining, of course, on a small scale ever since the beginning of the Prospect days, but here there were never less than fifty people at the smallest dinner party, and often a hundred or more attended her informal teas. But she knew how to delegate responsibility and allow the housekeeper and the household staff to perform

229

their long-established duties, unhindered by too many orders from her. She managed, however, to make even the huge receptions more homely and gracious, supplying the refreshments and punch which had been omitted in recent years, and strolling informally about with father among the guests, after the long ordeal of the receiving line was over. She wanted, as she said, to keep even "functions" both beautiful and simple.

And she never forgot old friends, often inviting them to come for a visit, when she and father somehow managed a quiet evening by the fire where they talked about books and grew intense over the discussions they loved.

My sisters and I plunged into a mad social whirl, but to my dismay, Belle insisted that, in order to distribute the White House favors, we must not go to the same parties. I was panic-stricken at the thought of going without Margaret or Jessie—from earliest dancing-school days I had clung to them, and not even my loveliest new frock or most devoted swain compensated me for their absence.

Night after night I sat in dressing rooms, powdering and re-powdering my nose, fussing with my hair, anything at all to postpone the awful moment when I must make my entrance. A butler would throw open a door with a flourish and solemnly announce, "Miss Eleanor Wilson." Then I must run the barrage of lorgnettes and curious eyes, walk across what seemed like miles of shining floor to my hostess, and stand stiffly while dozens of people I had never seen before were presented. It was sheer agony!

In those pre-war days almost every party ended with a dance, and as soon as the dancing started I was all right, although at first the dowagers used to stare at my feet as I passed, surprised that a "highbrow" could dance without falling down on her nose. But I knew that I danced well, and I was safe from one of the worst feminine terrors. The men had to dance with me!

One night at a dinner I heard a man say about another guest, "That woman is really a beauty, but no one knows it. She comes into a room like a mouse, quietly and meekly, and people take her at her own valuation." The observation stayed in my mind, and I resolved to try an experiment. I knew that I was no beauty, but if I could sail in with my head high, pretending to myself that I was perfectly fascinating, it could do no harm, and might keep people from knowing that I was dying of fright. The experiment was a great success. At once I began to lose much of my self-consciousness. I don't know what effect it had on my audience, but it made life much easier for me. Also it amused me enormously, and to a certain extent, became a habit. I have continued my little act throughout my life, to hide my unconquerable shyness. Once someone said to me, "You're a terribly conceited person, aren't you?" and I was delighted. I had put it over! Margaret and Jessie always seemed untroubled by such problems. They must have had their moments of shyness too, but they were both so vividly intelligent and interested in other people that they could not be self-conscious.

I was often comforted by the knowledge that father had fought shyness all his life. He wrote once, "Is there anything more hateful, or more unhandsome and ridiculous than self-consciousness? I would rather have the small-pox.

231

It is as fatal to any genuine action as any kind of disease is to acting at all." *

I began to enjoy the social whirl so much that I found it almost impossible to remember that I must often be the first to leave a party. According to the strict rules of Washington etiquette, no one could go home until the guest of honor saw fit to do so. Belle Hagner scolded me over and over, as she constantly heard groans from weary souls who had been out until two or three in the morning, because "Eleanor Wilson was dancing her head off, with no thought of the time." Belle suggested a wrist watch, and mother bought me the first I had ever had. I was very proud of it, but seldom remembered to look at it, and continued my nefarious conduct.

One night I was invited to a big dinner party and a charity performance at the theatre afterwards. After coffee we just sat and sat until at last I got nervous and blurted out, "I thought we were going to the theatre." At once everyone sprang up and dashed for their coats and wraps, and I realized that I had slipped again.

I protested to Belle, "Good Lord, can't they even go to the theatre unless I remember and make a sign?" But she had no sympathy for me, reminding me that there were responsibilities from which there was no escape, and I must take them more seriously. Margaret was an equally serious offender and, perversely enough, on the rare occasions when we all went together, and watching the clock was her responsibility as the oldest sister, I was acutely conscious when she committed the same crime. I remember making frantic signs to her one night when a desperate hostess

* Letter to Mrs. Hulbert.

strode out into the middle of the room, and stood there just glaring at the clock, while Margaret utterly oblivious, continued to murmur with a fascinating young diplomat in a corner.

The young army and navy officers were my particular beaux. There were thrilling dances on the "Mayflower", the President's yacht, and at the War College; dinner-dances at Chevy Chase, Washington's famous country club; small theatre parties when we dressed in our best and sat grandly in the stage box, and *thé dansants* almost every afternoon at private houses—we were not allowed to go to hotel dances. I ruined dozens of pairs of slippers, flirted outrageously, took moonlight walks by the Potomac, and fell off Charlie Rockwell's horses, one after another, in Rock Creek Park.

The world seemed a wonderful place, and for a time I was free from the old terror that some harm might come to mother and father.

Father loved the theatre, managing to see almost every play that came to Washington, and often sat laughing aloud at Keith's, the old vaudeville house. He was a devotee of the Washington stock company, and was beloved by every actor and actress who came to the city, for his sympathetic and uncritical enjoyment of their performances.

The White House receptions were not much fun. We all rather dreaded them; two or three thousand people passing in line to shake hands with father and mother and the Cabinet wives; afterwards just standing around for hours, talking and eating, reluctant to tear themselves away. All the food and wine were paid for from the President's own salary, but there is a sum added each year to the appropriation

233

for White House expenses to take care of the raids of souvenir hunters. Silver spoons, napkins, even small dishes were often missing after a big party.

I liked the diplomatic receptions because of the gorgeous foreign uniforms, and the grand manners of the Ambassadors and their entourages; but even then my own excessive politeness eventually bored me. Finally I devised a plan of escape. After an hour or two, I whispered to a few young and frivolous souls, and we crept up the back stairs to the Oval Room where we danced to the victrola until discovered by Belle or Helen, or an envious young aide.

The White House aides contributed greatly to our enjoyment. Chosen for their good looks and *savoir-faire*, and considering it part of their duty to see that we were well looked after, they gave us a comfortable feeling of protection on all occasions. We were told that if we ever wanted an escort, all we had to do was to call them, and they would be there; it would be a breach of etiquette to refuse an invitation from the White House. We never used this privilege, but it was nice to feel that we could, if an emergency arose.

One night at a dinner party I noticed an empty chair, and asked my host who was missing. He said, "Ed Greble. I can't imagine what's happened to him." After a while Ed dashed in and, without looking at any of the other guests, explained quite grandly to the hostess that he had been unavoidably detained; he had had a call from the White House "to escort Miss Eleanor to the theatre." There was a shout of laughter, and he looked around in bewilderment, to see me grinning at him from the other end of the table. While we were dancing together later, he told me that he had forgotten the dinner engagement, that a summons to the White House was his favorite excuse to cover such lapses of memory, and this was the first time he had been tripped.

Belle Hagner gave a tea party one day, and invited Alice Roosevelt Longworth to meet us. I watched her with curiosity when she came in: a quite fascinating woman with the most complete self-assurance I have ever seen. When she was introduced to me, she said, "I've been told that you and I look alike," whereupon we glared at each other like two cats on a back fence, equally displeased that anyone could have made such an absurd statement.

Neither of my sisters gave herself up to frivolity as I did. Margaret kept up her singing, and Jessie was active in the Y. W. C. A., sometimes making speaking trips to raise funds. Frank Sayre was Assistant District Attorney in New York, and when he came down to see Jessie they were radiantly happy, sometimes escaping the eagle eyes of reporters by meeting on the banks of the canal, and slipping off in a canoe.

Mother told me one day that she thought I should do something more than just amuse myself. I said that I was quite happy and didn't want to do anything else, but she persuaded me to go on the board of a charity organization, and once a week I spent a few hours working in a day nursery. But I was a complete failure; my heart was so obviously not in it that I am sure the committee was delighted when I finally resigned.

Mother herself had begun, three weeks after the inauguration, to give every spare moment to an attempt to improve the wretched living conditions in the slum areas of

Washington. To the casual observer, there were no slums in the Capital City, but hidden away in almost every quarter were narrow alleys, disgracefully filthy and overcrowded.

There were ninety-six thousand Negroes in Washington, one-third of the population, and philanthropists had tried for years to get Congress to do something about improving and rebuilding the places where they lived. In spite of her enormously increased social duties, her huge correspondence, her never-ceasing vigil over the health and happiness of her family, mother undertook this new burden. She said once, * "I wonder how anyone who reaches middle age can bear it, if she cannot feel, on looking back, that whatever mistakes she may have made, she has on the whole lived for others and not for herself."

She visited the alleys many times, often taking groups of Congressmen with her. She talked to the people, helped them with food and money, held numerous conferences, and insisted with her own peculiar gentle firmness that something be done at once. In the end a bill was passed which practically eliminated the slums, and no one doubted that it was she who had brought it about. She also spent long wearying hours inspecting conditions in the public buildings and, finding in some of them no rest rooms for the Government workers, managed to have these installed. Day after day she came home worn and white, but she never complained, changing her dress and coming down to the Red Room to receive her guests with her sweet calm smile and never-failing courtesy.

We were all worried about her, knowing that she did

* To Florence Hoyt.

not have the strength to stand work that would have taxed even the strongest and most unimaginative person. Her intensity and sensitiveness to pain in others was a terrific drain on her, but she felt that it was all a part of her duty, and the philanthropic women would not let her alone. I grew to hate the sight of one of them, a tall angular woman who was constantly arriving at the White House, and pounding at mother, tearing her tender heart with tales of woe.

She was busy from morning to night, but she always had time to help father in any way he needed, following with eager interest the progress of his program before Congress, discussing with him every important move and going carefully over his prepared speeches. Often she suggested an idea which he invariably used. He told us that it was always her passages that made the strongest impression in the whole speech.

The gardens were a great joy to her. There were two, one on either side of the south portico, and she got an appropriation from Congress to remodel them. One she planned herself, calling in a landscape architect for the other. They were both beautiful, but mother's had a suggestion of Italy, a lovely illusion of vistas that made it by far the more attractive of the two. Tall cypresses at one end led up to a statue of Pan, and at the other, a small terrace with a curved marble bench was enclosed by clipped hedges. There were roses in profusion, and masses of small multicolor flowers bordering the paths. She could look down into it from her own room, and I often saw her standing at her window, smiling with pleasure.

Helen Bones was the greatest possible help and comfort

to mother. She took care of all her personal correspondence, managed the private account books, and relieved her of many worries and cares, giving at the same time devoted love and companionship. Helen was very popular in every overlapping circle of Washington society, and I don't know how any of us could have gotten along without her. She helped us all in a thousand ways, and fitted perfectly into the family group. Her room was always a sort of rendez-vous; the door was open all day long, and we drifted in and out, sometimes ending the day with an impromptu tea around her fire—mother, relaxed in the corner of a big sofa; father, teacup in hand, standing before the fire; Belle Hagner shouting with laughter, and my sisters and I tell-ing the day's adventures. I made her my confidante, pour-ing all my problems, romantic, sartorial and otherwise into her patient ears.

Sunday was still kept as much as possible a day apart. We always went together to a Presbyterian church, came back to a quiet family lunch, and rode horseback or went for a drive in the afternoon. Only intimate friends or rela-tives were guests on that day, and father didn't like us to go to even the simplest Sunday night supper party.

Distinguished visitors to Washington were always enter-tained at the White House, and often there were at least two or three guests at the luncheon table. When father played the role of host, I always recaptured somewhat the same feeling I had had in Mrs. Reid's drawing room when I was a little girl. He was a dazzling stranger, and I couldn't bear to miss a word he said. Pretending to listen politely to my neighbor, I always had one ear cocked in his direction.

Our guests appeared at their best too, as father had a

way of promptly making them forget their first shyness in the presence of the President. His own sensitiveness made him acutely aware of other people's emotions, and taught him how to put them completely at their ease. And he was not only charmingly aware of his guests, but always of his family too—a quick flashing look of understanding or amusement, when we had not even spoken, telling us that he was always interested in our reactions.

All our lives we had loved his stories, often prompting him to tell one of our particular favorites. He never forgot one or stumbled in telling it, but one day, to my astonishment, I heard him stop in the middle of a pet anecdote and say, "By Jove, I've forgotten how that ends." It was the story of a man who asked an Irishman for whom he intended to vote. The Irishman replied, "Sure, I'm going to vote for that man Wilson Woodrow." His friend said, "You mean vice versa, don't you?" and Mike answered indignantly, "I do not. I'll not vote for a damned Italian." When he paused I couldn't believe my ears and opened my mouth to prompt him, but shut it just in time. Afterwards I asked him about it, and he said, "Why, didn't you see? Our Italian guest didn't understand English very well, and certainly could not have got the Irish brogue; all he would have heard was 'damned Italian', and his feelings would have been injured."

Mr. Balfour came from England and stayed a few days in Washington, making a speech before Congress and lunching afterwards at the White House. I was puzzled by a sort of hesitancy in his way of speaking, a distinct diffidence in his manner, and mentioned it to father after Balfour had gone. Father said, "Yes, I noticed it, too. He is one of those people—there are not many in public life—who see both sides of every question so clearly that they are never quite sure which is right. I have struggled with that myself. It is difficult to convince other people if one is not oneself a strong advocate."

There were often concerts after the big dinner parties, and one night Paderewski played. Margaret found him just before the concert, pacing excitedly up and down the Rose guest room. When she asked him if there was anything he wanted, he said nervously, "May I have a bowl of hot water? Feel my hands—they are so cold." She brought the water herself and held it in front of him like a votive offering, while he soaked his fingers, and then led him, a little calmer, to the East Room.

We saw him that night perform an act of pure courtesy and thoughtfulness that I shall never forget. One of the Senators had had too much to drink, and in the middle of a beautiful soft passage, rose and, striding up and down between the chairs, talked at the top of his voice. Margaret quickly persuaded one of his colleagues to lead him out, and in five minutes things were quiet again. But during all those bad moments Paderewski never even turned his head, or faltered in his divine playing. By a man who was famous for not being able to stand the least noise during his concerts, it was a fine exhibition of consideration. We all fell in love with him, and father and he began a friendship that night that was to last all their lives and lead, indirectly, to Polish freedom.

Father looked extraordinarily well and vital during these first weeks. When I saw him come out of his study and stride down the hall toward us, I noticed that his walk had acquired more than its usual buoyancy. His eyes were strikingly clear and bright, and there was a sort of chiseled keenness in his face. He was finer looking in those days than ever before in his life. A friend said, "God set out to make Woodrow Wilson ugly, but Woodrow has made himself handsome."

He thought very little about his own appearance, but I know that he considered himself a plain, almost an ugly man. He often said that he looked like a horse, and his favorite limerick was:

> *"For beauty I am not a star*
> *There are others more handsome by far.*
> *But my face—I don't mind it,*
> *For I am behind it.*
> *It's the people in front that I jar."*

Things were moving swiftly and smoothly, although the ever-present problem of patronage was troubling him considerably. Hungry Democrats, out of office for sixteen years, were clamoring at the gates, but on the day after the inauguration he had announced that he would deal with appointments only through the members of his Cabinet. He had told us that he wanted to make a careful, personal investigation of every man appointed to an office of any importance, but he soon found that, with the best intentions in the world, this was utterly impossible.

There were fifty-six thousand postmasters alone to be chosen, and he would have had to neglect practically everything else if he had undertaken to know personally about every one. Burleson had pointed this out to him, but was not until he had seen that it took two strong men merely to carry into his office the recommendations and information about a handful of applicants that he gave up. But he made the most important appointments himself, taking infinite pains to be certain that each one was "honest and capable and forward-looking". He was bitterly disappointed when President Eliot of Harvard, Richard Olney, who had been Secretary of State under Cleveland, John R. Mott, leader of the Y. M. C. A., and finally Harry Fine, his old friend, all declined Ambassadorial posts for financial reasons.

It was the old story of a rich country refusing to pay its representatives to foreign countries enough to live on properly, making it necessary to appoint rich men.

Father had no narrow-minded prejudice against rich men, but it was hard to find one who stood for his ideals of democratic simplicity and open diplomacy. In one or two instances, as in the case of Walter Hines Page, whom he sent to England, he had to get contributions from friends to help support them. It was difficult and discouraging, and Mr. Bryan, an old-fashioned politician in this respect, was on his back all the time with requests to reward "deserving Democrats", regardless, often, of their qualifications. He was so anxious to give the "faithful" a chance that he wrote to father suggesting that appointees should be asked to serve for only a short time so that "we can pass the offices around".

Father's affection for Mr. Bryan made him more than patient, but he was adamant in his determination to appoint only the best men. He insisted that many hitherto appointive offices be placed under the Civil Service, tightened up

242

the regulations and refused to dismiss men from office merely because they were Republicans.

He was able to make one appointment that pleased him greatly. On a trip to England in 1896 he had met Charles A. Woods, a young lawyer from South Carolina. They were instantly attracted to each other and Woods, admiring and enthusiastic, had predicted a great future for his new friend. Father had told him when they parted, "Well, if you're right, I'll put you on the Federal Bench when I'm President." Woods had had a fine career since then, and father was as pleased as a boy when he was able to keep his promise, made in jest.

Henry van Dyke, who had strongly opposed him in the Princeton controversies, he appointed Minister to the Netherlands. When father's letter reached him, van Dyke was astonished, and came down to Washington at once to thank him. He was a dignified little man and, as a child, I had always been very shy with him; now I was surprised, as I watched him talk with mother, to see that there were tears in his eyes.

When McCombs was offered the Ambassadorship to France, he declined and accepted at least a dozen times before finally turning it down with childish petulance. He had wanted to be in the Cabinet, and never forgave father for not putting him there. Father bore all this with patient good humor, but it irked him dreadfully to have his attention so distracted when he was eager to get on with his great program of reform.

He was pleased with his Cabinet, and on the friendliest terms with its members. At the meetings he called on each man in turn, but encouraged general discussion, and never

243

insisted on strict rules of procedure. If there were jealousies, they concealed them in his benign and courteous presence.

He called Burleson "the Cardinal", because of his priest-like appearance and the round "shovel hat" he affected, and later in his letters to Colonel House and his private conversations with his family, referred to Mac as "Pythias", to Bryan as "Primus", and to Garrison as "Mars". His loyalty to his official family never faltered. In the years that followed he defended and upheld them through many bitter attacks. However, he was, to all intents and purposes, his own Secretary of State, always consulting with Mr. Bryan but, in the end, making the final decisions himself, on all important foreign questions.

The Mexican problem was a legacy from Mr. Taft's slow-moving administration. Huerta had murdered Madero, the idol of the Mexican peons, and two factions in the United States, one for immediate intervention and the other for recognition of Huerta and a hands-off policy, were loud in their advice and demands. During the first months in office, he handled this situation and controversial matters with China and Japan, Nicaragua and Panama, with skill and almost dramatic sincerity. By May he had received the verbal consent of five countries to what were called "the Bryan Treaties—Treaties for the Advancement of General Peace". His repudiation of Dollar Diplomacy and his simple, direct statement of policy and principle, especially the principle of "the consent of the governed" with which he calmed the fears of Latin-America, brought a wave of excitement and commendation. Almost every newspaper in the country was with him.

One day I spoke to him exultantly about his enormous

popularity and he put his hand affectionately on mine and then, as though he hated to disillusion me, said, "Remember, the pack is always waiting near at hand to tear one to pieces. Popularity is the most evanescent thing in the world, and the most unimportant."

CHAPTER FIFTEEN

The White House

Precedent-loving Washington was shocked when, early in April, father delivered his first message to Congress in person. For a hundred and thirteen years the President's messages had been droned off with expressionless speed, by a Congressional Clerk, while the gentlemen to whom they were addressed chatted and yawned.

When he called a special session and announced that he would appear before them to consider the tariff, there was a wave of excitement and protest that amused us considerably. There were fiery speeches at the Capitol and even some of his Democratic friends protested, saying that it would be like a "speech from the throne". But to father it was just the simple and natural way, and he paid no attention to the outcries.

He always disliked to read his addresses from manuscript, but a Message to Congress could not, of course, be made extemporaneously. He had his own peculiar method of preparing his speeches; first writing the substance on a single sheet of paper, partly in script and partly in shorthand, then again entirely in shorthand, making the final copy himself on his own typewriter on small sheets of

246

thick paper. There were usually a few corrections, made in his fine, neat writing between the lines.

Mother and my sisters and I sat in the gallery of the House of Representatives where the joint session was held. It was jammed with people, and outside in the corridors there was a noisy crowd clamoring to get in. Washington society was well represented, coming all dressed up as if it were a "First Night".

The Vice President and the Senators marched solemnly in; the members of the Cabinet, looking a little nervous, settled themselves on one side of the Speaker's desk, and at last the Clerk announced, "The President of the United States".

Everyone rose as father walked briskly in at the head of the committee appointed to escort him. There was scattered, half-hearted applause from the floor, and then his old rival, Champ Clark, who was Speaker of the House, introduced him in an almost unintelligible mumble. Father stood quietly for a moment with a little half-smile on his lips, and then began, his voice very clear and untroubled.

"Mr. Speaker and gentlemen of the Congress: I am very glad indeed to have this opportunity to address the two Houses directly, and to verify for myself the impression that the President of the United States is a person, not a mere department of the Government hailing Congress from some isolated island of jealous power, sending messages, not speaking naturally and with his own voice; that he is a human being trying to cooperate with other human beings in a common service. After this pleasant experience, I shall feel quite normal in all our dealings with one another."

Then, in ten minutes, he covered the ground, presenting

247

a general outline of his plan for a revision of the tariff and
his reasons for advocating it. The speech was simple, con-
cise and so brief that when he finished, I was startled. There
was a moment of silence, and then a burst of spontaneous
and enthusiastic applause. It was another triumph, but the
unfriendliness at the start had upset me and I found, to my
surprise, that I was trembling as we rode down in the elevator.

As we drove home together mother said, "That's the
sort of thing Roosevelt would have loved to do, if he had
thought of it", and father laughed and answered, "Yes, I
think I put one over on Teddy."

One of the newspapers had the same thought, for the
next day it published a cartoon, showing Teddy biting his
finger nails and exclaiming, "Why didn't I think of that?"

With father, however, it was not an attempt at self-
dramatization, but was dictated merely by his instinct for
direct approach and his belief in responsible leadership in
a democracy. He told us that he had been terribly nervous
in the first few moments, but we had heard that before. All
his life he suffered from "stage fright", but it left him as
soon as he began to speak and lost himself in the earnestness
and sincerity of his thoughts.

Ever since, as a student at the University of Virginia, he
had made a speech on the subject of the tariff, he had been
interested in the problem and had made it a lifelong
study. He was, therefore, well equipped to deal with it
now, but he called in many experts and consulted at length
with Oscar Underwood, chairman of the Ways and Means
Committee, and with members of the Congressional Finance Committee, before the bill was finally introduced.

He had set forth the general principle of the measure in a speech he had made in 1908 when he said, "The power of the Government to tax ought never to be used to confer privileges upon individuals or groups of individuals, but should be used always and only to secure general benefits, the benefit of the taxpayer as a whole, or of the nation as an organism."

But he was a thorough student of the principles of economics and knew that too violent a remedy would cause havoc with American business. He argued that "existing protection should not be suddenly withdrawn, but steadily and upon a fixed program, upon which every man of business can base his definite forecasts and systematic plans". It was not, therefore, a free trade measure that he advocated, but one that would reduce duties on more than nine hundred articles and eliminate the "doling out of privileges" to special interests.

Economists all over the country approved it as both necessary and sound, but there was a howl from Big Business, and the fight was very bitter. Lobbyists poured into Washington bringing pressure to bear on the Senators and Congressmen, through insidious threats and promises and predictions of disaster. It was well known in Washington that "lobbying" had been used for many years to defeat measures unwelcome to the interests but it was always carried on with such secrecy and cleverness that it was difficult to uncover. Father handled this with the same courage and audacity that he had used so effectively at Princeton and Trenton. He made a public statement in which he said that Washington "had seldom seen so numerous, so insidious a lobby"—that "great bodies of astute men seek to create an artificial opinion and to overcome the interests of the public for their private profit". It was a bold move, because he knew that it would be almost impossible to prove that what he said was true, and his statement caused a great stir throughout the country. But it was instantly effective. From then on many Congressmen were afraid to oppose the bill for fear of being suspected of yielding to undue influence.

In only one month the House passed the measure by a large majority; but the struggle in the Senate lasted all through the long, hot summer.

At Cornish, in the New Hampshire hills, Winston Churchill, the American novelist, had built a lovely brick Georgian house and called it "Harlakenden". Mother and father rented it "sight unseen", having fallen in love with the photographs and glowing description of friends. When, in June, the heat grew oppressive we were eager to go, but put it off week after week, hoping that father could get away too. He was anxious for mother to have a rest, and urged us not to wait for him, but she was never really happy away from him and always felt that no one could take care of him as well as she.

At last, in July, he prevailed on us to go, promising to make flying visits as often as he could, but adding, "I can't be cool and comfortable at Cornish while Congress perspires here all summer at my request".

He expected at least to take us up there, but at the last minute had to change his plans because of some urgent matter. All he could do was to come down to the station to see us off, and after the train pulled out, mother cried and would not be comforted, lying in her berth with closed eyes, refusing to eat.

But she was pleased with Harlakenden and the winding river and blue hills, and she knew that Cary Grayson was staying at the White House, watching over father like a mother with an only child, and the next day she was able to smile again.

There was a studio on the place, a simple, barnlike affair, but she was delighted with it, and sending at once for her painting things, set to work with almost childlike zeal. Helen, my sisters, the servants and I all conspired daily to see that she had a few hours alone, and that no outsider ever knew where she was. Father wrote to her often, and again she read his letters aloud to us. And although she still skipped the "sacred parts", we knew by the tender pride in her face that after all the years together they remained the poetic messages of a lover.

We all had a beautiful time at Cornish, with climaxes of real happiness when father came for brief visits and we took long drives with him and, sitting on the terrace through the long twilights and starlit evenings, listened to his vivid and humorous account of what was going on in hectic Washington.

Our life at Cornish reminded us a little of our happy summers at Old Lyme. Our neighbors included a delightful group of artists, poets and writers, among them Maxfield Parrish, Homer Saint-Gaudens, Norman Hapgood, Percy MacKaye and Witter Bynner. They came frequently to Harlakenden and father and mother were able to relax in their pleasing and undemanding company.

Margaret, Jessie and I went to simple, lovely parties, listened to poetry and discussions of art and literature and gave our days to tennis and picnics.

Ernest Harold Baynes, the naturalist, was trying to establish a sanctuary for birds in a lovely grove in the hills, and Percy MacKaye conceived the idea of writing a masque and presenting it there to raise money and awaken the interest of the community. For weeks we were absorbed in preparations and rehearsals. I was the Bird Spirit, Witter Bynner, the Hunter, Harold Bayne and MacKaye himself had important parts and Margaret was a spirit voice, singing from a bush.

Father came up from Washington the night of the performance, and people drove in from all over the state, more, I think, to see him than the Bird Masque.

I had a headdress of white wings and, twenty minutes before the play was to begin, found that I had left it behind at Harlakenden. I was in despair for I thought the wings very becoming and was certain that I couldn't possibly speak my lines without them. White, the swiftest of the chauffeurs, was called in and promised that he could make the ten miles there and back in time. He was as good as his word, complaining, however, that he had had a hard time getting back because he "came all the way in his own dust".

After the performance, the cast, feeling very gay, drove home together. Passing through a tiny New England village we saw that there was a country dance in progress in the small town hall. We had the same idea almost simultaneously. Stopping the car a little way off, we approached stealthily and, without warning, appeared on the floor among the startled natives. Percy MacKaye, in his long blue hooded gown, leaned with folded arms against the wall, gazing at the scene like a necromancer who had himself created it. Witter Bynner in his leopard skin mantle and tall feather headdress, I in my white robe, Ruth Hall and three others dressed as birds, in brief, bright costumes we glided and swooped three times around the hall while the village people stood against the wall in a daze. Then we disappeared as silently as we had come. I have never known whether they thought us a dream, or a visitation from an insane asylum.

Marie Dressler, who had a summer home in Vermont across the river, asked one day if she might come and entertain us. Father was pleased, and we looked forward to an evening of laughter, but for some unexplained reason she insisted upon singing only lugubrious ditties about little, lost children, weeping mothers or blighted love. It was a sort of prelude to the "blues" that were to sweep America in later years. Toward the end we rebelled, politely, and she swung into her "Jamboree" song, and then told us a few amusing tales, but somehow the gloom was not dispelled.

Father's visits were depressingly few and far between, and one day mother decided to run down to Washington to see him. At my urgent request she took me with her, and father's face when we walked in and surprised him, made the long hot trip more than worth while.

I was surprised when Mac, calling on father that night, asked if I would play tennis with him the next day. He had singled me out two or three times at receptions, and seemed to like to dance with me at parties, but this was something

253

special. I dashed downtown and bought myself a tricky tennis costume, and we had a very amateurish and chatty game and tea afterwards in the garden. Father and mother were amused and teased me about it that night at dinner.

Father looked very tired. The controversy in the Senate over the tariff bill was fierce and exhausting and, having already introduced his proposed currency bill, he was in the midst of conferences and difficulties with the House of Representatives over this also highly controversial question.

We could hardly bear to tear ourselves away again, but Cary Grayson told us that father would worry too much about us if we stayed there in the scorching heat. He promised that he would make him play golf three or four times a week and drag him forcibly away to Cornish if he showed signs of breaking down.

We were having a hard time keeping newspaper reporters from invading Harlakenden. Jessie's engagement had been announced, and they all wanted "human interest" interviews. Poor Frank's past life was investigated in minute detail; if he had had anything to conceal it would have been difficult, if not impossible, to do so, and every time he and Jessie went out for even a walk or drive, they were tracked down like fugitives from justice. It was fine, however, to be able to take him openly into the family circle. We all loved him, and even father said, "He's almost good enough for Jessie." But we hated to think about this first break in the closely knit web of the family, and when mother consented to let them be married in November, I sulked for days.

We went back to Washington in October and plunged

at once into another round of parties. I was beginning to get my bearings, to look about me with some discernment, some understanding of the undercurrents of Washington life. It was interesting, but it was also disillusioning. Jealousy was the prevailing note, for the place was seething with ambitious people, and the gossips were busy from morning to night. I learned very soon that the few really important men and women there were invariably the simplest, the easiest to talk to.

I sat one night at dinner with Lord Bryce on my left and a young attaché of the British Embassy on my right. I was in awe of Lord Bryce; he was famous and old; he wouldn't want to talk to me. The attaché was not much older than I, so I began to chatter gaily with him. In five minutes I was bored to death by his self-opinionated air and eventually got up the courage to turn to Lord Bryce. He beamed at me and began to talk in the simplest and most charming way imaginable. It was not a monologue either, but a conversation. I talked as I had never talked before, expressed opinions, swapped stories, mentioned my travels in connection with his, and never even looked at the boy again.

But I was rapidly becoming a youthful cynic. Unless, like Lord Bryce, they already had a high position, I began to suspect people of wanting something. I had some reason for this: the begging letters, the requests for jobs, and the "freak letters" poured in literally by the thousand. I said one day to father, "Is everybody in the United States either crazy, or wanting us to do something for him?"

He laughed at my intensity and said, "My dear little girl, there are ninety million people in this country—these

few thousand don't represent America", and he talked to
me very seriously about not allowing myself ever to become cynical and suspicious. "Most people are fundamentally honest and good—of that I am sure. Don't let the
few cheap and dishonest ones hurt you. You have understanding and intuition; use them." He himself never lost
his faith in human beings, and over and over I have heard
him say, "When the American people know the truth, they
always decide right."

But he himself was often annoyed by the Washington
atmosphere. He spoke of it many times to us, and in letters
to friends. "Washington is, I should judge, the worst place
in America to keep normal. One's perspective goes wrong
along with one's nerves, and there are a lot of people here
who get on your nerves." He said once, "People never
remain the same after they come to Washington. They
either grow or they swell—usually the latter." And he was
constantly asking for the frank opinion of friends, who did
not live in Washington. "How does the game look to you,
and the actors in it—as you sit at a distance and look on
at it? It is more important to me how it looks outside of
Washington, than how it looks inside. The men who think
in Washington only cannot think for the country. It is a
place of illusions. The disease is that men think of themselves, and not of their tasks of service, and are more concerned with what will happen to them, than with what will
happen to the country.

"I am not complaining or scolding or holding myself
superior; I am only analyzing, as a man will on Sunday
when the work pauses and he looks before and after. My
eye is no better than theirs; it is only fresher and was a

thoughtful spectator of these very things before it got on the inside, and tried to see straight there." *

Thinking of himself and his own ambitions was a disease from which father never suffered. Lack of self-interest accounted for his clarity of vision and was, I think, the chief element of his greatness. It was also one of the things that few people realized about him and for which, almost subconsciously, they often hated him. He was not like themselves; he looked beyond personal aims to the far horizon.

One evening when we happened to be all together in the Oval Room, Brown appeared at the door, and announced in a booming voice, "De Secretary of de Treasury". Father looked around surprised, because he had not expected Mac, but Brown added, obviously restraining his own astonishment, "Fo' Miss Eleanor".

There were shouts of mirth and banter, and I dashed quickly from the room to hide my mounting color, and with a beating heart went down to receive Mac in the Green Room.

The second time he called, Brown marched a few paces into the room before he made the announcement in a lower voice. After that the frequency of Mac's visits and the proportionate progress of his suit were disclosed by Brown's increasing discretion of manner. Each time he advanced further into the room, and each time his voice dropped lower until he almost whispered his refrain, "De Secretary of de Treasury". Finally one night he appeared as usual and, amid the delighted silence of the family,

* Letter to Mrs. Hulbert, Sept. 28, 1913

257

marched over to me, his big feet turned outward, bowed low from the waist, grinned, rolled his eyes in the direction of the door, and made his exit without a sound.

The next day mother asked me how serious it was and if I had forgotten that I was supposed to be engaged; whereupon I wept and stammered that I didn't want to be engaged. She looked at me, puzzled, but left it at that, following her rule since we were grown, of not insisting on confidences.

Belle Hagner had a grand time with me, telling me with an innocent expression about the rich widow who, according to the gossips, was pursuing Mac and filling the Treasury office with roses. But I was so flattered by his attentions that nothing bothered me much.

One night he began to talk about the currency bill and I was in a panic. He would discover my abysmal ignorance an any subject related to finance. I quickly assumed the well-known feminine attitude of the rapturous listener and was enchanted when he told me that my comprehension of this complicated problem was little short of miraculous. The next day after lunch I took father aside and made him promise not to tell on me. He gave me a curious look, half enquiry, half quizzical amusement, and answered, gravely, "Wouldn't it be simpler to make a real study of the currency problem?"

The tariff bill had passed the Senate on the ninth of September, and the House had voted for the currency measure on the eighteenth, but there was still no respite for father, struggling with recalcitrant Senators, in the face of the unfair attacks of big business. But although he was

258

swamped with work, he was, I know, enjoying it; the Irish fighter was never very far from the surface.

He wrote to a friend, "Of course, I find a great zest in it all. Hard as it is to nurse Congress along and stand ready to play a part in guidance in anything that turns up, great or small, it is all part of something infinitely great and worth while and I am content to labor at it to the finish . . . So far things go very well and my leadership is most loyally and graciously accepted, even by men of whom I did not expect it. I hope that this is in part because they perceive that I am pursuing no private and selfish purposes of my own. How could a man do that with such responsibilities resting upon him! It is no credit to be sobered and moralized by a task like this." *

On the third of October he signed the tariff bill. Quite a ceremony was made of it. Members of the Cabinet, the men who had led the fight in Congress, the family and a group of friends stood around his desk in the executive offices and watched him. He wrote 'Woodrow' with one gold pen and 'Wilson' with another and gave them, still wet with the "unmitigated proof" of his signing, to Congressman Underwood and Senator Simmons after whom the bill was named. Then he made a little speech and everyone applauded. He looked almost jubilant. This was not a personal victory, but a triumph for the American people—the first step in "setting the business of the country free".

As November twenty-fifth, the day set for Jessie's wedding, approached we drowned our mounting depression in

* Letter to Mrs. Edith G. Reid.

a sea of preparation. Mother and I went with her to New York to order her trousseau and comforted each other as we watched her radiant face and delicious indifference to her own beauty, surrounded by enthusiastic saleswomen and fitters.

She didn't want a big wedding, but we found that it was impossible to avoid it without hurting everybody's feelings. We were all appalled, however, when we saw the list of people who "had to be invited". Margaret was to be maid of honor, and Jessie had chosen me and six of her own particular Princeton and college friends as bridesmaids. I had a grand time planning their costumes, making sketches and sternly imposing my own views on even the bride herself.

The bridesmaids' dresses, made in New York, were of charmeuse in four different shades of rose, from palest pink for Margaret to deep rose for me and the other tallest bridesmaid. They had Elizabethan ruffs of silver lace, and the skirts were draped in the prevailing mode, almost touching the floor in the back but, in front, daringly showing four inches of silk stocking through silver petticoats. There were head-dresses too—little rose velvet caps with silver lace, wired and standing up in the Russian manner. I thought them triumphs of simple chic!

Such a flood of wedding presents poured in that even in that big house it was difficult to find a place to put them. A committee was chosen in each of the Houses of Congress, to buy Jessie something really impressive. When the gifts arrived, a massive silver service from the Senate and a magnificent diamond pendant from the House, she sat down suddenly in a near-by chair, something like consternation in her face. "What shall I do with these? What can a poor professor's wife do with such things?" she cried.

Frank had accepted a professorship at Williams, his own college, and Jessie was rejoicing over the prospect of returning to the simple life of a college town.

The day before the wedding the bridesmaids arrived, and the dresses, and we all tried them on together. It was a bad moment: the head-dresses, which I had thought a stroke of artistic genius, were complete and hideous failures. The bridesmaids looked at me accusingly, and I was sunk in despair. But Margaret and I and the ladies' maids, went to work and, after sitting up most of the night, remade them entirely. They were nothing to boast of, even then, but at least they weren't too awful.

I woke up the next morning without a voice. A sore throat and my self-assumed responsibilities had deprived me of everything but a whisper. All day I felt like a ghost, unable to make myself heard above all the chatter and excitement.

The ceremony was to be at six o'clock, and at five mother, Margaret and I barred the door to everyone else, so that we might be alone with Jessie while she dressed. Her hair was like a wide golden fillet above her calm brow, and the long satin gown fell in soft lines to the floor. She looked half angel, half Grecian statue, and she had that lovely shining look that always brought a lump into my throat.

Mother pinned the veil on, smiling into Jessie's eyes with no sign of the grief that this parting meant to her. I was very busy on the floor, pretending to arrange the train, and not daring to look at Margaret for fear we should both burst into tears. I could only think how beautiful she was, and wonder how we could ever be a happy family again, without her.

The Marine Band, in their gorgeous scarlet coats, were tuning up in the entresol when we assembled in the big dining room. Father looked very distinguished in his dark grey cutaway, as he drew Jessie's arm through his and smiled gravely down at her.

Then we marched, two by two, down the long hallway to the East Room, crowded with people and blazing with lights. Dignitaries and their wives, diplomats, Army and Navy officers in full dress uniform and all their medals; then the familiar faces of old friends—I saw it all in one swift glimpse while I slowly paced at the end of the procession.

The big east window was banked with flowers and ferns and, between tall candelabra, there was a little satin-covered prie-dieu on a white rug of soft vicuña fur that had been sent as a wedding present from the Peruvian Minister. Frank's dearest friend, Dr. Grenfell, of Labrador fame, was best man, and his solemn, ascetic face lighted up as he looked at Jessie. He and Frank had shared many hardships at his mission and he loved him like a son. Dr. Beach, who had been our pastor in the Presbyterian church in Princeton, performed the ceremony.

In the midst of his solemn words I was conscious of a curious accompaniment, and stealing a side glance toward the front row of guests, had a vision of little Auntie Blanche, almost concealed under beads and bracelets and rings, and the famous serpent belt. Her dream had come true! She was taking long, ecstatic breaths, and every jewel and bead was clashing like a tiny cymbal.

Suddenly the Marine Band blared out in a triumphant march and Jessie turned and, seeking mother's face, smiled like a happy child. I saw the room and the crowd through a blur of tears and, clinging blindly to a young usher's arm, managed to make a more or less dignified exit.

But soon everything was gay again. Mac sought me out and I took him into the Blue Room, and gave him lessons in one-stepping and fox-trotting, my enforced whispering making me feel very intriguing.

Cousin Lucy presided in the Oval Room where the wedding presents were displayed, showing positive genius in her ability to put names, faces and gifts together with precision and dispatch. Knowing that everyone invariably looks first for his own contribution to the array, she managed to have each gift in a prominent position the moment she caught sight of the donor. Some of the presents were pretty awful, and these had been placed behind the door. There was one huge and ghastly oil painting, and how little Cousin Lucy contrived to heave it up on the mantelpiece just before the proud searcher discovered it, was a mystery.

Father and mother and the bridal party had supper in the big dining room, and then we all ran down the corridor to the main staircase where, standing halfway up, Jessie threw her bouquet down among the laughing bridesmaids. I saw her catch my eye and then deliberately aim the flowers in my direction, nearly tumbling me over with the weight of them.

Once more we four were alone in Jessie's room, pretending to be very jolly while we helped her to change into her violet-colored "going-away" dress, with its little velvet hat to match.

Father and mother had always disliked the old noisy rice-throwing custom and, as Jessie and Frank were anxious to avoid the newspaper sleuths hanging around outside, their departure was very quiet—almost clandestine. Leaving by the south entrance, they escaped in an automobile without the White House emblem on the door, and drove to a place in the Maryland hills, lent to them by a friend.

As we turned away, father put his arm about mother's shoulders and, drawing her close to him, walked slowly back to the elevator.

He went off soon to keep an appointment, but there were still friends and relatives milling around, so mother, Margaret and I took long breaths and tried feebly to entertain them. I even turned on the victrola and suggested charades, the old childhood cure for the blues, but my hoarse whispering was not exactly a merry sound, and nobody really wanted to do anything but talk about Jessie.

I heard mother say, with a little rueful smile, "I know; it was a wedding, not a funeral, but you must forgive us— this is the first break in the family."

CHAPTER SIXTEEN

The White House

THE BATTLE FOR CURRENCY REFORM had already lasted five months, and the debate was still raging in the Senate. Everyone was worn out and demanding a recess for the Christmas holidays. But father, knowing well the danger of deferred action, was adamant. He himself needed a holiday badly, but insisted that he could not rest nor enjoy himself until the bill was passed.

He had been studying this most complicated of all domestic problems ever since 1897, when he had said that "nothing but currency reform can touch the cause of the present discontents". He told us that he knew very little about the technical problems of banking and finance, but men who had talked with him and listened to his speeches on the subject, knew that he was extraordinarily well grounded in the fundamentals.

In Bermuda he had spent many hours studying proposed legislation, and carrying on a correspondence with economists and bankers. On his return to America he had asked Carter Glass, a member of the House Banking and Currency Committee, and for many years an advocate and student of banking reform, to come to Princeton for a con-

265

sultation. He had spared no effort, no time, in trying to work out a solution.

When I remember the countless hours he spent, then and later, talking to men from all over the United States—not just taking advice when it was offered, but seeking it—I am astonished that he could ever have been accused of arbitrary indifference to other people's opinions.

In his message to Congress in June he had, as in his tariff message, gone to the heart of the matter in a short lucid speech.

"We must have a currency, not rigid as now, but readily, elastically responsive to sound credit, the expanding and contracting credits of everyday transactions, the normal ebb and flow of personal and corporate dealings. Our banking laws must mobilize reserves; must not permit the concentration anywhere, in a few hands, of the monetary resources of the country or their use for speculative purposes in such volume as to hinder or impede or stand in the way of other more legitimate, more fruitful uses. And the control of the system of banking and of issue, which our new laws are to set up, must be public, not private: must be vested in the Government itself, so that the banks may be the instruments, not the masters, of business and of individual enterprise and initiative. . . . I am at your service without reserve to play my part in any way you may call upon me to play it in this great enterprise of exigent reform which it will dignify and distinguish us to perform and discredit us to neglect."

The Republicans had passed the Aldrich Vreeland Currency Act in 1908, a plan which provided for a great central bank, owned and controlled by private banking institutions. It concentrated the control of credit in the hands of small groups of capitalists; a far cry from the Democratic ideal of developing the country's business by individual initiative.

It was only after months of effort, complicated by the fact that in addition to the bitter opposition of the big interests to any change at all, Mr. Bryan and his followers were insisting on too radical reform, that a measure was evolved.

The bill, as it finally passed, provides for what is now known as the Federal Reserve System. It consists of twelve Federal Reserve banks in twelve different sections of the country of which all National banks are members. State banks and trust companies are permitted to join if they wish.

A Federal Reserve Board was established in Washington to supervise the whole system. The member banks must keep a certain percentage of their cash reserves in the Reserve banks and the Government may deposit its funds in these banks, at the discretion of the Treasury. The Reserve banks issue currency, as loans, to the member banks against notes of their customers or against other securities acceptable under the Act.

Obviously the system provides for currency "elastically responsive to sound credit", because the pooling of part of the reserves of many banks, in a few central banks under strict governmental supervision, makes possible the quick loans needed by business for expansion which, when business was dependent on the resources of small local banks only, or on the favors of a few powerful banks in New York, were often not available.

267

There was a howl of indignation from the bankers when they heard that theirs was not to be the controlling voice on the Federal Reserve Board; the President was to appoint all but the two ex-officio members! They were not appeased by the provision that at least two had to be "persons experienced in banking and finance."

One evening father told us about a conference he had had that day with the Currency Commission of the American Bankers Association. They sat around the table in his office and quite peremptorily insisted upon banker representation on the Federal Reserve Board. He listened patiently until they finished, and then asked, "Will one of you gentlemen tell me in what civilized country of the earth there are important government boards of control on which private interests are represented?" There was a minute of complete silence, and then he added, "Which of you thinks the railroads should select members of the Interstate Commerce Commission?" He was amused by the suddenness with which they dropped that particular point.

There were many days when it looked as though the bill could not possibly pass. Big business brought all its guns into action; the radicals in Congress threatened to bolt; Colonel House was alarmed and pessimistic, but father, Mac, Underwood and Carter Glass labored incessantly, and at last on the nineteenth of December the Federal Reserve Act was passed by the Senate.

We at once made plans to get away for a real vacation and, wanting to go as far away as we could, chose Pass Christian, a sleepy little place on the Gulf of Mexico. We could hardly wait to get off, but it was not until the twenty-third that the Senate and House were able to iron out their small differences, and present the bill to father to be signed.

There was an even larger group of invited guests in the Executive Offices than when the tariff bill was signed, and the elation in the air was exhilarating. I came back from a *thé dansant*, ran along the corridor in a frenzy, for fear I would be late and, arriving breathless, saw to my dismay that Mac wasn't there. There was still time to inquire, and I found that he was at the door of the building, waiting for his daughter who was late.

I ran back and whispered to mother, "Ask father to wait a minute—Mac's daughter hasn't arrived." She flashed me a glance of intense amusement and murmured, "I'm to ask your father to hold up the currency Act because the McAdoo child isn't here?" But when father sat down to sign, Mac was beside him—minus his daughter—and the three gold pens that were used, were presented to him, Underwood and Glass.

The house at Pass Christian had been built before the Civil War. I felt as though we had been suddenly transported to the far-away days at Colonel Stribling's; there were the same tall white columns, romantic balconies, soft-voiced Negro servants and the gentle consideration of the neighbors. But here the garden was a mass of luxuriant bloom, the trees festooned with moss and, riding through the woods, we were constantly coming upon little winding rivers and still green bayous.

On Christmas morning we had a big tree, but it seemed strangely out of place with warm sun streaming through the windows, and we spent the rest of the day picnicking.

We were very happy; there was a deluge of praise from all over the country, approval of the new bill, and admiration of father as a great leader and administrator. Even Republican newspapers and erstwhile opponents expressed their commendation.

Father was particularly pleased with a published tribute from Mr. Taft, commending the Democratic Party for fulfilling its promises made in the platform, and saying that this was due to "Mr. Wilson's masterful personality and attitude".

Floods of messages came from friends and followers.

Father dictated and wrote four hundred letters in the three weeks of our stay, but he managed also to rest and relax, playing golf, riding horseback, loafing on the water in a little slow-moving launch. We celebrated his fifty-seventh birthday on the twenty-eighth of December, and I thought, watching his clear eyes, his eager almost boyish expression as he unwrapped his presents, still carefully untying the ribbon and folding the paper, that he looked amazingly young. What a goose I was to have worried about him! He had gone through a grueling summer and the terrific strain of the last few months, and was well and vigorous and looking forward with undiminished eagerness to the next step in his program.

It was characteristic of him that he never for a moment rested on his laurels, always and immediately looking ahead to more accomplishment. He was, even during this holiday, considering the next tasks: trust legislation, and a wisely planned budget system, and framing his next message to Congress.

There seemed to be only one black cloud; the situation

in Mexico was still extremely disturbing. There was a mysterious visit from John Lind, father's special agent to the southern republic, which interested me considerably. Father met him on a cruiser in the Gulf of Mexico, one day, and came back looking very troubled. Lind, he told us, had had nothing very new to offer in the way of information, but had urged action against Huerta as the only solution, even suggesting the seizing of Tampico.

Intervention in Mexico was the one thing father had been trying to avoid and we knew, although he did not say so, that he would continue if possible to avoid it; but we were all upset that night.

The Smiths came from near-by New Orleans to visit us and we welcomed them joyously. Father could hardly wait for them to take their hats off before insisting that they sit down at once and tell him all their latest "darkey stories". "I've told all I know," he said. "Please give me a new supply. What has Susie been saying lately?" Susie had been their cook for many years and, when later I went to the Twelfth Night ball in New Orleans and stayed with the Smiths, she gave us a new story that delighted us for years. She was very much interested in the new White House family and had made a large collection of newspaper pictures. On the morning of my arrival she brought my breakfast up to my room and then, standing at the foot of the bed, folded her arms and nodded her head solemnly, up and down. I said, "Susie, what on earth's the matter with you?" and she replied, "Miss Nell, I'se gwine tell all my friends dat you ain't half as ugly as dey say you is."

We were all rested and in fine spirits when we got back to Washington. One day Margaret and I decided to carry out a long-deferred plan to ride "incognito" on a "rubber-neck wagon". Every day they drove around the White House on their tour of the city and many times, driving in or out of the gates, we had been subjected to the scrutiny of tourists as the gentleman with the megaphone pointed us out.

We dressed in old clothes, draped veils over our hats and took a taxi to the bus depot where we clambered aboard, finding seats in front beside the driver. We were a little worried for fear we should be discovered, and were very quiet at first, but after a while we recovered our adventurous spirits and began to ask questions. Margaret assumed a high nasal voice and a Midwestern twang, and kept up a running fire of comment.

When we reached the White House she cried, "Oh, mister, can't we go in? I want to see where the Wilson girls sleep. Please take us in . . . Why can't we go in?" He soothed her condescendingly, explained that she would have to have a pass and promised to get it and take her through himself, but for all her pleas, he said that she couldn't see the bedrooms. Weak with laughter, I dragged her off as soon as I could.

Toward the end of January Jessie and Frank came back from an extended honeymoon trip in Europe, and stayed with us for a few days. They had had a wonderful time, but all the things they had seen, the people they had met, the grand parties at the Embassies, seemed to have slipped from their minds. All they could talk about was the little house waiting for them in Williamstown, and their plans and hopes and dreams for the future.

We hated to let them go again. I was desperately homesick for the old days, most of all for the long nightly confidences with Jessie, as we lay in bed in the dark.

I began to be terribly troubled about my long engagement. Mac and I had formed the habit of taking walks every afternoon at dusk; he was sending me flowers, and at dances refusing to allow anyone to "cut in", while we whirled about together. He would scowl and say severely, "It's not etiquette to cut in on a Cabinet Officer."

Washington was beginning to gossip about us, and mother's amusement was mixed with definite concern over what looked like double dealing on my part. At last I told her that Mac had proposed, and that I was shedding tears every night over having to refuse him. She was adorably sympathetic, but urged me to break my engagement at once, and think it all over very carefully. Also she told me to tell Mac that we must be *incomunicado* until his return from his trip to decide upon the locations of the Federal Reserve banks.

I obeyed in both respects except for an occasional exchange of messages with Mac by what we called the "epaulette route"; reports on each other's health and activities, relayed by a friend in the navy. While I was dancing one night with a great friend of mine, he asked me suddenly what was the matter; whereupon I buried my face in the gold braid and brass buttons on his chest and wailed, "Oh, I'm so lonely." He led me behind some palms, wiped my eyes and advised me, a little grimly, to go home. When Mac returned I was so glad to see him that I accepted him on the spot.

Then began the difficult business of keeping our engagement a secret. There was a second performance of the

273

"Bird Masque" at the Waldorf Hotel in New York and while I was there we wrote every day, Mac's letters always arriving covered with registered mail and special delivery stamps. In the end one letter was opened, carelessly stuck together again and remailed to me. In a few days our secret was placarded all over the front pages of the newspapers, and on the thirteenth of March we were forced to make an announcement.

Father had established the custom of receiving the Washington corps of newspaper men twice a week. No President before him had done this, but he told them that he wanted to take the people of the country into his confidence, and asked them "to go into partnership with him" and "to lend him their assistance as nobody else could", in spreading the truth about what was going on in Washington. In many ways it was successful, most of the correspondents responding to his frankness and trying hard not to color their reports to please the prejudices of their papers, but there were a few who betrayed his trust, and he was constantly irritated by personal questions fired at him almost daily by those who seemed interested only in our private lives.

He was very patient, however, answering their queries whenever it was possible, with courtesy and sincerity, and only on one occasion losing his temper. He was angry because my mail had been opened, and they had also been publishing absurd rumors about Margaret's engagement to any number of men.

He faced the group one day with fire in his eyes. "I am a public character for the time being", he said, "but the ladies of my household are not servants of the government and they are not public characters. I deeply resent the treatment they are receiving at the hands of the newspapers at this time. Take the case of my oldest daughter. It is a violation of my own impulses even to speak of these things, but my oldest daughter is constantly represented as being engaged to this, that or the other man in different parts of the country; in some instances, to men she has never even met in her life. It is a constant and intolerable annoyance. These things are printed without any attempt to verify them by communications to the White House and, when explicit denials are received from persons who are known to tell the truth, and to feel bound to tell the truth, those denials are not respected in the least. On the contrary they are represented as avoidances. If this continues I shall deal with you, not as President, but as man to man."

He frightened the correspondents to such an extent that for some time they let us alone.

Father was sternly opposed to any form of nepotism, refusing, although it often hurt him to do so, to appoint even a distant relative to any office. So when Joe Tumulty came to me and asked me, quite solemnly, if I had realized that, if I married Mac, I was putting both him and father in an awkward position, I was aghast and ran at once to mother.

She assured me that nothing could be more absurd. "Your father appointed him to the second highest position in his Cabinet before you even thought of marrying him," she said. "What more could he want, or your father give?"

I had had a bad shock when I got back to Washington

after the play. Father and mother met me at the door of
the Oval Room, and mother looked white and ill. Father
said, "She gave us a scare. She fell in her room a few days
ago and she won't stay in bed and rest." Mother smiled at
me and said she was all right. "This goose keeps worrying
about me for no reason at all." But as he led her down the
corridor, supporting her with his arm around her waist,
my heart suddenly sickened and the old fears crowded
back thick and fast.

Helen and Margaret and I had a long talk that night. I
raged against the social workers who were demanding too
much of her, but Helen said that there was nothing to be
done about it; that mother had her heart set on getting the
bill for better housing conditions in Washington passed
by Congress, and that she would not spare herself. Then
too, the Mexican situation was very bad, and we knew that
she was terribly worried about it.

A British mining man had been executed in Mexico and
England was excited. British financial interests were using
the incident to insist on American intervention. Father had
had to order two regiments to Texas to calm the outraged
feelings of border citizens who had been subjected to raids
by Mexican bandits. It was one of those occasions when a
spark might light a conflagration.

Father himself was deeply disturbed, but determined to
prevent war. He was convinced that "infinite patience and
infinite firmness" would solve the problem. Colonel House
said one day, "Get him to read his nonsense rhymes again;
try to inveigle him into evenings with the poets; he is
worrying more than you realize". Once in a while we succeeded, but he wanted no serious poetry in those days, and

confined himself to Stephen Leacock, "The Bab Ballads," James Whitcomb Riley and "Mr. Dooley".

I remember our rather weak laughter over one of Dooley's remarks. "Sure, with Mexico so contagious, we'll be takin' it soon whether we want it or not." Father told us one night that the worst part of it was that every report that came to him from Mexico was quite different, and yet that he was sure that those who sent the reports were telling the truth as they saw it. He said, "I listen carefully to what everyone says, and then piece together the parts that fit. Parts of truth always match."

In April we all went down to White Sulphur Springs for the Easter holidays. Mother had failed to get her strength back, and at the last minute father decided to take a nurse along to watch over her. It was a lovely interlude. Frank and Jessie and Mac joined us, and we played and rested together and managed for a few brief days to recapture the illusion that all was well.

But in Tampico Huerta's men had arrested a peaceful landing party of American sailors who had come, unarmed, in a Navy boat to take off supplies for their ship. They had been released later, but when word came that Admiral Mayo had insisted upon a formal apology, and demanded that the American flag be saluted with special ceremony by the military commander of the port, father had to leave us and go back to Washington.

He was intensely annoyed. Mayo's action seemed an unnecessary bit of drama in the midst of a situation that was already tense enough but he had, of course, to support the Admiral in command. Also it was not merely a question of one isolated incident. Huerta was a tyrant who had

277

come into power by deliberate murder; there was a great principle involved; the consent of the governed, the right of a majority of the people to choose their own rulers— a principle very dear to father's heart.

If the United States could do her part to save Mexico and other Latin-American republics from recurrent anarchy, it was all worth while. Yet armed intervention—the cry of rich men who wanted their interests in Mexico protected—was unthinkable. It meant a long war. It meant sacrificing the lives of American boys. For the first time in his life father couldn't sleep.

After investigating the situation in all its aspects, he informed Huerta that he expected "a prompt acceptance" of Admiral Mayo's terms, giving him until the nineteenth of April to comply, and came back to White Sulphur Springs very tense and troubled.

There was great excitement throughout the country, and hundreds of letters, most of them approving his action, poured in from all sides. The nineteenth came and went with no sign from Huerta, and that night we went back to Washington, a silent and depressed family.

The next day father addressed Congress, and this time even the galleries, defying the rules, broke into tumultuous applause as he appeared. He summed up the moment's crisis and concluded, "This government can, I earnestly hope, in no circumstances be forced into war with the people of Mexico. Mexico is torn by civil strife. If we are to accept the tests of its own constitution, it has no government. General Huerta has set his power up in the City of Mexico, such as it is, without right and by methods for which there can be no justification. Only part of the country is under his control. If armed conflict should unhappily come as a result of his attitude of personal resentment toward this Government, we should be fighting only General Huerta and those who adhere to him and give him their support, and our object would be only to restore to the people of the distracted Republic, the opportunity to set up again their own laws and their own government. But I earnestly hope that war is not now in question. I believe that I speak for the American people when I say that we do not desire to control the affairs of our sister Republic. . . .

"The present situation need have none of the grave implications of interference, if we deal with it promptly, firmly and wisely. . . .

"I, therefore, come to ask your approval that I should use the armed forces of the United States in such ways and to such an extent as may be necessary to obtain from General Huerta and his adherents the fullest recognition of the rights and dignity of the United States, even amidst the distressing conditions now unhappily obtaining in Mexico.

"There can be in what we do no thought of aggression or selfish aggrandizement. We seek to maintain the dignity and authority of the United States only because we wish always to keep our great influence unimpaired for the uses of liberty, both in the United States and wherever else it may be employed for the benefit of mankind."

That night he told us that the reaction to his message had not been very favorable and added, with a sort of grim sadness, "People seem to want war with Mexico, but they shan't have it if I can prevent it."

When I came down for breakfast next morning I was startled by father's expression. I said, "Oh, what's happened, darling?" And he told me that the Americans had landed at Vera Cruz, at his order, taken possession of the cable, post and telegraph offices and the customhouse, and that there had been unexpected casualties; four of our men had been killed.

I knew that he felt personally responsible for their deaths, and I had such a lump in my throat that I couldn't swallow my breakfast.

The days that followed were hard to get through, especially when we heard that fifteen more Americans were dead. Father was calm and managed most of the time to be optimistic, while mother concealed her intense concern for him behind a smiling serenity. As I watched her in those days, I remembered what Uncle Stock had once said about her. "She has a tragic capacity for suffering and being still about it."

War talk was beginning to spread through the country. Carranza, who had the moral support of the United States in his attempt to oust Huerta and give the Mexicans an opportunity to hold an honest and legitimate election, was making very little headway. The occupation of Vera Cruz had not, apparently, had much effect on Huerta, and things had reached a serious impasse, when suddenly they began to straighten out.

On the twenty-fifth of April three South American countries, Argentina, Brazil and Chile, ordered their Ambassadors to call on the Secretary of State and offer to mediate, and father accepted at once. Huerta also consented and made no protest, even later, when father insisted that the settlement should provide for the "entire elimination of General Huerta" and "the immediate setting up in Mexico of a single provisional government, acceptable to all parties."

We were all immensely relieved. There would be weeks of mediation and many difficulties to be ironed out, but armed intervention had been definitely avoided, and "personal aggrandizement" by American investors prevented. Father's enemies had sneered at his policy of "watchful waiting" but, in the end, he was to be vindicated.

CHAPTER SEVENTEEN

The White House

THE SEVENTH DAY OF MAY was the date set for my wedding, and I was busier than I had ever been in my life. Fearing that it would tire mother too much, I begged her not to bother about my trousseau, and went with Uncle John Wilson's wife, Aunt Ida, to New York for strenuous, happy days in the shops.

I was an especial favorite of the John Wilsons, because I looked like their daughter who had been killed in an automobile accident, and they were delighted with my choice of a husband. When I told Uncle John that I was engaged, he turned red in the face with indignation until I said, "But, it's Mac, Uncle John", whereupon he gave me a big hug and exclaimed, "Thank God—I was afraid it was one of those damned young whipper-snappers."

When I wasn't shopping and having fittings, I was sitting in the Senate Gallery, listening to impassioned oratory over the question of Panama Canal tolls, and watching Mac talk confidentially to Senators on the floor.

Whenever father wanted an important bill passed, Mac and Postmaster General Burleson worked day and night, arguing, calming, trying to convince uncertain Senators

282

and Congressmen. Father called them, privately, his "wet nurses."

The bill passed the House in March, by a large majority, but the Senate was very wrought up about it. The question was whether or not to repeal a provision of the Panama Canal Act, passed in 1912, which exempted vessels engaged in the coastwise trade of the United States from payment of tolls. America had signed a treaty with England in 1901, guaranteeing equality of treatment for the ships of all nations, and the exemption of United States ships was obviously a violation of solemn treaty obligations. Involving, therefore, a moral issue, father considered it a vital matter, not only of the moment, but for the future and enduring prestige of America.

Appearing before Congress on the fifth of March, he expressed himself with the especial ardor that questions of honor, either personal or national, always aroused in his idealistic nature. He said, "We consented to the treaty; its language we accepted, if we did not originate it; and we are too big, too powerful, too self-respecting a nation to interpret with a too strained or refined reading the words of our own promises, just because we have power enough to give us leave to read them as we please. The large thing to do is the only thing we can afford to do, a voluntary withdrawal from a position everywhere questioned and misunderstood. We ought to reverse our action without raising the question whether we were right or wrong, and so once more deserve our reputation for generosity, and for the redemption of every obligation without quibble or hesitation."

But there was strong opposition from big shipbuilders, with their own interests to serve, from violent anti-English Irishmen, and from people whose attitude was simply that the Canal was American property and we should do what we pleased with it. Theodore Roosevelt issued a bitter denunciation of father, and the Senate, before they finally yielded and repealed the provisions, filled one hundred and eighty-six pages of the Congressional Record with speeches. It seemed to me incredible that anyone could argue that America should go back on her word, and I sat in the gallery hour after hour, forgetting even my coming marriage, in seething indignation and astonishment.

We had decided to have as small and private a wedding as we could manage, in order to save mother from too much exertion. She insisted that this wasn't necessary, but we didn't want a big wedding anyhow, and finally convinced her. Only the Cabinet and their wives, Uncle Stock, a few other relatives, and my most intimate friends from Princeton were invited.

But the presents came flooding in just the same, and some humorist in Congress suggested that they should form a permanent committee to buy wedding gifts for the President's daughters. Again a huge silver service, complete with enormous candelabra, appeared at the White House—the gift of the House of Representatives; but I have always been sure that some clever woman chose the Senate's gift— an exquisite pearl and diamond bracelet.

Father and mother were devoted to Mac, but mother was a little worried because, as she told Mac privately, I was very young and she hadn't given me the training that would make me an efficient housekeeper, or fit me for the compli-

W. G. McADOO AND JOSEPH TUMULTY, WASHINGTON, 1913

W. G. McADOO AND ELEANOR McADOO
At Harlakenden on their wedding trip

cated business of being a Cabinet Minister's wife. She told me afterwards that this didn't seem to disturb Mac in the least.

The day before the wedding, the members of the Cabinet gave a stag party for him, and amid much persiflage and laughter insisted that he should make a speech. He told them the story of the young mountaineer who, on receiving a letter from his girl accepting him, walked out into the moonlight and, lifting his head to the sky, murmured, "Oh, Lawd, I ain't got nothin' agin nobody no more!"

Jessie and Margaret were my matron and maid of honor, and the only other attendants were two little flower-girls, Secretary Lane's daughter and Mac's youngest child. Cary Grayson was "best man".

Having learned from sad experience that, as a costume designer, I was not as clever as I thought, I accepted experienced advice, and the result exceeded my wildest dreams. My wedding dress was made of heavy ivory-colored satin, in an almost mediaeval style, and was trimmed with very old, real lace. Margaret and Jessie wore ethereal-looking gowns of blue and rose-colored organdie. They carried, instead of bouquets, tall shepherds' crooks with Cécile Brunner roses and lilies of the valley tied to the handles and festooning almost to the floor.

My bridal bouquet was of white orchids, gardenias and lilies of the valley and, to be on the safe side of superstition, I pinned a piece of blue ribbon inside my dress, with a tiny brooch borrowed from mother.

Before I dressed, I went to mother's room to help her for the last time. Her dress was made of creamy lace, with a little bunch of violets on the shoulder, and she wore a set of amethysts that father had given her. She looked so radiantly pretty that my heart grew light and I ran back to my room thinking, happily, that I had not a care in the world.

We assembled at the head of the main stairway, and we were prompt, as we had been all our lives when we knew that father would be waiting. But the Marine Band, for some unexplained reason, didn't start the wedding march on time and father frowningly sent word to Hoover to find out what was wrong.

At last they began, with startling loudness, and as I marched slowly down the stairs on father's arm, I suddenly remembered a day in Princeton years ago when Uncle Stock had taken me to hear Sousa's Band and had said, "When you're married, Nellie, have a big band like this play your wedding march. Everyone should have very loud music on that occasion, to keep up their courage."

As we made the turn at the foot of the stairs and started down the corridor to the Blue Room, I saw, out of the corner of my eye, that my long train had turned over, showing the chiffon lining and the little bunches of orange blossoms sewn here and there. But Hoover, always at hand in any emergency, was standing near by and I said, in a loud whisper, "My train, Hoover—turn it over—quick!" He sprang to the rescue and I felt father's arm shake, as he silently laughed at me.

The Blue Room was a mass of lilies and white apple blossoms, and Jessie's white vicuña rug was again in front of the little prie-dieu. Through the windows I could see, in the dusk, the Washington Monument and the blue Virginia hills.

286

THE WHITE HOUSE

After the ceremony I cut the huge wedding cake with one of the young aides' swords.

When I went upstairs and mother, Margaret and Jessie were helping me to change, I thought suddenly that I couldn't leave them—for one wild moment I couldn't imagine what had ever possessed me to think that I could—but they all laughed at my tragic face, and I put on the blue suit with the long, slit skirt, and the little sailor hat with one huge rose in front, kissed them wildly and went down the stairs, clinging to mother's hand until the last possible moment.

The reporters were determined that this time the White House bridal couple should not escape them, but Mac had devised an elaborate scheme to outwit them. His own automobile and the three White House cars were drawn up in various places, two in front and two at the south entrance, with the shades on the windows drawn down. Jessie and Frank dived into one, Margaret and Cary Grayson into another and two other couples into the third and fourth, and they all whirled madly out of the gates, pursued by wild-eyed reporters.

Then Mac and I slipped into an inconspicuous little automobile that no one had noticed and drove peacefully away. We were all in a gale of laughter, which helped me to live through the last few minutes. Father and mother stood, hand in hand, at the door and they were both smiling, but when I had kissed them good-bye, I noticed the little familiar quiver of father's eyelid and the unfamiliar firmness of mother's mouth, and I horrified my husband by dissolving into tears in the darkness of the car.

Father and mother had lent us Harlakenden for our

honeymoon, and Richard Green and the Irish maid from Princeton were there to welcome us when we arrived. Richard was very proud of his "Sec'eta'y", and joyful over my advent into the McAdoo family. He waited on us at meals with such an air of pomp and ceremony that even the spinach looked like ambrosia, and a glass of buttermilk like the nectar of the gods.

I had been told by a friend of my husband's that Mac was the most picturesque curser in Washington, but much to Richard's relief, he never allowed the women of his family to hear his repertoire. One night, however, he was telling me about an interview he had had with an insolent office-seeker. He showed me how he had brought his fist down on the table and said, "You're just a damned fool!" Richard, entering from the pantry, fried chicken held aloft, heard only the last words, and thinking that his hero was cursing his bride, turned and fled to the kitchen. Mac went after him, to find him shedding tears over the chicken. He said, "Richard, did you really think I was swearing at Mrs. McAdoo?" And Richard answered, "No suh, Mr. Sec'eta'y —not really—but it looked awful bad."

We had only a day or two of privacy. The newspaper men promptly tracked us down and visitors, messengers and telephone calls disturbed the quiet of the New Hampshire hills. I was terribly troubled when I heard that father was going to New York on the eleventh to attend the funeral of the nineteen men who had died at Vera Cruz. Mac, as head of the Secret Service, had been told that it was an exceedingly dangerous thing to do—there had been anonymous letters threatening father's life and if he rode in the procession he would expose himself to hostile demonstrations. Mac was unable to conceal his anxiety from me and I wrote to mother asking her if she couldn't keep father from going. Her answer came after he had left Washington. She told me that she hadn't tried to stop him. He felt responsible for the tragedy, he wasn't afraid and we mustn't be, and she reminded me of what he had said on another occasion, "I am immortal until my time comes".

But I was haunted by a memory. Standing on the sidewalk in Buffalo years ago, I had held father's hand and watched McKinley's coffin go by between lines of marching soldiers. Father had looked sad and grim and I had said, "Why did they kill him, father?" He said, "It was a poor crazed man—every president must face that risk". But that day in New York he walked at the head of a funeral procession and, amid the great crowds lining the streets, there was no sign of animosity.

Two weeks later Mac and I were back in Washington. I was enchanted with the victoria and the two prancing black horses which met us at the station. Congress had, for many years, provided each of the Cabinet members with two carriages, a victoria and a small barouche with a negro coachman and footman, officiating in resplendent livery on the box. The advent of automobiles had not moved the budget makers to further generosity, but I loved the feeling of stately leisureliness it gave me to lean back on the cushions, with a gay parasol over my head, and drive along the wide, tree-lined streets, to the jaunty accompaniment of trotting hoofs. Not even the White House automobiles had made me feel so dignified.

That night I called Hoover on the telephone, asking to speak to mother, and was puzzled by the slightly evasive answer he gave me. He said that she had gone to bed. Could I call in the morning? Father was having a conference, and Margaret and Helen were out; they hadn't expected us until the next day. I was worried and by nine o'clock the next morning, I was up and dressed, and at the White House, knocking at mother's door.

She was still in bed and overjoyed to see me, but my heart sank when I looked at her. She had changed—she looked very small and white, and all her lovely color was gone. But she wouldn't let me ask her any questions. She was "all right". She was interested only in me and she looked at me happily, and patted my hand. "I needed only to see your face, as I did Jessie's, to know that you are happy", she said.

Father came in smiling, but I knew the instant that he embraced me that he was troubled. Before I left I had a few moments alone with him, and he told me that mother had been really ill—that he was terribly worried, but that the doctors had told him that it wasn't too serious—that we mustn't be frightened.

I went every day to see her. Sometimes she got up, but most of the time she lay on her sofa, and she had to give up all her activities. She talked a great deal about father in those days, tender pride in every word she said, but she was anxious too—anxious about his many problems, about the fearful strain he was under. One day I found her sitting at her desk writing indignant little letters, which she never sent, to Senators who were attacking him. Sometimes she would lie there happily and reminisce, dwelling on her girlhood and the early days in Princeton.

In June the Smiths came from New Orleans. She had,

herself, urged them to come to "cheer up Woodrow" and, for a time, after their arrival she seemed much better.

Except for the easel and the paint box, it was like old times to come in and find the three of them sitting together, Cousin Mary reading aloud, or Cousin Lucy telling one of her long, delicious yarns and father running in, between engagements, to stand before the fire with his cup of tea. But as he talked and laughed, his eyes seldom left mother's face and he always held her close for a moment before he went out of the room.

My social duties as a "Cabinet wife" were rather overwhelming. It was a blow to find that I had to spend every afternoon, from three o'clock until six, paying calls. The Cabinet ladies made the first call only on the wives of Ambassadors and Ministers and the "Senate ladies". Everyone else, including Congressmen's wives, was visited only if she had called at the Cabinet houses. But practically everyone did call on us, which ran the appalling list close to a thousand.

Mrs. Lane, wife of the Secretary of the Interior, took me under her wing and coached me in the practical aspects of the job. I thought it all perfectly absurd, for we sometimes made twenty or thirty calls a day, and never stayed more than five or, at the outside, ten minutes. To walk into a house, say "How do you do?" sit down, remark on the weather and the price of eggs and depart, seemed to me little short of inane. But I understood that bills had sometimes been defeated because of a little matter like an unreturned call or a broken engagement, and I primly made the rounds, longing for my irresponsible afternoons at races or tea dances.

One day a Senator, visiting Mac at the Treasury Department, invited us to a party he was giving at the Chevy Chase Club. Mac accepted, but under the terrible pressure of Government business, forgot all about it. A week later he suggested that it would be a pleasant relaxation to go out to Chevy Chase by ourselves, have supper and dance. When we were ushered to a small table in the dining room, I noticed a large dinner party going on in the center of the room, and wondered vaguely why there were two empty chairs. After we were seated, the head-waiter touched Mac on the arm and whispered, "But, Mr. Secretary, Senator — waited an hour for you. Aren't you joining his party?" Mac looked at me in consternation. We joined the party, but what could we say except that we had forgotten? The Senator never forgot or forgave us, and for some time made things difficult for Mac whenever an opportunity arose.

The Cabinet women had a "day at home" every Thursday, and usually two or three hundred people arrived during the afternoon. Almost always there were one or two pathetic figures, sitting against the wall, silently stuffing themselves with food—old retired Government clerks, whose only recreation was attending "at homes". It was a difficult business trying to remember all the names and to say the right thing. My memory was atrocious and I spent hours beforehand going over lists and imploring Belle Hagner or Anne Lane to describe people to me, and put the names and faces together.

The big White House receptions which I had never really enjoyed became dreadful ordeals. The Cabinet officers could wander about, but their wives must stand in line. I could no longer run away to the Oval Room to dance, but must shake hands for hours—murmuring banal remarks and growing dizzy as the endless procession passed by. I tried all sorts of tricks to amuse myself. I was sure that no one ever heard a word that anyone else said, so I experimented. Instead of the monotonous "How do you *do*—I'm *so* glad to meet you", I smiled politely and muttered, "One two three *four* five six seven—A B C D E F G," and was caught only once. A large maternal-looking woman said, "What did you say, my dear?"—and when I stammered and blushed, asked me if I was feeling ill.

The first large dinner party I gave developed into a nightmare. I made the beginner's mistake of inviting both members of the Cabinet and Senators, and then discovered, to my horror, that I was "rushing in where angels feared to tread". There was an ancient controversy which had never been settled, as to which should come first in the Order of Precedence—Washington's notorious bugaboo—and experienced hostesses always avoided trouble by never asking them to dinner at the same time.

I frantically called Belle Hagner and the special official at the State Department who gave advice on these important matters, and after many hectic consultations, they told me to put the Senators first, but before we went in to dinner, to go to each Cabinet member in turn and explain to them that I was treating them like members of my own family, and beg them to understand and forgive me. They were amused and kind, but by the time I sat down at the head of the long table, I felt like a wounded veteran of the wars.

On another occasion we gave a stag dinner for a group

of Senators. I spent many hours in preparation—conferring with the cook, discussing wines with Richard, and arranging the flowers sent to me from the White House greenhouses. I surveyed my table with pride—masses of flowers, tall candelabra, cut glass and shining silver; then I rushed upstairs to dress and chat with Mac while he battled with his tie. Richard had tried at the beginning to prevent me from going to Mac's room during this ceremony. The first time he had nervously approached me and murmured, "Miss, would you mind just steppin' outa de room a minute?" I said, "Why, Richard, why should I?" and he replied in anguish, "Oh, Miss, please go, just until de Sec'eta'y finish tyin' his tie." But he sooned learned that the proverbial masculine language over a recalcitrant tie could be controlled by a Southerner in the presence of a lady.

One of the Senators failed to arrive for the party and the others insisted that I should dine with them instead of disappearing, as I had intended, when dinner was announced. When the first course was passed I suddenly noticed something strange occurring at the other end of the table. Richard was presenting the platter to Mac, but pulling it away every time he reached for it. After two unsuccessful attempts to help himself, I saw Mac grab the edge of the dish, frown at Richard, and take a piece of fish. Richard rolled his eyes in my direction and heaved a tragic sigh. Then I realized what the trouble was. Trying to economize, I had provided only one piece of fish for each guest, and some of the Senators had helped themselves to two, so there were only a few pieces left.

I relapsed into silent despair and Senator Swanson, sitting on my right, asked me what was the matter. I pointed

helplessly at Richard advancing slowly and hopelessly with
an almost empty plate held tremblingly in his hands. Senator Swanson began making a loud outcry, "You pigs, you
gluttons! Why do you have to be so disgustingly greedy?
This child provides you with plenty of food, and you
heap your plates with extra fish. Now, divide up!" Everyone laughed and joked and passed fish across the table, and
I too managed to laugh. I decided that Senator Swanson
was a really great man.

Every morning Mac and I walked to the Treasury Department where I left him, to return in the late afternoon
and walk home with him. It was his only form of exercise,
for he was busier than any three men. He had much to do
with the organization and administration of the new laws
and was, with father, deeply concerned with new ones that
were pending. There was a feeling in the very air of Washington in those days—a feeling of great achievements already accomplished, an assured and vital interest in more
to come. We all felt that America had already stepped
across the threshold of a great future. Idealism, altruism,
all the fine hopes and dreams that fill men's hearts seemed
realities, and no one imagined that in a few weeks our
pleasant, dependable world was to collapse about us.

CHAPTER EIGHTEEN

The White House

In July we began to be really frightened about mother. Each time I went over to see her she seemed a little weaker—a little less interested in what was going on. I paid no attention to the murders at Sarajevo, and rumors of war in Europe seemed far off and unimportant compared with the doctors' reports.

Helen was sick, too, and one day I arrived to find that Cousin Mary Smith had been taken to the hospital with a dangerous attack of appendicitis. Cousin Lucy was very brave, but we were all anxious, and the whole house seemed suddenly dark and silent. We were hiding our secret fear about mother from one another—all stubbornly pretending that she would soon be well again; but I remember waking up one hot morning with a dreadful sense of oppression—of intense terror. I could hardly wait to dress and get over to the White House where I sat for hours outside her door as she slept. Then I saw father coming down the long corridor. His step had lost its swing and, when I saw his face, gaunt and gray, etched with deep lines, I sprang up and ran and clung to him desperately. We sat hand in hand on the sofa near mother's door, and he told me that he had not for a moment lost hope—that the doctors kept reassuring him; but in my heart I knew. The old fear had caught up with us at last.

Every day mother insisted that father should go out and play golf—he must not feel that he had to be with her when he needed exercise. He always assured her that he would go and then, instead, sat very quietly outside her room trying to work, tiptoeing once in a while to lean against her door and listen.

Mac had been sure for some time that war in Europe could not be avoided but when, during the last week in July, it actually began, I found it hard to believe. I think that father felt the same way. At lunch, on the day that Austria declared war, he said in a low voice, "It's incredible—incredible." Then he added, "Don't tell your mother anything about it." I asked him to tell me what he thought. Would the whole world be involved? But he stared at me as if he were dazed and then, suddenly, put his hand over his eyes and said, "I can think of nothing—nothing, when my dear one is suffering".

By the thirty-first the extent of the catastrophe was apparent to everyone, and the air was tense with excitement. Early in the morning J. P. Morgan called Mac on the telephone at our house, and told him that the governors of the New York Stock Exchange were considering closing the Exchange doors that day. They wanted Mac's advice. I heard him say, "If you really want my judgment, it is to close the Exchange", and my heart skipped a beat. Was it really as bad as that!

August second fell on a Sunday, and before noon newsboys were shouting extras up and down the quiet streets—Germany had delivered her ultimatum to Belgium!

Mac had gone to the Treasury Department and I drove, in a sort of panic, to the White House, but father was working in his study and mother was asleep. I sat beside Helen's bed for a long time. She was too ill to speak, and I stared out of her window and wondered vaguely if this was the end of the world. Then Mac called me on the telephone. Some of the big New York bankers had just called him up to say that they were afraid there might be a run on the New York banks the next day, which would mean a disastrous panic; they begged him to come up immediately and talk with the Clearing House Committee. He would probably go, if father approved, and he wanted me to go with him.

We were met at the Pennsylvania Station by a group of some of the most important financiers in New York, and I was startled by their white faces and trembling voices. Were these America's "Great Men"? Mac greeted them cheerfully, took me to the hotel, told me not to worry, that he had already deposited fifty million dollars of emergency currency in the Subtreasury in New York, and departed for the conference.

But I couldn't sleep and sat up reading until one o'clock, when he returned and told me all about it. They had asked for emergency currency and were enormously relieved when he told them that it was already there, but such currency could be issued only to National banks, Mac paced up and down the room. "My God, why couldn't this have happened a little later?" he said. "Just a few months and the Federal Reserve system would have been in operation, and taking care of a situation like this."

There was only one thing to do—go back at once to

ELLEN AXSON WILSON IN ENGLAND IN 1906
Portrait by Fred Yates

Woodrow Wilson with Ellen Wilson McAdoo
(three weeks old) in 1915

Washington and get Congress to pass an amendment immediately, giving him the right to issue currency to any state bank or trust company that had "signified its intention to join the Federal Reserve system, and could deposit satisfactory collateral."

It all sounded like Greek to me, and I wondered if even father and Mac could get Congress to pass anything immediately. But we dashed back to Washington and, in twenty-four hours, it was done and the panic averted.

I went straight from the station to the White House, and, when I saw the faces of Brown and Mays at the door, and Hoover sitting silently at his desk in the little anteroom, I knew that things were blacker than ever. Margaret told me that Jessie and Frank and Uncle Stock had been sent for, and that Doctor Davis, father's old friend and classmate, was on his way from Philadelphia for a consultation. We sat all day waiting. Every time Cary Grayson came from mother's room we searched his face for some sign of encouragement, but we never found it. It was like a terrible nightmare: Europe in flames, and all hope fading from our own hearts.

On the fourth I watched father as he sat beside mother's bed and struggled, in the midst of his own despair, to write a message to the nations at war, tendering his "good offices in the interest of European peace". She was sleeping, and I was thankful that she knew nothing about the world tragedy.

It was Doctor Davis who told us the truth at last—that mother could not live. Father did not speak, but for the first and only time in my life I saw him weep.

Mother must have known for some time, because she

had asked many times about her bill for the poor people in the Washington alleys, and had said that she hoped they would hurry so she would know that her work had been accomplished. Friends sent word to Congress and the bill was passed at once. When father told her, she smiled her radiant smile and lay peacefully holding his hand, but we knew that by then her heart and mind were filled only with deep concern for him.

She seemed happy when he was with her, and restless in the brief intervals when he was not there, saying over and over, "Is your father looking well?" At the last, just before she left us, she murmured to Cary Grayson, "Promise me that you will take good care of my husband."

Years afterward, as father lay ill in Lincoln's great carved bed, I closed the book I was reading to him and watched him lying with his eyes shut, apparently asleep. He had been sick for weeks and spoke very little—facing patiently and calmly whatever was to come. Someone had sent him a dwarf pine tree—a beautiful little thing, with the graceful symmetry of its larger brothers. He had it placed where his eyes would fall on it whenever he awoke and, at night, kept a light burning above it, telling us that he could imagine himself in the forest if he looked at it long enough. Suddenly he opened his eyes and smiled at me, the live, happy smile of the old days. "I was back on the island at Muskoka", he said, softly. "Do you remember our picnics there, and your mother reading poetry under the pines? I wish I could hear her voice." We were silent for a little while and then he said, "I owe everything to your mother —you know that, don't you?" and he began to talk about

300

their life together, how brave and radiant she was, how she had devoted her life to him and to us, with no thought of herself—how she had never failed him. I said, "I wish I could hand her torch on to my own children", and he answered, "You can—tell them about her. That is enough."

THE END